Dina Julia

Diva Julia

The Public Romance
and Private Agony
of Julia Ward Howe

VALARIE H. ZIEGLER

TRINITY PRESS INTERNATIONAL
A Continuum imprint
HARRISBURG • LONDON • NEW YORK

Trinity Press International, P.O. Box 1321, Harrisburg, PA 17105

Trinity Press International is a member of
the Continuum International Publishing Group.

Cover art: Close-up portrait of Julia Ward Howe © Bettmann/CORBIS

Cover design: Laurie Westhafer

Library of Congress Cataloging-in-Publication Data

Ziegler, Valarie H., 1954–
    Diva Julia : the public romance and private agony of Julia Ward
Howe / Valarie H. Ziegler.
    p. cm.
    Includes bibliographical references (p.) and index.
    ISBN 1-56338-418-3
    1. Howe, Julia Ward, 1819-1910. 2. Women and literature—
United States—History—19th century. 3. Authors, American—
19th century—Biography.   4. Feminists—United States—
Biography.   I. Title.
PS2018.Z54   2003
818'.409—dc21

                                                              2003008778

Printed in the United States of America

03 04 05 06 07 08   10 9 8 7 6 5 4 3 2 1

Dedicated with love to Bill

True like ice, like fire

Contents

Acknowledgments

I owe so many people so much for their assistance with this book that it is a relief and pleasure to have the opportunity to thank them. First, I want to recognize those who helped provide money and release time: at DePauw University, President Robert Bottoms, Provost Len DiLillo, Dean Anita Solow, Vice President of Academic Affairs Neal Abraham, Barbara Steinson, Martha Rainbolt, Bob Garrett, and the Faculty Development Committee; at Rhodes College, Harmon Dunathan, Michael McLain, and the Faculty Development Committee. I enjoyed a wondrous sabbatical at Emory University under the auspices of the Dana Foundation. Bob Detweiler administered the grant and led our Dana "fellows" through an exciting and absolutely enjoyable year of mischief and scholarship. Bob, you are the best.

I owe intellectual debts to many, particularly to the leaders of the Young Scholars in American Religion at Indiana University-Purdue University Indianapolis: Director Conrad Cherry and our two mentors, William Hutchison and Catherine Albanese. The Young Scholars program urged me to get an agent and to write the manuscript so that it would be accessible to a general audience; without that advice, this book would have been very different indeed. I am especially grateful to the Young Scholars program for providing me with a cohort of supportive and incisive colleagues: Madeleine Duntley, Tony Fels, Matt Glass, Rosemary Gooden, Laurie Maffly-Kipp, Andy Manis, Joel Martin, Gerald McDermott, Keith Naylor, Roger Payne, John Stackhouse, and most especially, Betty DeBerg and Tom Tweed, who were incredibly generous with their time and expertise when I was looking for a publisher. It has been a kick to see the publications that our group has produced, nurtured by our conversations in Indianapolis. That none of us has been drafted by the NFL remains a surprise, given what we showed the scouts, but I am confident that in time we will surely reap fame and fortune from our mind-numbing talents in ritual performance and obscure television theme songs. And we'll always have Muncie.

Outside the confines of Indianapolis, I received valuable assistance from a number of people. I especially want to thank Danny Smith of Gardiner, Maine, for his generosity in initiating me into the Yellow House Papers. He remains the Howe family historian par excellence, and generations of future scholars will be indebted to him for the marvelous cataloging job he has done in the Howe family archives. At DePauw, Barbara Steinson of the History Department has been incredibly and energetically helpful; in the Religious Studies Department, Bernie Batto and Leslie James offered unqualified support; and Roni McMains was a super secretary. Given the forearm overuse and computer problems I had in the last stages of this manuscript, I particularly to want to thank three people at DePauw who worked hard for me: Bonnie Crawley and Paul Schmitt in Personnel and Nelson Greenwell in Computing, as well as all the folks at Greencastle Physical Therapy who tried to put me back together: Ken, Chet, Valerie, Karen, and Candace. And for keeping my morale high, special appreciation goes to Dan Reck and the Tiger Pep Band/Tiger Pep Band Maniacs, to whom Marvin's delivers and from whom the fateful challenge, "What have you done to beat Wabash today?" ever flows.

I want to thank Brooks Holifield from Emory University as well; like the faithful friend he is, Brooks has always made time to read my work, even when he was working hard on his own. Congratulations to Brooks on his magisterial study of the history of American theology. My agent, Ted Weinstein, believed in this manuscript and in addition to working amazingly hard for it provided astute critical analysis. I learned so much from him. And Henry Carrigan, my editor at Trinity Press International, gave me years of thoughtful advice about this manuscript long before he ever read it or decided to publish it. Amy Wagner at Trinity guided me through the process of manuscript preparation with skill and good humor. I also want to thank Gary Williams, professor of English at University of Idaho. Neither of us expected to run into someone else working on Julia Ward Howe's unpublished hermaphrodite novel, and I cannot imagine having come to know a more gracious person or a more elegant writer. Last, Bill Eckerle, the best historian Fort Thomas, Kentucky, has ever produced, has been a mentor and friend since I first studied American history with him at Campbell County High School in 1970. Wilson!

Librarians all over the country gave me access to the archival sources that form the backbone of this manuscript. From the Manuscript Room at the Library of Congress, to the Houghton Library at Harvard, to the Schlesinger Library of American Women's History at Radcliffe College, to the Swarthmore College Peace Library, to the Yellow House Papers at Gardiner Public Library in Gardiner, Maine, and at Colby College, and to the rare book room at Brown

University (where librarian Mark Brown was personally concerned to see that I found what I needed), I traveled the Eastern seaboard, enjoying the resources of institutions with which I had no formal relationship. I am grateful to each of them. Nick Noyes and Stephanie Philbrick of the Maine Historical Society (where the Yellow House Papers housed at Colby College were relocated after I drafted this manuscript), Anne Davis at Gardiner Public Library, and Wendy Chmielewski at Swarthmore were especially kind. I confess that I begged for housing at Episcopal Divinity School in Cambridge so often that I promised to list the EDS housing office in the acknowledgments to this book. They deserve it.

I want to mention three friends who were great. My dear friend Barbara Rossing let me live with her for months at a time while I was working at the Houghton Library, and I also got to visit her at Holden Village. I enjoyed every minute of the time we spent together. Kris Kvam and Linda Shearing and I co-authored a book on Genesis 1–3 and the social construction of gender while I was working on this manuscript, and I can never repay them for the sisterhood. God knows we have shared enough dinky hotel rooms for a lifetime, but there is no way I would have missed a single one of our consultations. Kris and Linda: many thanks in honor and in memory of the bonds of womanhood.

Finally, I want to thank my family. Joye Patterson and Bill Nunn, Sr., took us on vacation, opened their house for many memorable weekends, and were always eager to talk and think about Julia Ward Howe. A stalwart crew gathered annually at Hatteras Island and shared a glorious cruise in Alaska. So to my Sandcastle/Vollendaam/Alien Nation housemates, thanks beyond measure go to Harold and Ruth Ziegler; Beulah Jean Combs; Cindy and Jim Combs; Dale and Pam Allen; Carole Ziegler and Evan and Teddy Roach; Susan, Scott, and Iris LeCates; and of course our matriarch Dona, who makes the best "bidkits, Gammaw." They say that 2003 is the summer of the martini (again!). Remembering our good friends Black Jack and Deacon, I dedicate this book to Bill Nunn: by your patience, by your love, by your insight, and by your sparkling wit, I am blessed.

Introduction

"There never were more devoted and tender parents. . . .
Every day and all day, people of all kinds and all nations
were coming to my father and mother for help, or comfort,
or pleasure; but the happy home was always there for
children."[1] —*Laura E. [Howe] Richards, 1911*

"Only a year ago, Julia was a New York belle. . . . now she is
a wife who lives only for her husband, and a mother who
would melt her very heart, were it needed, to give a drop of
nourishment to her child."[2] —*Samuel Gridley Howe, 1844*

"Is it selfish, is it egotistical to wish that others may love us,
take an interest in us, sympathize with us, in our maturer
age, as in our youth? . . . in giving life to others, do we lose
our own vitality and sink into dimness, nothingness, a living
death?"[3] —*Julia Ward Howe, circa 1846*

If the female inmates at the Charlestown, Massachusetts prison were excited to learn on April 23, 1865, that the evening's reading would be given by Julia Ward Howe, the elegant Boston matron who had written "The Battle Hymn of the Republic" three and one-half years earlier, no record of their enthusiasm remains. Julia's typical sermon on such occasions would have stirred few listeners, awash as it was with exhortations to "listen now for the music of silence." Rather than rail at their confinement, Julia would advise, the prisoners should learn to hear within it God's invitation to "lead you in green pastures, and beside still waters." In her mind, prison was an ideal setting in which to answer God's call. "This spiritual journey you can make within these walls, as well as any where—perhaps better," she insisted.[4]

This was easy advice for a free person to give, and undoubtedly more than a few of the inmates found it gratuitous. Julia's refined appearance and her delicate voice, with its precise diction and melodic delivery, hinted of a life of wealth and privilege that her listeners had never enjoyed and had hardly even imagined. What could such a woman know of prison? She had grown up in one of the wealthiest families in America, she had traveled widely, and her friends included famous figures like Charles Dickens, Oliver Wendell Holmes, and John Jacob Astor. The governor of Massachusetts had routinely dined in her home. Yet the best wisdom she could offer her Charlestown listeners was that they seek spiritual freedom within the very cells that confined them. How glib was that counsel for one who lived in the heady atmosphere of New England Brahmin culture, and how self-serving it seemed.

If the prisoners had only known Julia's story, however, they would have realized that she was preaching as much to herself as she was to them. No one knew better than she what life governed by an unyielding warden could be. Julia Ward Howe had spent her entire life in confinement, first by her controlling father and next by her tyrannical husband. Despite furious opposition from her husband and children, she had chosen to spend this evening—her twenty-second wedding anniversary—at the Charlestown prison rather than at home with her family. She knew her husband would excoriate her for courting publicity when she returned home, and she anticipated with dread what her second oldest daughter might add to the list of her mother's crimes. "I feel utterly paralyzed," Julia wrote in her diary that night.[5]

It was not the first time in her marriage that Julia had gone to bed alone and miserable. Like the inmates she had just visited, she was desperate to find autonomy and respectability in her life. Many days she despaired that the demands of marriage and motherhood had stripped her of her true self, and for years she struggled mightily to break the shackles that bound her to the private world of the home that Victorian women were expected to occupy. In time, however, Julia would achieve the public acclaim she so desired, becoming by the end of the nineteenth century one of the most famous and beloved women in the United States. In numerous books, including a wide-selling autobiography, and in countless newspaper articles and speeches, Julia had the opportunity to share with the nation the agonies she had endured on the road to celebrity. Yet the public account she gave of her life was an altogether different tale. Once Julia succeeded in escaping the confines of the home and launched a legendary career dedicated to social and political reforms, she worked tirelessly to depict herself as a genteel homemaker who lived to extol the joys of domesticity.

What does it mean for a woman to base her career on a rhapsodic description of motherhood—a description that meshed with popular notions of womanhood yet violated her lifelong efforts to achieve autonomy? This is one of many questions raised by the life of Julia Ward Howe, celebrated author of "The Battle Hymn of the Republic." The sheltered daughter of a wealthy New York family, Julia married the dashing Samuel Gridley Howe in 1843. She was twenty-three. By all accounts, it was a romantic match. Samuel—known as the "Chevalier" or simply "Chev," in deference to his volunteer work in the war of Greek independence—struck a majestic pose on the black horses he favored. He had won national fame for his work with the handicapped in Boston, particularly for the success he enjoyed with the blind and deaf Laura Bridgman. Handsome and well-known, at age forty-two Samuel had never been married. Once he met the elegant Julia Ward, however, his bachelor days came to an end.

Julia was pretty, bright, and accomplished. At the time of her marriage, she was already a published author. Their match was a social and romantic success, much envied. As the Howes set sail for Europe to enjoy an extended honeymoon, they seemed, as much as any other couple of the Victorian age, to be embarking on a fairy-tale marriage.

Unfortunately for both, such bliss was not to be. From the beginning, their marriage was a clash of wills. Chev expected his wife to be faithful to the traditional canons of domesticity. She should give up her writing and devote herself entirely to family life. Julia, on the other hand, wanted not only to continue publishing; she dreamed of becoming famous. Chev hoped that the arrival of children would convince Julia that her place was in the home, but the demands of six children only made her more anxious to enter public life. She wanted to write poems, plays, philosophical treatises, and works of theology. She wanted to give lectures and to receive the same kind of respect and adulation accorded Chev's renowned male friends like Henry Wadsworth Longfellow, Theodore Parker, and Charles Sumner. She wanted, in short, the one thing that her husband was determined she ought not have: a life of her own, separate from his.

Not surprisingly, the Howes' marriage was tumultuous, marked by daily hard feelings, lifelong grudges, and occasional outbursts of temper so severe that each feared for the other's sanity. Gradually, Julia reentered public life. In 1854, without Chev's knowledge, she published a book of verse entitled *Passion-Flowers*. The next year, her play *The World's Own* was produced in New York, and in 1857 she produced another volume of verse entitled *Words for the Hour*. In 1859, she published a travel account of a journey to Cuba. In 1861, while visiting Federal troops in Washington with Chev as a part of his work with the Sanitary Commission, she stumbled into fame by penning the words to the soon acclaimed "Battle Hymn of the Republic." Later in the war, despite Chev's opposition, Julia began giving lectures on philosophical topics. In 1870, she reached a turning point, finding herself converted both to the cause of woman suffrage and to international peace. Julia would spend the rest of her life in the public sphere, working for a variety of social reforms and becoming one of the most famous and revered women in the United States. Chev never reconciled himself to this turn of events, but his death in 1876 made it easier for her to put any lingering misgivings aside.

In the pages that follow, I will trace two key themes in the life of Julia Ward Howe: her desire for autonomy and her desire for respectability. Family dynamics within the Howe household provide a rich source for just such an examination. Julia's childhood and early married life were marked by her attempts to establish herself as an agent independent of the men who ruled as head of her home: first, her father, and then, her husband. No woman of the Victorian age found it easy to establish an autonomous existence apart from the men in her life. Moreover, once Julia was married and had children, she found, as primary caregivers always have, that parenting involved sacrifice and a relinquishing of focus on the self.

Other factors also stood in the way of her pursuit of autonomy. Julia Ward Howe passionately wanted to establish herself as a literary figure; yet, she came of age at a time in American history when such an ambition was unconventional and even unseemly for women. Proper women confined themselves to the domestic sphere. They did not openly publish books nor did they expose themselves before "promiscuous" audiences containing men as well as women in order to lecture or to read poetry. Such activities were immodest, even scandalous. If Julia wanted to be respected as an author (or, as many nineteenth-century Americans would have said, an "authoress"), she would have to buck convention.

She would also have to battle her husband, as well as find ways to reconcile her children to the reality that, though she loved them, she needed an identity apart from them—no matter how angry that made their father or how much it disrupted family harmony. And in the midst of all that, Julia was determined to protect and maintain her own and her family's public respectability. Despite the literary ambition that distinguished her, Julia Ward Howe was in many ways a thoroughly conventional woman, proud of her family heritage and concerned to maintain her own position in polite society. She was also exceptionally ambitious: she wanted fame *and* respectability, autonomy *and* public acceptance.

In the years prior to Chev's death, Julia's desire for autonomy—her insistence on finding and using her own voice—dominated her literary work. The poetry and plays that she wrote in the 1840s and 1850s were, for those who knew how to read them, remarkably personal; indeed, they revealed her innermost agonies and struggles. The philosophical essays she composed in the 1860s were no less concerned with issues that loomed large in her relationship with Chev—titles like "Limitation" and "Polarity" described her marriage as well as philosophical concepts—but such works appeared cooler, less emotional than her earlier writings. After Chev died in 1876 and Julia turned to the lecture circuit for her income, her public utterances continued to be more generalized and less obviously personal, though anyone who knew her well could read between the lines.

Similar dynamics appeared in the voluminous private papers Julia generated. In the 1840s and 1850s, her correspondence to her sisters and her husband was full of pain and frustration. The tone was frequently impassioned and the details exceedingly intimate. Her unpublished literary work from the period (poems and a sensational novel tracing the life of a sexually desirable hermaphrodite) recorded powerful inner experiences—the lure of sexual desire, the agony of hating one's husband, and the fear of losing one's self. Diary entries in the 1860s and 1870s continued to disclose scenes of fierce family warfare—of children loyal to their father and furious with their mother, of a wife so distraught with her husband that every moment in his home was filled with agony—but after Chev's death in 1876, the tone both of Julia's diary and of her letters to family members moderated. The days of pouring out her heart (and giving the details of the latest fracas at the Howe home) had largely ended.

The nation's political climate had changed as well. By the turn of the century, many of the rights for women for which Julia had struggled had become attainable. Access to college and graduate education, openings in the professions, equal guardianship of children, opportunities to speak and write publicly—all these things that had seemed unreachable to Julia in 1840 were available to women in 1900. Woman suffrage had not yet been established, but the grave danger of appearing unwomanly simply for publishing a book had passed.[6] By that time, Julia had little reason to worry about her reputation. Americans at the beginning of the twentieth century lionized Julia Ward Howe as the most gracious and cultured of women, as a role model for others, not a pariah. Ironically, Julia's daughters would feel chagrined not because their mother was a public figure—a fact that initially had caused them some embarrassment—but because they were unable to match her literary and political accomplishments.

Once Julia's public reputation was firmly established, it became increasingly possible for her to rewrite those early days of struggle and to cover them with respectability. While her daughters or granddaughters took charge of the everyday details of her home, Julia was free to establish herself as an expert on domesticity and to give advice on housekeeping to the many women who listened to her lectures or read her speeches. Fewer and fewer people remained who had personally known her husband; to later generations, Samuel Gridley Howe was a heroic figure of the past, not a mercurial personality with whom Julia persistently clashed. Removed from the heat of their encounters, Julia could reinvent herself, casting herself as the prototypical Victorian wife and mother.

Given the frustrations that marriage and motherhood caused her, we might expect that in championing women's rights, Julia would have stressed women's autonomy, defining women as persons valuable in themselves, apart from their traditional domestic roles. Admittedly, such advocacy would have gone against the cultural grain. The Victorian era proclaimed a doctrine of "separate spheres" that relegated women to the domestic realm.[7] The public world of business and politics was understood as men's world—a savage and brutal place, ruled by cutthroat competition. Only the fittest men were thought to prevail. And in the midst of their worldly success, these men found themselves brutalized, inured to the gentler virtues of Christian love and compassion. The remedy to such barbarism, according to nineteenth-century wisdom, was "true womanhood." Protected from the fierce world outside, the Victorian woman was an "angel of the home," ready to immerse her brothers, sons, and husband in the civilizing graces of Christian love as soon as they left the public world and returned to her nurturing arms. The key to this cult of domesticity was thus the assumption that women best communicated their moral character by confining their activities to the private sphere of the home.

Revisionist historians have cautioned that, while the doctrine of separate spheres may have functioned as a reigning ideology in the Victorian age, it did not in fact describe the lifestyle that vast numbers of women actually led. For the millions of working-class women who earned a living in factory or domestic positions or who labored in the fields, the doctrine of separate spheres could only have described an ideal life beyond their reach. Although they bore the burdens of the cult of domesticity—most careers were closed to them, and they could neither vote nor run for public office—such women enjoyed few of its rewards. They could emulate true womanhood by becoming good wives and loving mothers, but they could only rarely achieve the affluence that the notion of separate spheres presupposed.

If women of the limited economic means *literally* could not afford to confine themselves to their own sphere, there were numerous middle and upper-class women who *emotionally* found confinement in the home too stifling to bear. The reform fervor typical of nineteenth-century American evangelicalism created a distinctive piety that combined perfectionism with a commitment to social justice.[8] American Christians assumed that it was their task to mold their culture into a social order so attuned to the divine will that the disparity between heaven and earth would gradually dissolve, and the kingdom of God would dawn. Longing to take their place in the great work of the millennial age, a succession of relatively affluent women would leave the home to labor with their brothers on behalf of an array of reforms such as abolitionism, temperance, peace, and woman suffrage.

Women who entered the public sphere were, by that very act, defying the cult of domesticity. Frequently they justified their rebellion by arguing that it was necessary to apply their influence outside the sphere of the home if the American public were to receive the full benefit of their moral wisdom. Women who wrote books championing the canons of domesticity typically invoked this strategy. Such books were so prevalent that they formed a recognizable genre in the Victorian age, but the very act of publishing a book—even if the book were a litany of the joys of domesticity, and even if the author hid her identity behind a pseudonym—was a violation of the doctrine of separate spheres. Ironically, then, a genre intended to champion domesticity simultaneously undermined it. As Mary Kelley has shown in the case of Harriet Beecher Stowe, female authors were not necessarily unaware of the paradox. Stowe, while not rejecting woman's sphere, chafed under its constraints and used her literary success to gain power within her own family.[9]

But not all women who entered the public sphere did so under the guise of supporting the cult of domesticity. Some women explicitly rejected it. Dorothy Bass has argued that, as they worked for peace, the abolition of slavery, and universal suffrage, the women associated with the New England Non-Resistance Society not only insisted that men and women were social and political equals, but also denied the predominant notion that women's "nature" inclined them to be domestic and peace-loving, while men's "nature" pushed them into aggression and worldliness. In light of those convictions, Sarah and Angelina Grimke endured the wrath of the Connecticut clergy in their 1837 antislavery lecture series, defying social convention by addressing "promiscuous audiences" of both men and women.[10] After the Civil War, some reformers rejected use of the separate-spheres doctrine in the cause of woman suffrage. These reformers advocated extending the vote to women on the basis of *human* rights, not on the grounds of the peculiar duties incumbent upon women in their roles as mothers and wives. After all, these reformers noted, every woman did not marry, nor did every woman become a mother. Yet the fundamental human rights of liberty and equality remained.[11]

Thus, women who entered the public sphere had the choice of appealing to the cult of domesticity or of rejecting it when they strove to explain what had prompted them to violate the convention of separate spheres. In her career as a reformer, Julia Ward Howe seemed to champion traditional notions of the sublimity of motherhood. Yet there were more radical elements in her rhetoric. In her peace activism, for example, she theorized that women were superior to men, because the nurturing love instinctive to them as mothers was truer to the character of God than was the aggression typical of men. She concluded that civilization's only hope for evolutionary progress was in allowing women to enter public life, where their divinely inspired predilection to love others would gradually extinguish the male propensity for violence and war.

Casting God as a mother was a potentially subversive move, and certainly, Julia hoped that her rhetoric about motherhood would make people rethink their prejudices about gender conventions. Nevertheless, in characterizing women as cheerful matrons overflowing with kindness, Julia was hardly offering a theory that would free women from being defined by the roles of mother and wife. Moreover, she was describing motherhood in ways that ran counter to her own experience. Julia loved her children, but she railed repeatedly against the loss of autonomy that birthing, breast-feeding, and raising six children cost her. Chev rejoiced in the children, believing with each new arrival that Julia would at last resign herself to her exalted position as wife and mother and find fulfillment in living only for the family. Julia was never convinced. "It is a blessed thing to be a mother," she noted in 1847, "but there are bounds to all things, and no woman is under any obligation to sacrifice the whole of her existence to the mere act of bringing children into the world. I cannot help considering the excess of this as materializing and degrading to a woman whose spiritual nature has any strength. Men, on the contrary, think it glorification enough for a woman to be a wife and mother in any way, and upon any terms."[12]

Since motherhood for her was as much an exercise in self-denial as in fulfillment, it was significant that Julia chose, in her public rhetoric, to present motherhood in lofty, majestic images. Undoubtedly practical considerations were involved. Julia Ward Howe wanted to shape the social customs as well contribute to the literary arts of American culture. Quite simply, she sought power. As Carolyn Chute has pointed out, "Power is the ability to take one's place in whatever discourse is essential to action and the right to have one's part matter."[13] Victorian society, however, was not about to cede that type of authority to women. Victorians could not perceive a woman as ambitious and powerful and still consider her ladylike and respectable. Ambition was the antithesis of respectability. Julia Ward Howe would not sacrifice her ambition, nor could she afford to relinquish her respectability. If she wanted a public hearing, she would have to couch her views in language that did not reject the traditional gender roles dictated by the dominant cult of domesticity.

But Julia did have considerable control over the way she framed such a discussion. She toyed with two different models of the new woman. The first model, which Julia ultimately rejected, was that of the exceptional woman, who through her own considerable abilities acquired gifts and graces that crossed gender lines. More accomplished than her peers, the exceptional woman was an isolated individual who dared to impinge on the male world of privilege simply because she was talented enough to do so. Such an individual threatened the status of other women, as well as that of men. In the initial years of her marriage, Julia was attracted to this model because she regarded herself as unusually gifted. But the model of the exceptional woman had real drawbacks. It depended on the peculiar talents of an individual woman, talents that others might characterize as "manly." That was the last way Julia wanted to think of herself. Moreover, as she became involved in the woman suffrage movement in the 1860s, for the first time Julia joined with other women in a common cause of gender uplift that she was convinced would benefit humanity as a whole. The paradigm of the exceptional woman was useless to describe this vision.

Accordingly, Julia turned to a second understanding of gender, a model that viewed maleness and femaleness simply as two different poles of human experience. In this view, God created maleness and femaleness as counterpoints to one another. Together the two genders were an outpouring of the divine nature, designed to work in partnership with one another for the development of the human race. Though men and women were different from one another, neither maleness nor femaleness was a static entity. Instead, united in purpose and resolve, men and women could learn from one another and expand their own experiences and abilities. While key biological features would never change—women would never father children, and men would never give birth—emotionally and intellectually women and men could come to appreciate and incorporate the rich realities of the other. In this model, the new woman was not an isolated individual, nor did her accomplishments make her "manly." Neither did the new woman set herself in opposition to man. Rather, she worked to create a world in which all women were free to explore the fullest expression of their natures, so they could offer to men the most abundant resources for their own evolution. Fully united in partnership with men, the new woman sought human progress, not mere personal aggrandizement. Together, man and woman could be transfigured into images more reflective of their shared divine origins.

This model of gender relations, Julia believed, would allow her to extol the traditional virtues of womanhood without limiting women to conventional gender roles. It also permitted her to argue that women's rights were not in opposition to men's prerogatives but rather a complement to them, since it was only in mutual growth that man and woman enjoyed progress as God intended. Still, the clash between Julia's public, more theoretical descriptions of womanhood, particularly of the experience of being a mother, and her private lamentations about marriage and motherhood, were striking. In the body of this book, I will examine in more detail the circumstances that prompted her to pursue a public career by championing a form of domesticity that she at times characterized as a "living death." I will draw upon themes from Julia's life and her literary work as they illuminate the interplay between her private and public descriptions of the joys and sorrows of being a woman in the Victorian age.

I will also call upon the work of Julia's children, whose writings about their parents constituted a virtual cottage industry. Every one of Julia's five children who lived to adulthood became authors. Three of the daughters—Flossy, Laura, and Maud—lived well into the twentieth century and published on a variety of topics. Laura alone produced more than eighty books. But a favorite theme that each repeatedly explored was the Howe family. From 1894 to 1944, these three women produced more than two dozen volumes on their mother, father, and other family members, with titles ranging from the whimsical *Flossy's Play Days* to the stultifying *Uncle Sam Ward and His Circle*.[14] They also managed the vast collection of private family papers produced by years of correspondence, journal entries, and rough drafts of literary projects. Ultimately, the final word on their mother's character—and, for that matter, on their father's—belonged not to Julia or Chev, but to their children, particularly to their daughters.

By the time Julia's daughters were adults, the question of their mother's autonomy was not a burning issue. To them, she was a legend. No work was necessary to establish her as a public figure with a distinct voice. The question of respectability, on the other hand, *did* matter to them. In presenting to the larger world the image of family life that they wished to perpetuate, the children searched for ways to describe their parents that would capture the high points and disguise the enmity. They wanted to tell noble truths, to uplift their readers, and to conceal the unlovely. They were not braggarts—Laura would deliberately exclude scenes from her autobiography that might have appeared boastful—but they did write with moral purpose.[15] As Flossy put it, "the memory of heroic deeds, of noble sayings, is the most precious inheritance of mankind. . . . To pass on to our descendants the lighted torch received from our predecessors . . . is for us an imperative duty and a splendid privilege."[16]

But before Julia's daughters could pass on their sacred memories, they had to sort them out. Growing up, the Howe children had found themselves caught between their father and their mother, determined to love both, but puzzled and pained at the tumult that marked their parents' relationship. Naturally, the children took sides from time to time, blaming one parent or the other for various imperfections. Those dynamics are part of every family. What was highly unusual, however, was the Howe children's access, once they determined to become family historians, to an array of letters, poems, and diaries that revealed their parents' innermost secrets. Laura began working on her father's papers the year after his death in 1876;[17] by 1886, she had acquired her deceased sister Julia Romana's correspondence and had read as well some of her mother's most sensitive letters.[18] After Julia's death in 1910, her papers went to Laura. Sisters Maud and Flossy would collaborate with Laura in writing their mother's biography, and brother Harry agreed to pay a private secretary to transcribe and type the family archives (a work of years, not months!).

As a result, Julia's daughters/biographers knew as much about their mother as any children could possibly know. They had their own memories; they had the benefit of discussing those memories among themselves; and they had access to tens of thousands of pages of private documents that replayed significant events from innumerable angles. They could compare what their father, their mother, and her siblings thought and said to each other over the course of many decades. They could read about themselves, too, in those documents. And in and through all the words and the many perspectives, the Howe daughters wove their own family story. It was an uplifting narrative of service to humanity, of obstacles overcome, and of enduring parental devotion. Despair, anger, resentment, and fear played no significant role; in her daughters' telling, Julia Ward Howe was not merely respectable, but positively inspirational. When the 1916 biography upon which her daughters collaborated won the Pulitzer Prize as the "best American biography teaching patriotic and unselfish services to the people, illustrated by an eminent example," they could consider themselves successful.[19]

In the chapters ahead, I hope to portray the heady process by which Julia Ward Howe's search for autonomy and respectability produced a literary tradition that established her as an American icon. The archival materials, united with the many books the Howes published about themselves, afford us the rare privilege of examining two different sides of Julia Ward Howe: her private reality and her public persona. More than that, we also glimpse the ways in which Julia's children experienced her and can view, as well, the fascinating process by which they sought to create a suitably heroic public image of their mother. Her children's desires to celebrate their remarkable family in such a way as to resolve—as much for themselves as for others—the deep divisions that had tortured their parents' lives and disrupted their own is as much the subject of this book as is Julia Ward Howe.

This study of Julia Ward Howe, then, traces the ways in which Julia (and later, her children) struggled to invent sufficiently celebratory public images of themselves. In giving a hearing to Julia's private voice and in listening as well to her family's responses, I have written an intellectual and cultural biography. I have highlighted those aspects of Julia's life related to her own and her family's quest to see Julia Ward Howe established as an eminent public figure. In particular, I have focused on the ways in which the Howes molded more complex private realities into the public image of a noble Victorian family. Julia's story illustrates dramatically the obstacles Victorian women faced in their search for political power and personal autonomy.

I hope that readers will resonate with the frenetic lifestyle of a nineteenth-century woman who struggled, as women continue to do in a new millennium, to "have it all." As one hard-working and perpetually sleep-deprived author/ wife/mother in Spokane advised college women recently, "You *can* have it all— but it will kill you."[20] The dilemmas that Julia faced—how to be her own person and yet belong to others too, how to raise children and carve out a life with her partner without imperiling her career—are all too familiar to contemporary Americans. What is intriguing to observe in the life of Julia Ward Howe are both the particular compromises she made in the choice between autonomy and respectability and the concentrated efforts she and her children expended to hide those compromises from public attention. The Howes were masters of "spin" before politicians had invented the term. But even their eminence could not spare them from experiencing the kinds of doubt and guilt that typical American families endure in every age. What made the Howes special was their fierce denial of such ordinary human failures and their astonishing determination to conceal them.

Given my desire to examine such issues, it is inevitable that my focus is selective in this biography. For example, I do not provide a day-by-day or even a year-by-year account of the life of Julia Ward Howe; rather, I trace critical themes that characterized her life. Nor do I provide a systematic examination of Julia's literary works. Instead, I cull from her writings the elements relevant to the story that I am telling, highlighting family dynamics as well as discrepancies between public and private realities. Finally, in most instances I will not interrupt the flow of the narrative to consider debates in the secondary literature regarding the issues raised in the text. Endnotes provide references and further information of interest to scholars, but in the narrative itself, I will attempt to construct a story line that allows the Howes to speak for themselves. The Howes' testimonies to their conflicts over Julia's quest for autonomy were candid, explicit, and—given the vigor and wit typical of the family—unforgettable. More than discussions of the scholarly literature could ever hope to do, the Howes' voices bring to life the myths and the realities of the Victorian age.[21] Available materials on gender in nineteenth-century America are voluminous. In the pages ahead, I will not attempt to provide comprehensive bibliographical data on secondary texts. Rather, I will limit my citations of secondary texts to materials quoted or borrowed.

In examining the life of Julia Ward Howe, then, we see not only the troubled gender dynamics that she negotiated as a Victorian women; we also glimpse the remarkable ways in which she and her children managed their own history. The Julia Ward Howe that we know today—indeed, our understanding of her entire family—was the careful creation of Howe family members. In the end, at least in their telling, she had it all: autonomy, respectability, refinement, and the acclaim of a grateful nation.

Chapter One

Julia Ward Howe was born on May 27, 1819, to a wealthy New York family. Her mother died when she was five, and her father, a strict Calvinist, assumed control of the family's domestic life. From then until her husband's death in 1876, Julia would be under the influence of men who dominated her. Like other Victorian women in similar situations, she learned to assert her own wishes by subverting those of her superior's; that is, she learned to listen meekly to orders and then quietly to do as she wished. Not until she was in her fifties would she find a voice that allowed her to speak with authority—rather than at her father or husband's sufferance—regarding her own views and desires. At that, she was lucky. Most Victorian women never found that voice.

Two other significant traits characterized Julia's childhood: isolation and intellectual seriousness. Her father secluded her from the wider world, permitting little social interaction outside her extended family. Julia received much of her schooling at home from private tutors. Though she had three rambunctious brothers who longed to introduce her to fashionable New York society, her father largely confined her activities to the family home. Moreover, he expected her to be serious, not frivolous or playful. As Julia's own daughters later observed, when she was nine Julia's "dolls were taken away from her, that she might realize more the dignity of her position as 'Miss Ward,' the eldest daughter and sister. She was always addressed as 'Miss Ward' by servants and masters; and tried hard to be dignified, poor little girl!"[1]

Julia eventually applied her seriousness to intellectual matters. Writing poetry, reading philosophy, learning foreign languages, and studying music were acceptable outlets for a precocious girl. She read Paley's *Moral Philosophy* and Bunyan's *Pilgrim's Progress* (both at age nine), enjoyed her father's excellent art gallery, and received the best musical education available in New York City. Instead of playing with dolls, she wrote poetry. Urged to take herself seriously, she learned to cherish her intellectual gifts. In her own words, she developed "a sense of literary responsibility which never left me, and which I must consider to have formed a part of my spiritual makeup."[2]

In short, Julia's father dominated her early life. He isolated her from the larger social world and urged her to regard her intellectual pursuits with great seriousness. All of these themes—domination by powerful men, isolation from women outside her family, and an earnest intellectualism—would mark her later life as well.

CHILDHOOD DAYS: LIFE WITH FATHER

Julia was the fourth child born to Samuel and Julia Cutler Ward. Her two older brothers were Samuel and Henry, and her older sister Julia died just before her own birth, "leaving me," she explained, "her name and the dignity of eldest daughter." The family referred to the departed daughter as "the first little Julia." A brother named Francis Marion (the family was descended from the great revolutionary hero "Swamp Fox") and a sister named Louisa followed. In autumn 1824, Julia Cutler died giving birth to her daughter Annie. Married at sixteen, Julia Cutler was just twenty-seven when she died, having brought seven children into the world.

Though she was only five and a half when her mother died, Julia retained vivid memories of her "first and dearest of friends." She remembered how her mother taught her to sew, and how she chided Julia when she struggled to say "mother" rather than "muzzer." She remembered, too, that her mother had been an intelligent, refined woman, devoted to literary arts. "She had been a pupil of Mrs. Elizabeth Graham, of saintly memory," Julia explained, "and had inherited from her own mother a taste for intellectual pursuits. She was especially fond of poetry and a few lovely poems of hers remain to show that she was no stranger to its sacred domain."[3]

Julia cherished the memory of a family trip taken when she was four. Hoping to improve Julia Cutler's health, her older sister Eliza accompanied her and the children on a journey up the Hudson River. From Albany they went overland to Niagara Falls. During the trip, her mother took Julia to meet Red Jacket, a Native American chief. Little Julia impulsively ran up to Red Jacket and threw her arms around his neck—a gesture of familiarity that the dignified Red Jacket appreciated not in the least. The Ward children and their mother spent the summer before her death at a picturesque estate outside New York City. Julia recalled that summer as an especially happy period. A tutor from the city gave Julia and her brother Marion French lessons in an elegant green bower, and often Julia and her mother took walks in the garden, where her mother picked flowers that she would arrange "with great taste."[4]

When they returned to the city, tragedy struck. Though Julia, in her own autobiography, remarked only that "one bitter morning, I awoke to hear the words, 'Julia, your mother is dead,'" her own daughters described the occasion in more detail. Given the Wards' adherence to the doctrines of election and predestination—a faith Julia later described as "the savage theology of the old school" with its "undivine Deity of vengeance and hate"[5]—the impending death of Julia Cutler raised considerable apprehensions. "Her life," Julia's daughters declared, "had been pure, happy, and unselfish; yet her last hours were full of anguish. Raised in the strict tenets of Evangelical piety, she was oppressed with terror concerning the fate of her soul. . . . It is piteous to read of the sufferings of this innocent creature, as described by her mourning family; piteous, too, to realize, by the light of to-day, that she was almost literally *prayed to death*."[6]

Julia's father Samuel was so distraught at his wife's death that it was days before he would consent even to hold the infant whose delivery had been the occasion for such grief. Unwilling to remain in the house without his wife, Samuel moved the family to Bond Street into one of the finest houses in the city. Julia Cutler's sister Eliza agreed to look after the children. Samuel's father and his brothers Henry and John soon bought houses on Bond Street within a block of Samuel's. This extended family was the basis of Julia's social life for years to come. As she explained, "the early years of my youth were passed in seclusion not only of home life, but of a home life most carefully and jealously guarded from all that might be represented in the orthodox trinity of evil, the world, the flesh, and the devil. My father had become deeply imbued with the religious ideas of the time. He dreaded for the children the dissipations of fashionable society, and even the risks of general intercourse with the unsanctimonious." Samuel concluded that six children, with the help of an extended family, ought to provide company for one another, and tutors could take care of their educational needs.[7]

Eventually, Samuel did allow the children to attend neighborhood schools, although Julia was not permitted, as she wished, to enroll in dance school. As the years passed, Samuel's notions of religious duties increased. By the age of seven, Julia had attended two operas, but after them, she was not to visit the theatre again until she was an adult, because her father decided that the theatre was too worldly. This dictum came as a great disappointment. When Julia had learned to read, one of the first works she had perused was a tale called "The Iroquois Bride," which she had promptly dramatized for her siblings. She had played the part of the bride, and her brother Marion had been her lover. Both had climbed on a stool and stabbed each other, in accordance with the plot.

That bit of drama, however, "was not approved by Authority, and the book was promptly taken away." Nevertheless, Julia's enthusiasm for drama was undiminished. At age nine, she wrote her first play. She also found herself eagerly anticipating the occasional concert and oratorio, performed by a local musical association, which interrupted her daily school routine. She discovered, however, that an "intense melancholy" invariably seized her after those performances. Returning to her accustomed isolation was distressing. When her musical training had advanced to the point that her tutor advised that she would benefit from playing trios and quartets with other instruments, a similar depression would follow those performances. "The reaction from this pleasure," she contended, "was very painful, and induced at times a visitation of morbid melancholy which threatened to affect my health."[8]

One safe outlet for this discontent was intellectual activity. Julia was not supposed to play with dolls, but she was allowed to write. This she did with great enthusiasm and seriousness of purpose. On at least one occasion she attempted to convince her younger sisters to give up the childish game they were playing and join her in improving their minds by composing verse.[9] The solemnity with which she regarded intellectual endeavors such as writing is evident in the following note that she wrote at the age of eight to her cousin Henry Ward, who was suffering from a childhood sickness:

> I hear with regret that you are sick, and it is necessary as ever that you
> should trust in God; love him, dear Henry, and you will see Death
> approaching with joy. Oh, what are earthly things, which we must lose
> when we die—to our immortal souls which never die! I cannot bear the
> thought of anybody who is dying without a knowledge of Christ. We may
> die before tomorrow, and therefore, we ought to be prepared for death.[10]

Obviously Julia was a precocious eight year old who had appropriated theological doctrine and rhetoric, but it is evident, in addition, that when she put pen to paper she had a strong sense of her own authority. Her letter to her ten-year-old cousin Henry was indistinguishable from a letter that his pastor might have sent him. She did not ask how Henry felt, or express any longing that he might get better, as a note of personal concern to a first cousin might do; rather, she took the occasion of Henry's illness to write an elegy to death. The focus of the letter was herself, and her exalted notions of death. As her daughters later commented, "this was scarcely cheering for Henry," but at least he was to live for another half century before he had to make the preparations for eternity that Julia had urged upon him in childhood.[11]

In 1831, Julia composed a book of poetry for her father. In dedicating the volume to her "beloved father" and beseeching him to "LET ME BE THINE!" she again displayed a facility with words and a sense of the importance about her work:

> Expect not to find in these juvenile productions the delicacy and grace
> which pervaded the writings of that dear parent who is now in glory. I am
> indeed conscious of the many faults they contain, but my object in present-
> ing you with these (original) poems, has been to give you a little memorial
> of my early life, and I entreat you to remember that they were written in the
> eleventh, twelfth, and thirteenth years of my life.[12]

For Julia, her poems were a testimony to her life. She took them seriously, as she did all her intellectual endeavors. She entered a neighborhood school at age nine, but left at sixteen so that she could "study in good earnest." Her discipline was remarkable. Devoting much of her time to language study, relieved by intervals of practicing instrumental and vocal music, she studied German (she was already fluent in French) until she was "able to read with ease the masterpieces of Goethe and Schiller."[13]

It is difficult to overstate the importance with which Julia regarded these studies. To avoid distractions, she would tie herself to a chair and give orders that she was not to be set free until the hour she had previously designated. This sense of urgency never left her. As her daughters observed, "She was always a student. . . . The chain of habit once formed was never broken, and study was meat and drink to her. Her 'precious time' (which we children saucily abbreviated to 'P.T.') was as real a thing to us as sunrise."[14] Julia's father encouraged her intellectual development by hiring expensive tutors, providing a large assortment of books, and purchasing the best works of art available in New York City. Consequently, intellectual endeavor, particularly writing, became essential to Julia's sense of self. As her daughters asserted, "we have seen that from her earliest childhood Julia Ward's need of expressing herself in verse was imperative. Every emotion, deep or trivial, must take metrical shape; she laughed, wept, prayed—even stormed—in verse." Although women writers were rare in the early nineteenth century, Julia nevertheless developed in childhood "the vision of some great work or works which I myself should give the world. I would write the novel or play of the age."[15] From her earliest memories, she regarded literary expression as not only necessary to her identity, but as also comprising what was most valuable in her.

If Samuel Ward's parenting helped form Julia as a literary creature, there were other parts of his personality that imperiled her aspirations, because it was in her father's home that Julia experienced what it was to be dominated by the male head of the house. As her daughters pointed out in their biography of Julia, "Mr. Ward's anxious care for his children's own welfare extended to every branch of their conduct."[16] His children chaffed at this domination. Julia's brother Marion wrote their brother Sam in 1838, complaining: "Father's peculiarities are becoming more and more striking. Yesterday we were in high glee, singing, laughing, talking, when in comes Father. His first words were 'Henry, my son, take off that cap. You may admire yourself in it, but it's too black-guardish for me. Children, stand from before the fire. I don't see why you can't sit down quietly, instead of standing all together on the rug.'" The effect of such decrees was deadly. As Marion complained, "The Atlantic Ocean could not have thrown more cold water on us."[17]

In addition, the Ward children felt cramped by Samuel's insistence on separating them from fashionable society. Julia's older brother Sam once had a bitter argument with his father over the elder Samuel's refusal to "keep in view the importance of the social tie." When his father scoffed that he indeed gave the social tie little account, Sam blazed back, "I will die in defense of it!" This rejoinder struck his father as so humorous that he repeated it later to a friend: "He will die in defense of the social tie, indeed!"[18]

Undoubtedly the remark was not nearly as funny to Samuel Ward's children. As his religious conservatism increased, Samuel emptied his cellar of dozens of bottles of expensive wine, serving only water at his table. He gave up cigars and ordered his sons to quit smoking as well. As young men, Sam, Henry, and Marion were freer than their sisters to escape their father's domination. They could and did enter fashionable society. Sam spent four years in Europe unfettered by his father's supervision and confessed to having enjoyed "various social, artistic, literary, scientific, gastronomic, and bacchic grades."[19] After returning to New York, he insured his independence by marrying a daughter of the John Jacob Astor family. For Julia and her sisters, however, there was no escape. Samuel had decreed that they remain at home, socializing with their own family, and at home they remained. Julia found this isolation painful, recalling: "I greatly coveted an enlargement of intercourse with the world." Stymied at that ambition, she turned to her studies. "I lived, indeed, much in my books," she explained. But expanding her experience through literature was not enough. "I seemed to myself," she concluded, "like a young damsel of olden time, shut up within an enchanted castle. And I must say that my dear father, with all his noble generosity and overweening affection, sometimes appeared to me as my jailer."[20]

Her father was not the only one who tried to run Julia's life. Her bookishness provided a battleground on which her brothers could dispute their father's authority. They thought Julia should devote more time to mothering her sisters than pursuing her studies, and they criticized their father for indulging Julia in her literary whims. In a letter written in July 1838, Sam upbraided his father for compelling Julia to remain with him in New York while her sisters summered in Newport. If her father had taken Julia under his wing earlier, Sam complained, she would never have formed such excessive habits of study. Her sisters would surely develop their own eccentricities unless Julia became a mother to them. "Julia writes all day and half the night," Sam complained. "One morning she wrote, in 5 hours, 16 pages. She is murdering herself. Yet she is forced to do this. In the tedium and heat of a large solicitude her restless mind must be at work." The answer, Sam concluded, was to send Julia to Newport and let her become for her younger sisters the mother that they needed.[21]

Julia's father sent her to Newport, but her behavior there proved no different than it was in New York. Her brother Marion wrote Sam, complaining: "Jule has locked herself up in her room this morning, to write, for how long I know not. This should not be, and yet she says it is very hard to be constantly interrupted by the girls. She will never be of service to them until she makes their improvement the first object of her life. Much does she seem revolving over some plan for literary distinction, but this, I hope, as she grows older and wiser, she will lay aside."[22]

On other issues, however, there was no question that Samuel Ward, Sr., was in charge. Before Julia left for Newport that summer, he made sure she was learning to cook. As Julia explained to her Aunt Annie, "By a strange and inexplicable caprice Papa took it into his head that I must make some pies. Alas, Auntie can perhaps sympathize with me in the miseries of pie making, of kneading and rolling out paste, or stewing, sweetening, stirring and worse still, tasting the gooseberries, of daubing one's self with butter, lard and flour—hands, face and clothes, of tearing the paste to pieces in trying to transfer it from the board to the dish!" The only consolation to be obtained, Julia concluded, was "that though I made them, Father will have to eat them and not I."[23]

In bowing to her father's will—a will that concerned itself with the smallest details of household life—Julia became accustomed to the caprice with which he wielded his authority. She learned that those in power could be self-centered, acting on their own wishes without considering hers. At meals, for example, Julia sat next to her father at the table. He "would often take her right hand in his left, half unconsciously, and hold it for some time, continuing the while to eat his dinner. Julia, her right hand imprisoned, would sit dinnerless, but never dreamed of remonstrating."[24] Thus, Julia developed a habit of surrendering her will to male authority, a habit that would later form a crucial dynamic in her relationship with her husband.

An even more painful exertion of capricious parental authority occurred at her brother Sam's wedding. Julia idolized her older brother and was excited to be chosen first bridesmaid when he married Emily Astor in 1838. The wedding was a grand affair, followed by an elaborate supper and an elegant ball. Resplendent in a dress of white moiré, a material of the most recent fashion, Julia was looking forward to a long night of dancing. Alas, she reported, "the evening was at its height when my father gravely admonished me that it was time to go home." Bitterly disappointed, she nevertheless left the merry assembly, acknowledging, as she later put it, "paternal authority was without appeal in those days." On an occasion after Sam's wedding, her father consented to take Julia to an evening party. Surrounded by suitors eager to talk to her, she had no choice but to break off the evening when Samuel summoned her to leave. As she turned, however, she waved goodbye over her shoulder to the most ardent of her admirers. After they had been home for a few days, Samuel mimicked her gesture, mocking her as flirtatious.[25]

If there was no way to appeal male authority, however, there were ways to subvert it. Julia learned this lesson early and never forgot it. When men commanded and would not accept any debate on the matter, it was always possible to nod obediently and then do as she pleased (at least, until she was discovered!). Her brothers had pioneered such tactics on several occasions. When their father told them to give up cigars, for example, they never smoked again—where he could see them. Unbeknownst to him, however, they continued to smoke as well as to drink alcohol outside the home.[26] Julia watched and learned from her brothers, seeking to discover ways to assert her autonomy while living in a household in which authority belonged to the patriarch.

At times, she could escape into her books, but on other occasions, she felt compelled to exert her will in the world of action. Her brothers repeatedly asked their father to allow them to introduce Julia into society, but always he refused. At last, in an event that her daughters described as "singularly characteristic of both father and daughter," Julia determined to have her own way. As her daughters wrote, "Julia was nineteen years old, a woman grown, feeling her womanhood in every vein. She had never been allowed to choose the persons who should be invited to the house; she had never had a party of her own." Julia told her disbelieving brothers that she intended to give a grand party. She received permission from her father to have a few friends over, and then she and her brothers conspired to produce a long guest list. "It was characteristic of her," her daughters pointed out, "that the plan once made, the resolve taken, it became an obsession, a thing that must be done at whatever cost." Accordingly, Julia proceeded to hire the best caterer and the most fashionable musicians in New York City. She rented a cut-glass chandelier for the evening. In short, she did everything that an ambitious hostess might do to compete with the Astors.[27]

When the night of the party arrived, Samuel Ward descended the stairs to find himself welcoming not a few friends, but "as brilliant a gathering as could have been found in any other of the great houses of New York." He was courteous and betrayed no surprise at finding the young people dancing to the music of an orchestra. Julia, on the other hand, was trembling with dread at his reaction. When the last guest departed, her brothers reassured her that they would speak to Samuel on her behalf. Nervously, Julia declined, insisting that the situation was her responsibility. When she went 'round to her father's room, however, he said nothing more than that her idea of "a few friends" differed so much from his own that in the future she should consult with him more carefully. Father and daughter kissed goodnight, and nothing more was said of the matter.[28] Yet Julia had verified at firsthand a valuable lesson: sometimes subversion worked. Even when she had no power, at times it was possible to ignore the wishes of her superior and do as she pleased. With luck, those acts of rebellion and independence would go unpunished.

DIVA JULIA: LIFE AFTER FATHER

In November 1839, Julia had, for the only time in her life until the death of her husband in 1876, the opportunity to exert her own will in her household. After a short illness, Samuel Ward died at the age of fifty-five. Julia was with him until the end, holding his hand. Her father's brother John then moved into the house to look after the five unmarried children. Although John Ward often chided Julia about her disinterest in housekeeping (on the occasion of her first publication, he remarked: "This is my little girl who knows about books, and writes an article and has it printed, but I wish she knew more about housekeeping"[29]), Julia nevertheless was free to make decisions about household routines that formerly had been her father's prerogative. Her family anticipated a loosening of the "Puritan feeling" that had prompted Samuel to declare Saturday night inappropriate for receiving visitors and to require the children to attend two services and two Sunday school meetings on Sunday. Surely, the young woman who had yearned to enlarge her world and enjoy fashionable society would put an end to the isolation and religious rigor that had been the hallmark of the Ward household.

Here, to their dismay, Julia continued her father's customs. Undoubtedly the death of her brother Marion in October 1840 played a role in driving her into the familiar territory of her father's Calvinism. In response to the losses she had experienced at home, she attended several revival meetings and found that the "angry and vengeful Deity" of Calvinism suited her mood of grief. Attempting to show how uncharacteristic this was of their mother, her daughters later observed, "these were days of emotion, of fervor, of exaltation alternating with abasement; thought was to come later."[30]

At any rate, Julia turned her theological principles upon family life with severity. She outlawed cooking on Sunday, serving only cold meat. That decree prompted her brothers and sisters to change her nickname from "Jolie Julie" to the "Old Bird," an appellation that was to follow her the rest of her life. Uncle John labeled the cold afternoon meal "Sentiment," and the hot tea she permitted in the evening "Bliss," but Julia was undeterred by sarcasm. She hovered over her family, spouting pious pronouncements and dispensing somber admonitions. Her emotional fervor was also heightened, her daughters believed, by a semi-engagement to a young minister who was in love with her. A visit to Boston, however, gave Julia some distance from her feelings, and she broke off the relationship. Nevertheless, the months immediately following the deaths of her father and her brother Marion were a time of retrenchment for her. The old authority, at which she had once chaffed, was gone, but in her grief and fear, she herself continued its reign.[31]

Custom dictated that Julia mourn her father's death for two years. At the end of that period, she was free to pursue the social life heretofore denied her. Ultimately, the lure of that lively world, combined with new theological understanding, conquered any remaining inclinations to pursue the restrictive lifestyle her father had favored. Julia's theological growth came largely from her reading. The ending line of an essay by Matthias Claudius: "And is he not also the God of the Japanese?" jarred her into considering that the divine being was operative and beneficent outside the limits of Judaism and Christianity. Then, after reading *Paradise Lost,* she "threw away once and forever, the thought of the terrible hell which till then had always formed part of my belief," cherishing instead "the persuasion that the victory of goodness must consist in making everything good, and that Satan himself could have no shield to resist permanently the divine power of the divine spirit."[32]

Having assuaged her theological fears with the assurance of a loving God, Julia was free at last to enter fashionable society. She made quite a hit. Indeed, even while her father was alive, she had caught the eye of any number of young men. As her daughters reported, "Her finely chiselled features, and the beauty of her hands and arms, made an ensemble which could not fail to impress all who saw her. Add to this her singing, her wit, and the charm which was all and always her own, and we have the *Diva Julia,* as she was called by some who loved her." With her sisters Annie and Louisa, the Ward women were known as the "Three Graces of Bond Street." One of her friends later told Julia's daughters, "Louisa had her admirers, and Annie had hers; but when the men saw your mother, they just flopped!"[33]

Thus, even during Samuel Ward's lifetime, suitors flocked to Julia, although she was forbidden to encourage them. As her daughters admitted, "she could not love them, she would not marry them, but she was very sorry for them, and—it must be admitted—she liked to be adored." Here Julia's considerable intellectual accomplishments served her well, providing a means to entertain her admirers as well as to encourage a modest degree of intimacy. As her daughters pointed out, "she sang duets with one, read German with another, Anglo-Saxon with a third."[34]

With Samuel's death, however, Julia was able to gratify her long-suppressed desires to enjoy the merry social life of the wealthy. Her brothers took a lively interest in her affairs and those of her sisters, offering advice that she did not always heed.[35] Ultimately Sam paved the way for her immersion in society. He introduced her to fashionable people in New York and Boston, and in a letter written from Boston to her sisters, she noted her fatigue from "having talked and danced for the two last nights" in the company of such agreeable people as Sumner (Charles Sumner), Longo (Henry Wadsworth Longfellow), and Hillard (George S. Hillard). Her daughters wryly observed that Julia "had come a long way from old Ascension Church, where Peter Stuyvesant, in a full brown wig, carried round the plate. . . . and where communicants were not expected to go to balls or theatres."[36] Indeed she had. Soon she was writing that Longfellow was an "enthusiastic dancer" who "hops about, as nimbly as a flea." She also mentioned meeting a man named Chev (Samuel Gridley Howe), with whom she did not talk, since he did not dance.[37]

Julia took her sisters to visit Boston in the summer of 1841.[38] It was then that she first ventured to the Perkins Institution to see Samuel Gridley Howe in his element. Born in 1801, Howe did not come from a wealthy family, but he had managed to attend Brown University and to receive his medical degree from Harvard. From 1824 to 1830, Howe had volunteered as a surgeon in the Greek war of independence, and he had returned to Boston with the reputation of a dashing warrior of righteousness. His friends then dubbed him the "Chevalier," and he did his best to live up to the name. Women found him attractive. As future suffrage reformer Anna Shaw Greene remembered those days, Howe "was the handsomest man I ever saw. When he rode down Beacon Street on his black horse, with the embroidered crimson saddle-cloth, all the girls ran to their windows to look after him."[39]

On his return to Boston, Howe took up work with the blind. Though medical knowledge of the day dictated that the blind were mentally defective, Howe determined to pioneer methods to prepare the blind to enter the sighted world as fully functioning citizens. Working at first without pay, he gradually built up his practice until he was able to establish a dormitory and a school. His greatest triumph was with a deaf and blind student named Laura Bridgman, whose progress seemed to Howe's admiring public to be miraculous. For a man as energetic and spirited as Howe to dedicate his life to working patiently with the "unfortunates" that polite society avoided earned him a considerable reputation. As Elizabeth Peabody, sister-in-law of Horace Mann and Nathaniel Hawthorne, put it, "I shall not, in all my time, forget the impression made upon me by seeing the hero of the Greek Revolution . . . wholly absorbed, and applying all the energies of his genius to this . . . work, and doing it as Christ did, without money and without price."[40]

Intrigued by the enthusiastic descriptions of the Chevalier that they had heard from Sumner and Longfellow, Julia and her sisters accompanied them to the Perkins Institution for the Blind to meet Howe. Subsequent family lore recorded this meeting as the epitome of romance, so dramatic that family members chose to depict it as the original meeting between Julia and Chev.[41] The visitors arrived while Howe was out, so they showed themselves around, observing Laura Bridgman and another blind and deaf student named Lucy Reed conversing in the finger alphabet Howe had taught them. Eventually, Sumner looked out the window and cried, "Oh! here comes Howe on his black horse." Julia remembered her reaction: "I looked out also, and beheld a noble rider on a noble steed."[42] She was not to forget the sight. Indeed, her daughters argued that no woman could have seen him and remained untouched: "The slender, military figure, the jet-black hair, keen blue eyes, and brilliant complexion, above all the vivid presence, like the flash of a sword—all these could not fail to impress the young girl deeply."[43]

For his part, Chev was also taken with Diva Julia. After getting to know him better, however, Julia feared that Chev was more attracted to Louisa. She wrote a prescient letter to brother Sam warning that Louisa would be disappointed in the position Chev could offer her, because "South Boston will not be Bond Street, and the Doctor will not be you."[44] Julia's fears about Chev's attraction to her sister proved unfounded, and in the winter of 1842–43, she and Chev were engaged. Brother Sam supported the match, writing Julia: "were I your Papa the alliance could not afford me greater pleasure. . . . You know I already esteem the Chevalier as a brother."[45] Accordingly, Julia became increasingly convinced that Chev was the man of her dreams. Years later, in her autobiography, she quoted with approval the preface to Franklin B. Sanborn's biography of Chev: "It has fallen to my lot to know . . . several of the most romantic characters of our century; and among them one of the most romantic was certainly the hero of these pages."[46]

Certainly there were aspects of the relationship that must have given Julia pause. Samuel Gridley Howe was eighteen years her senior, and he was also, as she pointed out after their first meeting, a man of "unusual force and reserve." He ran the Institute with a passion for detail, determined to direct every activity and make every significant decision. He resented her wealth and was determined to show her affluent family that he could support Julia without assistance. Soon Sam was writing to Chev, pleading with him that "you must not get angry with the old bird for having some $2000s a year of her own, because such circumstances help eke out amazingly."[47] Chev *did* find the income irritating and was particularly incensed that brother Sam was the trustee of Julia's estate. Eventually Chev compelled Julia to yield control of her estate to him. Julia complied, noting in a letter written to Uncle John that Chev "will not consent either to receive money through his [Sam's] hands, or to my receiving it in the same way." As Julia accurately concluded, Chev "is very sensitive, and accustomed to an independent course of action. Sam, on the other hand, is fussy, has a great love of power, and is fond both of finding fault and of giving advice, things to which Dr. Howe is not accustomed."[48]

Other difficulties emerged. Chev had unshakable notions of a married woman's place: in the home. Though he delighted in Julia's wit and poetry,[49] he believed that after marriage she should be devoted to him, not to literary endeavors. He would entertain no thoughts of Julia pursuing the publishing career she yearned for, nor would he allow her to work with the staff at the Institute.[50] If Julia married the Chevalier, she would have to return to the "enchanted castle" from which her father's death had so recently freed her.

Understandably, such a prospect worried Julia. She shared her anxieties
with brother Sam, who tried to play peacemaker. Arguing that literary aspirations made women fitter companions for men as well as better mothers, Sam
advised Chev to tread lightly in this matter; in time, Julia would come around.
"Love has given you authority," he counseled. "Let its influence work invisi-
bly—and do not strive to accelerate the approach of the not far distant day,
when every thought & desire will be stamped by your wishes, by insisting upon
a formal renunciation of tastes & impulses which so far from being rivals will
one day become your cherished friend. A woman cannot have too many qualities."[51] Chev was not convinced, but he was willing to concede that Julia loved
him. And she was optimistic enough to trust that all would be well.

Even if Julia chose to cast her fate with a strong-willed man, there were
compensations. She was marrying a hero of the age, a man whose idealism
inspired her love and admiration. And the Chevalier clearly loved her. As
Sumner wrote, "Howe has told me, with eyes flashing with joy, that you have
received his love. May God make you happy in his heart, as I know he will be
happy in yours! A truer heart was never offered to woman. I know him well,
I know the depth, strength, and constancy of his affections, as the whole
world knows the beauty of his life and character."[52] Sumner could have said
more; Chev would confide to him that he was almost "crazy with joy" at winning Julia. If, Chev said, "I have but the power to make her happy . . . I ask no
more of God in the world." Indeed, Chev concluded, Sumner too ought to
find such bliss: "if you would be blessed, go & win a woman like Diva! Go,
Sumner[,] go this very evening & begin to love—you have only to do it & be
beloved in return."[53]

Such enthusiasm would have been hard for any woman to resist. Chev
poured out his love in a series of letters to Julia, writing in one that he was
never alone, because her spirit was always present to him. In another, after
explaining that political duties kept him in Boston even though he would
prefer to be visiting her, he exclaimed that he was "no longer in love with
you[,] Julia—it is something more than love, & yet, adoration is not its name:
it seems that I have no longer any *me,* what formerly was *me* is taken away, &
you hold its place; I do not think of myself, of my own identity[,] but yours
seems to have monopolised [sic] mine. . . . I only know I shall not be restored
to myself until I am restored to you."[54] In yet another letter, he pointed to her
tendency to see the spiritual side of things, and promised to make the physical side of life and marriage worth savoring. "There are no lawful pleasures,
even those of sense, which, immortal though he be, man should ever despise,

for God's own hand places them before him," Chev explained. Life held great earthly pleasures for them to share:

> I give you fair warning; I shall not help you out of the cocoon state at all; you are a sweet, pretty, little mortal, & shall not be immortal if I can help it, this many a long year.
>
> I suppose you think you would look very beautifully emerging from the chrysalis state, & I should be proud to see a pair of wings sprouting out from your white shoulders . . . but no such thing, & I advise you not to show even a . . . feather, for I shall unmercifully cut them off, to keep you prisoner in my arms, my own dear earthly wife, who is to go forth with me through this pleasant world, until my wings grow also, where we shall fly away together.[55]

Julia's reply to Chev's letter has not survived, and it is hard to know how threatening (or enticing) she found his intention to confine her in the earthly prison of his arms. The vision of the two of them being transported to the angelic realm together, however, did not vanish with this letter. In her secret novel of the life of a hermaphrodite, written at the end of the 1840s, Julia would invoke the image of man and woman united and transfigured as an image of redemption and human transformation. Later, her philosophical lectures and suffrage addresses would use similar imagery when discussing the evolution of the human race. Chev had no idea that his rather ponderous promise or threat of earthly pleasures would prove so crucial to Julia's thinking about the progress of civilization. Neither, undoubtedly, did Julia.

To his credit, Chev did not ignore his own weaknesses. He knew he could appear uncaring. "It is very common with our cold Saxon race to conceal the feelings deep within; & it is my own wont too much to do so," he conceded. But he would do better, because "doubtless there are many husbands who love their wives devotedly but who treat them coldly even in the eyes of others; but this should not be . . . the husband . . . should not only love devotedly but also *seem* to love." Chev promised to be truly loving, assuring Julia that "my every day's study will be your happiness."[56] He asked, too, that she forgive him when he failed her. If she could but make allowance for "my impatience, my injustice if you will," she could unfailingly "count upon my love and & my determination."[57]

In the end, Julia took the chance, yielding herself to a man who, with all good intentions, would rule her life. She wrote her brother Sam: "The Chevalier says truly—I am the captive of his bow and spear. His true devotion has won me from the world, and from myself. The past is already fading from my sight; already, I begin to live with him in the future, which shall be as calmly bright as true love can make it. I am perfectly satisfied to sacrifice to one so noble and earnest the day dreams of my youth. He will make life more beautiful to me than a dream."[58]

In time, just a little time, Julia would learn that talk of self-sacrifice made for stirring poetry, but for poor living. William Astor had teased her at her engagement, saying, "Why, Miss Julia, I am surprised! I thought you were too intellectual to marry!"[59] It would not be long until Julia saw the truth of those words. Despite his joy in winning her, Samuel Gridley Howe would be unwavering in his insistence that Julia's role as his wife was to give herself completely to caring for him and his children. The duties of marriage and motherhood thus intruded on the study opportunities of a woman who still defined herself in terms of her intellectual accomplishments. Household cares also isolated her from the company of accomplished men—with whom she identified—and from the intimacy of other women, who might have helped her understand that she was not alone in enduring frustration and the loss of self as she attempted to become a Victorian "angel in the home." In short, Julia would discover that life with Samuel Howe was much like life with Samuel Ward: in both instances, she was isolated, dominated by men, and in search of intellectual achievements that could lift her above the lot that true womanhood had assigned her.

Chapter Two

THE LOVE BOAT

Julia began her married life with an act of independence, deciding to be known as "Mrs. Julia Ward Howe" rather than "Mrs. Samuel Gridley Howe."[1] She was to have her way in little else. After the wedding on April 23, 1843, the Howes set sail for Europe, accompanied by Julia's sister Annie and by newlyweds Horace and Mary Peabody Mann. Somewhat daunted by her new role, Julia acknowledged the "superiority of experience" that Chev's age awarded him, observing later, "my own true life had been that of a student and of a dreamer," while Chev's life was marked by "the practical knowledge which is rarely attained in the closet or at the desk." She was soon in need of that knowledge, as she found herself "stupefied with sea-sickness." After allowing her to suffer for two days, Chev descended to their room with a glass of brandy and commanded her to drink. "Magnetized by the stronger will," she confessed, "I struggled with my weakness, and was presently clothed and carried on deck."[2]

Julia wrote letters to her family describing marital bliss. "I cannot tell you how good my husband is, how kind, how devoted—he is all made of pure gold," she confided to sister Louisa. Even the struggles to gain her sea legs seemed humorous in retrospect: "I have had various tumbles. I confess that when the ship rolled and I felt myself going, I generally made for the stoutest man in sight, and pitched into him, the result being various apologies on both sides, and great merriment on the part of the spectators—a little of the old mischief left, you see."[3]

But behind the proclamations of merriment and joy lay darker emotions. In a set of bound poems entitled "Life is strange, and full of change," Julia was privately giving voice to doubts and grief that she shared with no one. In a poem called "La Veille des Noees," dated two days after her wedding, she said farewell to her family and asked her brother Sam to remember how they had sung together when she as "a vestal priestess . . . stood at the shrine of song." She spoke of a "strain of agony" in her heart and asked God to "gently bind the crown of thorns which must my forehead wreath," keeping "unstained and pure ... my virgin soul" until death. Equally gloomy was a poem called "Mary's Tears," written on April 29. There Julia described herself as having been anointed for death and burial.[4]

Other poems continued her melancholy themes. In a poem dated May 20, entitled "The Past Lives," Julia was more explicit about at least one of the anxieties that troubled her. She spoke of a love she had known and lost, a love in which "All heaven was centered in thy genial light" and in whose absence "All heaven departed." She mused: "was it guilty, was it innocent, / That mingling of my spirit's life with thine? / We touched not, spake not, but our thoughts were blent, / Our souls were wedded in one look divine." The poem's closing stanza revealed that whoever (or whatever) this lost love might be, she feared it would distract her from Chev: "Not for my own, but for another's peace / I plead, for him who slumbers at my side; / Let then thy daily resurrection cease, / Nor come at night, to claim another's bride."[5]

Perhaps Julia missed a former suitor; perhaps she simply grieved the circumstances that had transformed her from the popular Diva with a literary future into a dependent spouse. In "The present is dead," dated June 4, she confessed that since her marriage she had lost much of herself. "Fancies and penzies have all passed away," she remarked. "Methinks the soul is ebbing from the clay, / So little of itself remains behind. / I feel my varied powers all depart / With scarce a hope they may be born." Still, all was perhaps not lost; Julia looked to Chev for hope: "And thou, my husband, in whose gentle breast / I seek the godlike power, to keep and save / ... Come nearer to me, let our spirits meet, / Let us be of one light, one truth possessed."[6] Julia would not often find the harmony of spirits with Chev that she sought on her honeymoon, but she would continue to hold up that union of wills as her romantic ideal.

Julia pondered such thoughts as her ocean voyage came to an end. After their boat docked in England, the Howes commenced a lively round of socializing amid London's prominent denizens. Julia had tea with Thomas Carlyle, breakfast with the Richard Monckton Milnes, and gladly accepted tickets to plays at Covent Garden. Charles Dickens had written admiringly of Chev in his 1842 *American Notes* and was eager to function as tour guide, taking Chev, Julia, and Annie to prisons, asylums, and workhouses as well as to dinner.[7]

Both Julia and Chev made an impact in London—she for her wit and literary interests, he for his looks and reputation as a humanitarian. Julia wrote her sister Louisa: "Chev receives a great deal of attention, ladies press forward to look at him, roll up their eyes, and exclaim, 'Oh, he is such a wonner [sic]!' I do not like that the pretty women should pay him so many compliments—it will turn his little head!" In later years, Chev would rebuff Julia's pleas for outward shows of affection, rejecting her desires to be kissed. Something of this dynamic appeared during their stay in London. At one social function, she publicly addressed Chev as "darling." Charles Dickens reacted immediately, throwing himself "on his back on the floor, partly under the table, waving his legs in the air, and crying 'Did she call you darling?'"[8]

After touring Britain, the Howes proceeded to Switzerland, Austria, and Milan, coming at last to Rome, where they spent Christmas and much of the spring.[9] There they had a lively time, attending balls, going to musical parties where the "Diva sang to the admiration of all," and even being presented to Pope Gregory XVI, who was interested in Laura Bridgman. Julia was fascinated by the art she encountered. But the event that overshadowed all others was the birth of the Howe's first child on March 12, 1844. That birth was preceded by significant depression on Julia's part. Though her daughters observed that Julia's autobiography did not record the "languor and depression of spirits" that afflicted her in Rome, Julia's descriptions of the city intimated her emotional state. "The Rome that I then saw," she remarked, "was mediaeval in its aspect. A great gloom and silence hung over it." She noted as well her relief when, after the birth of her daughter, the Howe entourage took leave of Rome. That departure, she said, was "like returning to the living world after a long separation from it."[10]

Julia did not know, in 1844, that she would suffer similar depressions with the birth of each of her children. In Rome, she chose to blame her feelings on her environment. Later, she would identify the source of her depression as the process of motherhood itself. She did not have the benefit of twentieth-century psychological theories or therapists, who undoubtedly would have urged her to connect her fears and depression with the fact that her own mother had died while giving birth. A therapist might have wished to probe, as well, why Julia requested that her daughter be named Julia Romana.[11] Julia's own words indicated that she identified Rome with "gloom" and with being separated from "the living world." Yet Julia gave her daughter a middle name that would always connect her to Rome: Romana. It was a name that perhaps told more than Julia knew—a name that hinted at her ambivalence about her new role of mother.

In addition to her anxieties about pregnancy and motherhood, Julia was also continuing to struggle in her relationship with Chev. In an 1843 poem, she described herself as a person "not moved by common themes" who sang of "wondrous thoughts that come to her," and she asked to be heard with love as her interpreter.[12] Poems from 1844 indicated she was still pleading. In "The darkest moment," she complained that her soul panted for that sympathy that God never denied humanity, but which she did not expect to receive from Chev: "Hope dies as I was led / Unto my marriage bed." A poem optimistically entitled "The dawning of light," which Julia began in Rome and finished in England, addressed the conflicting feelings her marriage aroused within her. At times, she loved Chev dearly and wished nothing other than to conform to his will; at other times, she felt that their conflicts jarred the creation itself.

⁓

Often I turn away
From thee, to weep or pray;
I cannot rise on high,
My sad soul looks to God, and asks him why.

He says: "ye are not akin,
Your union was a sin;
Your natures meet and jar
And thus, the order of Creation mar.

⁓

Even in this situation, however, Julia professed to find comfort. The mysterious love that in earlier poems had threatened her devotion to Chev had faded; surely she would find her place with him and learn how to make both of them happy. All she had to do was kiss his feet and regard him as an angel, for then:

⁓

Regret departs, and love is born anew.

Then am I drawn to thee
By strongest sympathy;
Then grows the demon faint,
I kiss thy feet—thou art my house hold saint. . . .

When once I know my sphere,
Life shall no more be drear,
I will be all thou wilt;
To cross thy least desire shall be guilt.

Then, husband, smile on me,
Smile, and smile tenderly;
Pure angel that thou art,
Build up again the ruins of my heart![13]

⁓

Given the emotional anguish she was enduring, it was hardly surprising that Julia was, as she put it, unable to "give any very connected account" of the months preceding the birth of her daughter. Chev, on the other hand, did not share her nebulousness. Out of the sixty-two pages of her Reminiscences describing her honeymoon, Julia devoted only one paragraph to Julia Romana, whereas the birth of his first child was an epiphany for Chev. Months before the delivery, he assured his friend Charles Sumner that Julia did not bear an unequal burden in this great adventure. "Only a poor bachelor like you, could imagine such a thing," Chev advised. "No true woman ever considered it a burden to bear his [her?] infant."[14] On the day of the birth, Chev wrote to Julia's uncle John, observing, "the dear creature [Julia] suffered about eight hours, bearing herself with courage and confidence. I thought that nothing could make her nearer & dearer to me than she was," he added, "but I feel already that God in giving us new responsibilities has given us new bonds of affection."[15]

In a letter written four days later to Sumner, Chev considered at greater length the marvels of birth. He professed the affection Julia held for her child to be wonderful, remarking, "she said after she had been a mother only twenty-four hours, that should the child die, she had already tasted enough of the sweets of mother love to repay her all the inconveniences and all the pains." Julia, he said, had one "wish—one thought, one hope—to be enabled to continue to nurse her child herself, to fill its veins from her own." Chev believed that the profound experience of being a mother had already transformed Julia from a superficial young socialite to a single-minded, dedicated wife and caregiver. "How beautiful—how wonderful is nature!" he mused. "Only a year ago, Julia was a New York belle—apparently an artificial—possibly some thought a beautiful one; now she is a wife who lives only for her husband, & a mother who would melt her very heart, were it needed, to give a drop of nourishment to her child."

This perception prompted Chev to ponder anew the glories of motherhood. "To see her watching with eager anxious eyes every movement of her offspring: to witness her entire self-forgetfulness & total absorption of her nature in this new object of love," he said, "is to have a fresh revelation of the strength & beauty of woman's character, & new proof of their superiority over us in what most enobles [sic] humanity—love for others." He suggested that the long months of pregnancy were nature's way of preparing Julia for the sublimity of mother love. "This affection," he explained, "has taken deep root in the heart long before the child is born: all Julia's motions & actions have been for months regulated with a view to its condition."

Even the pains and terrors of childbirth were part of nature's grand design. "During the pangs of her confinement (and oh they were staunch & bitter)," Chev observed, "she seemed to have but one fear, lest her child should die; and the moment after its birth, while her whole system seemed to be giving way beneath the racking agony which had convulsed it, when she heard its first plaintive cry, she clapped her arms around my neck, & bursting into tears, sobbed out with joy & gratitude, 'oh! my child is alive! my child is alive!'" Thus, Chev cautioned, "dear Sumner, doubt as we may, suggest improvements as we may, it is, after all, indubitable that the apparently useless inconvenience of pains, preceding maturity, are seeds of beautiful and ennobling affections, & contribute much toward forming the tenderest of all human ties, the mother's love for her child."

The theodicy question thus dispatched, Chev declared that mother love not only revealed something sublime about the character of women; it actually pointed to the divine potential available to human nature. "Let me tell you," he lectured Sumner, "there's nothing more beautiful than the young affection of a young mother: it is so earnest, so tender, so devoted, that it is more than saint like, it is heavenly. . . . Who can doubt, when witnessing this love, that human nature has the element of God's nature, and under the most favorable of circumstances, may become angelic?" Chev himself felt ennobled by fatherhood but insisted that his feelings fell far short of Julia's. "I feel I could make any sacrifice for its [the child's] good," he confessed, "and still my love compared to hers is nothing: all woman[']s affections are stronger than man[']s, but all her other affections are weak compared to her maternal ones." Chev conceded to Sumner, "I have made much of this, but, thank God! I have lived to realize this new revelation of His benevolence & of human nature's beautiful capacities." Before mailing the letter, Chev added a note several days later, telling Sumner with satisfaction that Julia had "obtained complete control of the child, & is happy as the days & nights are long in being able to be *all* a mother to it."[16]

In discussing the birth of Julia Romana, Chev and Julia told two different stories. In naming her child after a city that represented gloom and death, Julia perhaps inadvertently expressed ambivalence about the turn her life had taken. Certainly she experienced fear and pain in delivery, as well as a more general depression in the months preceding and following the birth. Chev's letter to

Sumner, on the contrary, indicated that Chev felt elated at the birth of his daughter. He saw in Julia's sufferings a revelation of the divine love of which mothers, in his opinion, were uniquely capable. He also saw, or thought that he did, a transformation in Julia. Once she had lived for society, but now she would be "a wife who lives only for her husband." She was, in his mind, a mother who instinctively "obtained complete control" of her child, a woman who had no wish other than to be "*all* a mother to it."[17]

This was not the last time Chev would yearn for Julia to give herself up to her role of submissive wife and loving mother. Nor was he asking of her a sacrifice inconsistent with Victorian notions of female gender roles. Rather, his views were characteristic of the cult of domesticity; he wanted his wife to be what Victorians recognized as a true woman. But the private sphere of the home would never be large enough for Julia. No matter what she had promised before her marriage, she could not help but continue to covet a literary career. She was beginning to realize, moreover, that her wish to make a name for herself had just encountered an intractable obstacle. As a mother expected to nurse and care for her child, she was going to be confined to the home by demands that she could neither ignore nor escape. She could also expect, in the absence of reliable methods of birth control, to have more children. In a real sense, the "confinement" she underwent while giving birth to her daughter was just beginning.

The Howes' return visit to England prior to their voyage back to Boston could only have reinforced that message. At William Nightingale's request, the Howes spent a few days at Embly Park, the family home of the Nightingales. The Nightingales were worried about their daughter Florence. Twenty-four years old and ambitious, Florence had read of Chev's humanitarian work and desired to emulate him. Her family preferred that she behave conventionally. Chev and Florence retired for a private conversation, and Florence asked him if he thought it inappropriate for her to devote her life to works of charity, such as nursing, as Catholic nuns did. Chev opined that "it would be a very good thing." Whether he said more is unknown; Julia reported in her Reminiscences, "so much and no more of the conversation Dr. Howe repeated to me."[18]

Soon after this conversation, Florence commenced nursing studies and eventually achieved fame as a nurse in the Crimean War. Chev's interest in her career remained enthusiastic, and she grew close enough to the Howes that they would name a daughter after her. Chev predicated his approval of her work on the fact that she was unmarried, but still, the contrast between his support of Florence Nightingale and his desire to domesticate his wife was not lost upon Julia. Never was the price of marriage and children so clear as when

she looked at her unwed English counterpart. Florence Nightingale would provide the grist for a myriad of future arguments.

MY VOICE IS FROZEN TO SILENCE

Whatever apprehensions about her new life Julia endured on her honeymoon,
her return to Boston in September 1844 could only have been a most sober
occasion. She moved into Chev's home at the Institute, and found herself
more isolated from outside friendship or stimulation than she had ever been
in her father's house. As her daughters wrote, "from the bright little world of
old New York, from relatives and friends, music and laughter, fun and frolic,
she came to live in an Institution, a bleak lofty house set on a hill, four-square
to all the winds that blew . . . where three fourths of the inmates were blind,
and the remaining fourth were devoting their time and energies to the blind."
Forbidden by her husband to work at the Institute, she faced a life of domesticity that would seldom be relieved by trips to town, as town was virtually
impossible to reach. "The Institution was two miles from Boston," her daughters observed, "where the friends of her girlhood lived: an unattractive district
stretched between, traversed once in two hours by omnibuses, the only means
of transport."[19]

Physical isolation was not her only discouragement. She also faced long
hours of loneliness, as Chev was absorbed in his work and uninterested in pursuing social engagements. His daughters conceded that Julia's life in her new
home must have been lonely. Their mother, they confessed, had become "the
wife of a man who had neither leisure nor inclination for 'Society': a man of
tenderest heart, but of dominant personality, accustomed to rule, and devoted
to causes of which she knew only by hearsay; moreover, so absorbed in work
for these causes, that he could only enjoy his home by snatches."[20] Unlike the
obliging husband who had spent abundant leisure hours with his wife in
Europe, Chev in Boston would be preoccupied not only with his work at the
Institute, but also with various benevolent causes such as prison reform and
antislavery work. Julia would face many evenings like the one in which she
wrote despairingly to her sister, "Chev returned at one [a.m.], quite intoxicated
with benevolence."[21]

Finally, life in Boston brought with it the inevitable acknowledgement that
Julia and Chev were two very different people. Every intimate couple faces this
issue, but for Julia and Chev, acknowledging differences was particularly
painful. Each wished the other to change in ways that their personalities pre-
cluded. Chev wanted his wife to submit to his will and to find joy in domestic

affairs. Julia wanted her husband to be less absorbed in his work, more attentive to her, and enthusiastic about her desire to make a literary name for herself. It was hard, she observed, to go from being the "family idol" to "a wife
overshadowed for the time by the splendor of her husband's reputation." Years
later, when Julia entered the public sphere, coping with his wife's newfound
fame would drive Chev to distraction.[22] Each wanted to be the dominant force
in their relationship. They were fixed in their purposes, unwilling or unable to
accommodate to the other. It was probably best that they did not know, in the
fall of 1844, that they were entering into a cycle of bickering that would occupy
and at times consume them for the next three decades.

Julia began by deferring, insofar as she could manage, to Chev's wishes.
Chev liked to entertain old friends on a weekly basis and Julia did her best to
accommodate him, but her domestic proficiency left much to be desired. "I . . .
found myself lamentably deficient in household skill," she later admitted, and
even diligent application produced but "indifferent success. I was by nature
far from observant, and often passed through a room without much notion of
its condition or contents, my thoughts being intent upon other things." Chev's
oldest sister had served as his housekeeper before his marriage, and she continued to live with him after it. Unfortunately, as Julia observed, Chev's sister
"was averse to company" and typically absented herself on the days that guests
came for meals.

Consequently, Chev's dinner parties all too often became ordeals of humiliation for Julia. She did her best as cook, but weeks of studying Catherine
Beecher's cookbook produced little in the way of savory meals. Her daughters
conceded, "these dinners were something of a nightmare to Julia," concluding,
"this was not what her hand was made for." The absence of her housekeeper
was particularly telling, as Julia occasionally gave way to panic, not knowing
"where to look for various articles which were requisite and necessary." At one
dinner party, she was unable to find the frozen dessert (which a messenger had
delivered to a snow bank near the door), and was almost reduced to tears.[23]

In time, Chev's sister moved out and he hired a housekeeper, but Julia was
unskilled in overseeing servants, and the Howes would eventually go through
a succession of them. Governesses, cooks, and maids would come and go, often
performing unsatisfactorily, frequently leaving at inopportune moments, and
invariably furnishing the grounds for arguments over money and household
management. In 1847, Julia lamented to her sister Louisa, "I have spoiled a
good student, to make a most indifferent wife. The longer I live, the more do I
feel my utter, childlike helplessness about all practical affairs. Certainly, a creature with such useless hands was never before seen."[24]

Other words from Julia's pen indicated just how deep her despair ran. A scrapbook from her early years in Boston revealed the depth of her isolation. "I live in a place where I have few social relations, and all too recent to be intimate," she noted. Having no one to confide in, she despaired, "I am forced to make to myself an imaginary public, and to tell it the secrets of my poor little ridiculous brain. . . . I have nothing but myself to write about for four months past. I have seen and heard only myself, talked with myself, eaten and drunk with myself, make a solemn bow to myself every morning and condoled with myself that I was about to be left to myself for another day. Oh cursed self, how I hate the very sight of you!"[25]

Such isolation meant more than boredom punctuated by loneliness. It also threatened her ambitions as a writer. Living with one of Boston's eminent reformers put Julia in an odd position. Some of Boston's foremost talents were eating dinner in her home at Chev's invitation. Julia, however, was becoming acquainted with people like Theodore Parker not as a literary colleague, but as his hostess, and a novice hostess at that. Her guests were happy to discuss literature, philosophy, and theology at her table, but when they returned to their homes, they were free to publish, preach, and speak publicly. She was not. And so Chev's friends moved ahead with their careers, while she increasingly descended into inner turmoil and self-doubt. The girl who had confidently written theological exhortations to her cousin and poems to her father, who had tied herself to her chair, so great was her urgency in studying German, was becoming a woman plagued by misgivings. As she wrote her sister Louisa in January 1846, "My voice is still frozen to silence, my poetry chained down by an icy bond of indifference, I begin to believe that I am no poet, and never was, save in my own imagination."[26]

A DEBT WE OWE TO NATURE

In 1845 the Howes moved from the Institute to a nearby home that Julia dubbed Green Peace; unfortunately, their lives together did not mirror the idyllic existence suggested by that title.[27] Julia was still physically isolated from friends. And, as she had more children, the stress and anxiety introduced into her relationship with Chev by the birth of their first child multiplied. Both Chev and Julia found themselves caught up in a maze of incrimination, anger, and bewilderment. Neither had imagined that life with a partner initially loved and admired could be so difficult.

The tensions and misgivings that marked the first decade or so of Julia's life with Chev surfaced unmistakably in the letters she wrote to her sisters.

Julia's remarks revealed a bitterness marked by an abiding desire to believe that things were not so bad, after all. She hated her marriage, but also wanted to love it. Childbirth remained a source of unmitigated terror, and the demands of rearing children moved her to tears of sheer frustration on many days; but still a part of her needed to insist that she was quite happy.[28] Declarations of happiness following upon the heels of scathing denunciations of Chev, however, pointed at best to a deep ambivalence. The intimacies she enjoyed as a wife and mother could not mask the suffering that haunted her. Try as she might to resign herself to her lot, rage and a sense of loss were her constant companions.

Julia's letters from this period were peppered with reflections on marriage. She wavered between exalting marriage and bemoaning it. After her sister's Louisa's marriage in 1844, Julia asked, "Do you not feel the importance, the dignity of a married woman? I told Chev once that marriage was not desecration, but consecration, and made him very happy thereby." In July 1845, Julia was more inclined to count the cost of marriage. In becoming wives, "we have both had to give up something," she confided to Louisa, "but then we are fulfilling the destiny of woman, we are learning to live for others, more than ourselves."[29]

Living for others and ignoring her own ambitions, however, had its costs. In November 1845, Julia reported to Louisa that Sumner had been dining with them recently and that he and Chev had taken to "pitying unmarried women." This, Julia found absurd. "What a foolish mistake these impudent men make," she groused, "they think a woman's happiness is ensured, when she becomes tied for life to one of them—God knows one's wedding day may be worse than the day of one's death—one's husband may prove anything but a comfort and support."[30]

Julia linked marriage and death once again in 1846. Writing to her sister Annie about Annie's upcoming marriage, Julia first likened married life to war, declaring, "your marriage is to me a grave and solemn matter. . . . Some suffering and trials I fear you must have, for after all, the entering into single combat, hand to hand, with the realities of life will be strange and painful." Julia then advised Annie that "marriage, like death, is a debt we owe to nature, and though it costs us something to pay it, yet we are much more content, and better established in peace when we have paid it." After the wedding, Julia appealed to God to "keep dear Annie from suffering," remarking to Louisa, "I pitied her on the day of her marriage, for I thought how little she dreamed of the great changes which marriage brings."[31]

By 1846, Julia knew those changes all too well. Through her marriage, she seemed to have sacrificed all claim to the love and affection that she had, as

Diva Julia, taken for granted. "Is it selfish, is it egotistical to wish that others may love us, take an interest in us, sympathize with us, in our maturer age, as in our youth?" she asked Louisa. Again, she likened married life to death, asking, "in giving life to others, do we lose our own vitality, and sink into dimness, nothingness, and living death?" Julia despaired at the loneliness marriage had brought to her life. "Where shall I go to beg some scraps and remnants of affection to feed my hungry heart?" she asked. "It will die, if it not be fed. My children will, one day, love me—my sisters have always loved me—my husband? May God teach him to love me, and help me to make him happy."

This appeal indicated that she had not given up hope. If Chev could but understand and love her for the person she truly was, rather then insisting that she become someone else, then she could move beyond her resentment and labor to make him happy. "We must strive to come together," she said, "and not live a life of separation—we must cultivate every sympathy which we have in common, and try mutually to acquire those which we have not." As Julia described the effort required of Chev to regain marital concord, however, she laid out a program that did a better job of describing what he thus far had been unable to do than of predicting what heights he might achieve. "He must learn," she explained, "to understand those things which have entirely formed my character—I have come to him, have left my poetry, my music, my religion, have walked with him in his cold world of actualities—there, I have learned much, but there, I can do nothing—he must come to me, must have ears for my music, must have a soul for my faith—in my nature is to sing, to pray, to feel—his is to fight, to teach, to reason; but love and patience may bring us much nearer together than we are."[32]

For the most part, Julia recognized that love and patience were in short supply. A three-week stay with Annie in 1848 confirmed her belief that men rarely had the imagination necessary to understand their wives, much less to live with them in emotional and physical intimacy. Her study of Annie's marriage bolstered Julia's apprehensions of men's incapacity to be spiritual partners. As she wrote Louisa of her stay with Annie: "Like all of us, she has had to sacrifice many illusions—marriage is not what she expected, and men still less. Like us, after dreaming of perfect unions of minds, intimate sympathy, etc., she will have to fall back somewhat upon her own resources, and to find that, after all, the soul has but two possessions, itself and God."[33]

One of the biggest barriers in the way of reconciliation with Chev was the enormous changes that having children brought into Julia's life. Julia gave birth to her daughter Florence (named for Florence Nightingale) before moving to Green Peace in the summer of 1845.[34] In March 1848, her son Henry

Marion (named for Julia's brother Marion) was born, and her daughter Laura (named for Laura Bridgman) was born in February 1850. In November 1854, Maud was born. Finally, on Christmas day 1859, her last child, Samuel Gridley, came into the world.

In a set of remarkable letters, Julia and Chev shared their impressions of those births. It is hard to imagine how documents could reveal more dramatically the strains of family life. As with the birth of Julia Romana, the births of the subsequent children exposed the vastly different views Julia and Chev had of these events. The letters also depicted ways in which the feuding that was a daily part of their married life played itself out even in the terrifying and exhilarating process of childbirth.

Chev typically reacted to the birth of his children by remarking upon the ease of the delivery and expressing happiness at the new addition to the family. Julia, on the other hand, endured noticeable depressions with each pregnancy. Her daughters were open about their mother's despondency, observing: "[B]efore the birth of each successive child she was oppressed by a deep and persistent melancholy. Present and future alike seemed dark to her; she wept for herself, but still more for the hapless infant which must come to birth in so sorrowful a world." Her daughters believed, however, that Julia's dejection disappeared once each child was born. "With the birth of the child the cloud lifted and vanished," they claimed. "Sunshine and joy—and the baby—filled the world; the mother sang, laughed, and made merry."[35]

It may be true that Julia's demeanor changed after childbirth, and she may well have become at that point a more congenial companion for her older children. But her letters bespoke a portentous ambivalence toward her infants. Just as she was capable of comparing marriage to death at the same time that she proclaimed marriage to be consecrated, so she could announce her love for her newborns at one moment and refer to them in terms so derogatory as to be chilling the next. It is not unusual for mothers to feel resentful at the demands that infants make of them. But Julia's remarks about her babies indicated a disaffection that went beyond the ordinary. Her descriptions of them mirrored the bitterness she felt toward Chev at burdening her with the care of the children while he remained free to pursue his career. With each additional child, Julia feared that she became *"all"* and even solely a mother, powerless to be anything but "a wife who lives only for her husband."

Pregnancy was a time of depression for Julia, as she revealed to her sisters. Julia discussed her dread of pregnancy and delivery in a letter to her sister Annie, who was pregnant. "I cannot think of you without commiseration," Julia wrote. "These last months are so fearfully long," and accompanied "by such a death like weakness and stupidity, and then the crisis! . . . I always feel that this suffering must be some expiation for all the follies of one's life."[36] In contrast, Julia wrote to her sister Louisa in January 1847, remarking on the novelty, after bearing two children in four years, of not being pregnant. "I have waked up, for the first time in my marriage," she marveled. "You know that ever since that event, I have lived in a state of somnambulism, occupied principally with digestion, sleep, and babies. Thank God, this mist has been lifted from my eyes, for a time at least."

Julia celebrated her renewed ability to turn from death and somnambulism to the intellectual and artistic affairs that since her own childhood had formed the basis of her sense of self-worth. "I have again a soul, can again enjoy music and poetry, can again feel that there is in me something beside the clay which [is] every day approaching nearer to it's [sic] mother earth," she exulted. "Oh dearest Wevie, God only knows what I have suffered from this stupor—it has been like blindness, like death, like exile from all things beautiful and good." Julia recognized, however, that the respite was undoubtedly temporary, and that part of her depression had been due to her strained relationship with Chev, and not simply to the demands of motherhood. She commented, "I am so happy that it is gone, even if it be for a time only. I pray that I may suffer, may die, rather than lapse into that brutal state of indifference. . . . It is partly, dear child, the result of an utter want of sympathy in those around me, which has, like a writer's frost, benumbed my whole nature."[37]

By September 1847, Julia was writing Louisa to inform her that she was again pregnant. She related the usual spats with Chev, noting his refusal to allow her to visit Louisa in Rome before returning to Boston to give birth. "I have just been at Chev's feet, begging to go to you now, & come back in February," Julia explained, "but he . . . says that no woman in her senses would dare to propose such a thing." Asking Louisa to forgive the "uninvited stranger," Julia described her reaction to learning that she was once again to be a mother: "At first I cried & raved about it," she explained, "but now I am more reconciled to the idea. It will be a girl, and is already christened Dolores," because the pregnancy "so far, has been a very sad one. . . . How I do dread another nursing! it is so wearing and so uncomfortable."[38]

A January 1848 letter to Louisa indicated no improved spirits; as Julia put it, "The wretched little Dolores will be due in one month." Still, she was doing her best to believe that the "poor child which has come so unwished for, will yet bring me a certain consolation." Indeed, she reported with pride and relief that she had not had to ask Chev to make any allowances for her. She had taken no naps, had continued to attend to her studies, and had even carried the children around the house throughout her pregnancy. "I sit up until eleven," she reported, "and rise punctually at seven, and upon my asking Chev, the other day, if I had given him any trouble from my condition, he was forced to say that I had not claimed a single extra indulgence in these eight long months." Nevertheless, she had to confess that she was "weary and worn in spirit."[39]

Childbirth was always a harrowing experience for Julia, and nowhere was Chev's lack of sympathy for her more evident than in the culmination of this pregnancy. On a spring night in 1848, she gave birth to "Dolores"—who turned out to be their long-awaited son, Henry Marion, whom they nicknamed Harry. Earlier in the evening, she had been out walking while Chev entertained Sumner in the parlor. Julia went upstairs when she returned home. "Presently," Chev wrote to Julia's sister Louisa, "I heard the Old Bird singing from the top of the stairs in her sweet voice—Chev-ie-Chev-ie; so I went down and dispatched the man servant for the Doctor, sent Sumner for the midwife, & the girl for . . . 'chloroform.'" Julia moved quickly through labor. "Before a soul of them could get back," Chev explained, "I was holding my son in my arms & performing for him & his mother the various duties of surgeon, nurse, & midwife. I had got through the most important operations & was about to proceed to the ablutions when the nurse, doctor, apothecary & all came trooping in—but all too late."

Overjoyed at last to have a son, Chev summed up the experience as "very pleasant . . . absolutely an enjoyable affair which began with a laugh at 1/4 before eight o'clock, soon grew into a growl, & terminated with one short yell on the part of the mother, and a continuous scream on the part of the boy who came into the world in less than twenty minutes." As he considered the event, Chev concluded, "never was a pleasanter time, except in the case of a woman whom I knew when a boy at school in the country. Stoddard was her name—a hale, hearty, vigorous mother of seven fine boys, some of whom I used to fight with." Continuing the story, Chev recounted, "Mother Stoddard was at the edge of the woods, cutting up brush, to heat her oven, when she was heard to shout for her 'help,' & her help, a big girl, went to her. Here Sally, says she, you take up this baby that I have just dropped & carry it to the house, and I will bring in the faggots & the axe."

After the birth of his first child, Chev had decided that the pains of labor were God's way of strengthening the ties of mother love. After his son's birth, he concluded that labor was fearsome only to women who were timid and out of shape. "A woman of good constitution, good training, good habits, & good courage need not anticipate & will not have a formidable delivery," he told Louisa. "Depend upon it, it is all wrong & wicked for women to make such delicate things of themselves & the pains & perils of child birth are meant by a beneficent creator to be the means of leading them back to lives of temperance, exercise, & reason."

Comforted that labor was not, after all, so very trying, and elated at the role that he had played in his son's delivery, Chev assured Louisa that mother and son were doing splendidly. He predicted great things for the baby. "Julius Caesar, Pericles, Brutus, & a few others may have been equal to our Harry," he conceded, "but I never met with any." As for Julia, she was doing well. Already she had begun "to receive her friends & to be as gay & brilliant as ever."[40] The entire affair was, in short, an event that left Chev feeling deeply satisfied.

Julia's letters told a different story. Like him, she was relieved and delighted that they at last had a son, but she did not find the delivery as easy as Chev implied. In fact, she considered him an unskilled midwife. "I suffered very little for the head," she told Louisa, "but as Chev did not know how to assist me, I had to make a tremendous effort for the shoulders, & gave one horrid scream, the only one of which I was guilty. Chev soon gave one himself: 'oh Dudie! it's a boy!' I couldn't believe it—we both cried & laughed." Julia acknowledged that the baby was "a prince," but she was far from being "as gay and brilliant as ever." Depressed throughout her pregnancy, she worried that Harry might "partake of the melancholy which oppressed me during the period of his creation." She also fretted that the demands of a new baby would take her away from her studies. "I have seen little of the world since his birth, and thought still less. I shall try to pursue my studies . . . for I am no good without them," she sighed, insisting, "[A]n hour or two for the cultivation of my poor little soul, I must have."[41]

The birth of the Howes' fourth child Laura was the occasion for even more ambiguity for Julia. A letter to Annie before the birth indicated Julia's misgivings. She noted that she wanted to visit Annie after giving birth but was hesitant to travel with four children. "Some one I must leave," she said. "I fear it will have to be Harry, since Chev intends that I should nurse the monster, which I do not want to undertake at all." That comment betokened Julia's state of mind quite well. Laura's birth came at a point of particular strain in Julia's relationship with Chev, and she resented his insistence that she breast-feed the new baby, rather than hire a wet nurse. Given Chev's earlier depiction of Julia as a mother whose only desire was to fill her child's "veins from her own," it was not surprising that Chev felt strongly about the issue. Breast-feeding fit his image of Julia as a mother who lived only for him and their children. Moreover, breast-feeding bound Julia to the baby and the home, as both she and Chev realized.

Julia, as ever, had had more than enough of the home. "I have spent a most monotonous winter," she complained to Annie, pointing out that Chev had largely deserted her. "My children have been my only companions, and needle work my principal occupation." Facing the prospect of another child-birth, Julia begged Annie to visit her in March, "when the little wretch is some ten days old." In a letter to Louisa, she observed that Chev had been in poor health and wanted to take a trip to Europe. Julia announced she would travel when the new baby was five weeks old, if she could hold her head up. "This makes me desire so much that the arrival of the unhappy monster may be punctual," she remarked.[42]

When the anticipated day arrived, Chev had little to say about Laura's birth, indicating only in a postscript to a letter to Louisa that "Annie-Laurie popped in upon us very unexpectedly, after a tap or two at the door, the evening before last. Julia was much surprised, but glad to see her; so are we all. . . . Julia is hardly well enough to write you today, but she will do so tomorrow if she can find time."[43] Julia, on the other hand, had a great deal to say. In a letter to Annie, she remarked that Laura's birth had been the easiest one yet, but she followed that comment with a description of the events surrounding the birth that depicted more indubitably than ever the depth of the antipathy between her and Chev, as well as her qualms about having yet another child.

According to Julia, she had been entertaining Theodore Parker when she went into labor. It was about ten o'clock in the evening. She called the nurse and went upstairs to bed. Chev was working downstairs. Julia asked the nurse to bring Chev to the bedroom. "Chev was summoned, but refused to remain," she complained to Annie. Apparently, Julia's screams in earlier deliveries had convinced Chev that nothing serious would happen until she gave voice to the pains of labor. "'I shall hear you down stairs before you will want me,' he said, and descended to the library, to finish a letter to Mr. Mann." Angry and humiliated, Julia said, "I sent for him again, however, and after half an hour of severe pain, the child was born. I had resolved not to scream, and did not. Chev tied the baby, and every thing was just right. The baby was of the smallest pattern— six pounds & a half in weight—she looked like an insect."

Perusing the appearance of this "insect" child, Julia conjectured, "I suppose she had been exercised almost to death—her arms looked as if they had been parboiled, this was because there was such an unusual quantity of water." Parboiled or not, little Laura quickly began to make demands of Julia. "She was born with a good appetite, began immediately to suck her fingers, and in the space of an hour I was forced to put her to my breast, where she thought fit to remain all night," Julia reported. Accepting her fate, Julia concluded, "I

love her very dearly, and am unwearied in nursing her." Two months later,
Julia wrote a poem for Louisa:

Oh! that the sofa were my dwelling place,
With one big nigger for my minister!
That I might forget the Baby race,
And, nursing no one, wallop only her![44]

Clearly, Julia's ambivalence about giving up her lifeblood had not been resolved.

So Fierce an Opponent

The strains of parenting did not end with childbirth. Bringing five children
into their home between 1843 and 1854 gave Chev and Julia much to do, and
inevitably, most of the work fell on Julia. Chev doted on the children, and they
loved him in return, but his experience of parenting was very different from
Julia's. Chev's career continued unabated throughout Julia's childbearing years,
while hers came to a halt. Chev was opposed to Julia's having a public life in any
case once he had married her, but the demands of childcare prompted her to
give up (or at least to postpone) literary aspirations that she might otherwise
have pressed. For her, the world of home and babies often felt like a prison.

Not that she lacked compensations. In an 1845 letter to Louisa (which
Chev read and commented on in a postscript), Julia told her sister that having
children would open up to Louisa "an ocean of love." She conceded that caring
for children could be overwhelming. "I have not been ten minutes this whole
day, without holding one or other of the children," Julia confessed. "I have to sit
with Fo-Fo on one knee and Dudie on the other, trotting them alternately,
singing, 'Jim along Josie,' till I can't Jim along any further possibly." Still, Julia
added, "I cannot tell you the comfort I have in my little ones, troublesome as
they sometimes are—however weary I may be at night, it is sweet to feel that I
have devoted the day to them." Although Chev suspected that Louisa would
think Julia was unhappy with her lot, Julia insisted that she hoped she was not.
"I should be very ungrateful," she added, "not to be satisfied with so kind a husband, and such beautiful children."[45]

Julia searched for additional ways to rationalize her unhappiness. In an
1847 letter to Louisa, she observed that Chev had recently been an indulgent
husband, allowing her season tickets to the opera. The children, too, were

"coming along famously. Julia, or as she calls herself, Romana, is really a fine creature, full of sensibility and of talent. . . . She is very full of fun, and so is my sweet Flossy, my little flaxen-haired wax doll. I play for them on the piano, Lizzie beats the tambourine, and the two babies take hold of hands and dance." Still, even when things were going well, Julia's life as a wife and mother just was not enough for her. She wanted more.

"'Is not your heart fully satisfied with such a sight?' you will ask me. I reply, dear Wevie, that the soul whose desires are not fixed upon the unattainable is dead even while it liveth, and I am glad, in the midst of all my comforts, to feel myself still a pilgrim in pursuit of something that is neither house nor lands, nor children, nor health." What was it that Julia longed for? She was not sure, but it was helpful to believe that the joys she sought were beyond the bounds of mortal life. "Sometimes," she told Louisa, "it seems to me one thing and sometimes another. Oh, immortality, thou art to us but a painful rapture, an ecstatic burthen in this earthly life! God teach me to bear thee until thou shalt bear me! The arms of the cross will one day turn into angels' wings, and lift us up to heaven."[46]

Julia knew that the temptation to defy Chev frequently surged within her, and she did her best to suppress it. Tired of the endless battle of wills over suitable living arrangements for the family, she at one point conceded the initiative to Chev, acknowledging, "I make no opposition of will or of temper, because it would be useless. Your letter gave me great sorrow, but my part is to bear—I cannot struggle with so fierce an opponent."[47] In an 1848 letter, she expressed disapproval of a woman she and Louisa knew named Clampit who openly opposed her husband. "Her state of rebellion and discontent is almost wicked," Julia proclaimed. She conceded, "I do not see why one should pretend to be excessively happy when one is not, or why one should try to say to oneself, 'I love this man,' when love is a matter out of the question." Still, she maintained, "marriage is not simply an affair of happiness, it does not promise us a boundless gratification of any taste or feeling."

Having confessed all the good things that marriage, despite her highest hopes, was not, Julia proceeded to a minimalist definition. Marriage was, she said, "a contract into which people, for the most part, enter voluntarily, knowing that it has certain advantages and certain disadvantages—it is a relation in which we assume grave obligations to other people, and it is quite as important that we should make them happy as that we should be happy ourselves." Left on her own, Julia was apt to lash out at Chev for neglecting her, but with Clampit as a safe target, she found herself defending Chev. "If we do not suit each other," she contended, "it is quite as likely to be my fault as his. I am grateful to him for many kindnesses, for much that embellishes and elevates my life, and he has certain rights & privileges, a certain supremacy and dignity, as a husband, which I wish him to retain, as much for my own sake as for his. If I could be free tomorrow, it would be difficult for me to find as kind a guardian, as pure and noble a man. The children, too, what a point of union do they make! I could ever leave them?"

Worried that Clampit might be justifying her rebellious ways with the anger that Julia had expressed on occasion, Julia insisted, "I do not think as Clampit does—my nature is a more contented, perhaps a gentler one. I cannot pretend to say that I am perfectly happy, or that there are not vast and painful longings of my soul which, in this life, will never be satisfied." Still, Julia contended, her ultimate goal was felicity in the life to come, "and I shall be more likely to attain happiness hereafter by cultivating in this life, a spirit of humility, of gratitude, and the love of uses, upon which my Swedenborg insists." Despite all the misery of married life, Julia was determined to find a way to rationalize her pain. "I still bear in my heart the traces of much suffering," she admitted, "but there was much good in it for me, and there shall be good for others."[48]

Julia particularly sought to find contentment in her duties as mother and homemaker. Although she enjoyed literary work far more, she diligently attempted to became better at the domestic arts. A letter written in November 1854 revealed the extent of those efforts. Written from the Institute, where, at Chev's insistence and against Julia's wishes, the family was spending the winter, Julia discussed with Annie the state of her household. Pregnant with Maud, who would be born later that month, and fearful as always that she might not survive the delivery, Julia reported: "one satisfaction I have—I am of use. I look after all household matters, and do it much better than in old times. . . . I feel so much the importance of the effort I am making, to my children and through them, to myself, that I do not really pause to think whether things are pleasant or not." For this, Chev had rewarded her. "Chev seems quite contented, for him," Julia confided. "He even kissed me tenderly, this morning, and said that I had grown so kind and patient, that he did not know what to do for me in return." In the midst of that relative peace, however, Julia was worried that after the baby was born, domestic tranquility would again prove elusive. "I may not be able to do as much as I now do—nursing makes me irritable, and Chev will not make much allowance for that," she fretted.[49]

Ultimately, Julia's efforts to repress her own desires in order to please Chev fell short. For one thing, she was not capable of the degree of self-annihilation that such a project demanded. Raising the children pushed her beyond the limits of her resources. When she had just Julia Romana and Flossy, she "used to sit with one upon each knee, and cry in very helplessness when they cried."[50] As the family grew larger, so did her frustrations. As she wrote Annie after Maud's birth, "Why should I add another chapter to the complaining of Job? . . . But oh! this weary, tasteless life, which is a waiting, without hope, love, or courage to help one to the future. While I could work, I had a least a great refreshment, and contentment of mind." Mindful that her complaints were rapidly mounting, Julia asked Annie to excuse her, urging her to "remember that wailing is as natural to me as crying is to a new baby."[51]

Caring for the children was difficult, and Julia resented Chev for not helping her more. At times, he needed as much attention as the children did. A confirmed hypochondriac, Chev had confided to Longfellow as early as 1845 that he was near death.[52] He suffered periodically from bouts of fever and headaches (assumed to be malaria) that were remnants of his volunteer days in Greece. When an attack came, he retreated to the sofa, lying "in his peculiar dead state, unable to speak or move," and expecting, as Julia said, "to be coddled." She reported to Annie on one occasion that Chev had "been sick as a dog, and still remains as weak as a rat," writing that various family members had held his head over a basin, "sympathizing deeply" with their "perfecta*bile* philanthropist."[53]

The children were accustomed to their father's fevers, although the drama of his sickness never failed to impress them. Laura remembered that Chev's room would be closed and darkened, while Julia crept about with cracked ice and hot "fomentations." A visitor who happened to be staying with the Howes during one of Chev's attacks was so unnerved that he told people that Chev was dying.[54] Julia suspected at times that Chev used his disability as a means to compel her to serve him, though after enduring a painful headache of her own, she confessed, "I lay on the sofa, thinking that it might, after all, cost you something to be amiable when you are similar." Whether Chev was healthy or ill, it seemed to her that his chief goal was to dominate her. His illnesses served the same purpose that his insistence on her breast-feeding the children had: they forced her to stay at home and give herself up to caring for her family. Her only defense was to subvert his aim, as she related regarding one of his spells: "I, making my self active in a variety of ways, bathing Chev's eyes with Cologne water by mistake, instead of his brow, laying the pillow the wrong way, & being banished at last . . . Am I not the most unfortunate of human beings? divil a bit. I enjoy all that I can."[55]

Humor thus proved to be one of Julia's most valuable defenses against Chev. Upset that he devoted his days to philanthropy, abandoning her to the brave the rigors of the nursery alone, she taught the children a song about their absentee father:

∽❧∼

Rero, rero, riddlety rad,
This morning my baby caught sight of her Dad.
Quoth she, "Oh, Daddy, where have you been?"
"With Mann and Sumner a-putting down sin!"[56]

∽❧∼

But on some occasions, even humor failed. In 1856, all five children came down with the measles. Julia was terrified, as well as frustrated that Chev insisted upon interfering with her attempts to nurse the children back to health. Their ongoing battle of wills found its way even into the children's health care. As Julia reported, Julia Romana spent three agonizing days retching. "When this ceased, a dreadful faintness set in—she implored most piteously for food." Julia wanted to feed her daughter, but Chev forbade her. "Chev would not allow a drop of gruel, or anything to be given her," Julia asserted. "I know she ought to have had something. I thought I should have gone mad. She crammed rags into her mouth and chewed them, so ravenous was she."[57]

In the end, Julia had no choice but to accept the alienation that marked her relationship with Chev. She had married him hoping for spiritual communion, and she had been willing to make sacrifices in order to be the wife that he wanted. After all her efforts, however, she felt isolated and bitter. As she wrote Chev after just three years of marriage, "[Y]ou have made me feel that, in spite of all your kindnesses, you could not take much interest in my spiritual experience, such as it has been. It has seemed to me therefore both wiser and kinder to sink all these things and to live only in the present and future, which are all that I have in common with you—these three years of married life have wiped out, as with a sponge, all living memory of the past."

Julia reminded Chev of the cost she had paid in choosing to be his wife. "I firmly resolved, when I married you," she insisted, "to admit no thought, to cultivate no taste in which you could not sympathize. You must know that my heart has been very loyal." Rather than finding intimacy, Julia discovered that in yielding herself to Chev she remained as isolated from him as ever. All that remained was for Julia to make the best of her life with Chev. "I will not expect too much of you," she declared:

I will enjoy all the moments of sunshine which we can enjoy together. I will treasure up every word, every look of your's [sic] that is kind and genial, to comfort me in these long, cold wintry days, when I feel that you do not love me. . . . When you are affectionate to me, I am too proud, too happy. . . . I long for the sound of your voice, for the sight of your face. I would say, for a thousand kisses, were I not afraid of vexing you, & making you say: 'get out, you beast.'[58]

Ultimately, unmet longing and dutiful submission were unsatisfying. Julia was too ambitious to surrender her will to Chev's for very long. She wanted marital happiness, but she wanted autonomy and self-expression as well. As she wrote to Chev while he was on a visit to Washington, his absence allowed her to give rein to her own desires for power and control. "I feel grand and independent—my right there is none to dispute," she announced. "The house is my house . . . of the absent Doctor, I speak quite cavalierly—he is my husband, my servant, the slave of my caprices . . . it is by my will that he lives in S. Boston, by my will that he goes to Washington—all his labours are labours of love for me, and when he comes back, and humbly claims the slight reward of a kiss, I turn my back upon him, exclaiming: get out, you beast."[59]

Being autonomous meant controlling her body as well. In a century when the most dependable form of birth control was sexual abstinence, Julia found it difficult to limit her pregnancies. She was of two minds about her children. On the one hand, she loved them; on the other, she despaired at the hours and the energy that childcare drained from her "precious time." It was hard to study Greek and write poetry while breast-feeding, entertaining, and nurturing children. Her reply to a letter from Annie, in which Annie confided that she had managed to abort an unwanted fetus, provided insight into Julia's struggles over motherhood. At first she declared herself appalled with Annie, asserting, "Your letter astonished me beyond measure. You, to be guilty of infanticide? You ought to be ashamed of yourself, and no doubt are." In her next sentences, however, Julia revealed just how intrigued she was with the notion of avoiding unwanted pregnancies. "How did you accomplish the wicked deed?" she asked. "By . . . James Clarke's female pills? or did you go on horseback? Well, poor Annie, you won't do so again, I know, and so we mustn't be too hard upon you—only I would like to know how the thing is done."[60]

More than marriage itself, becoming a mother had taken control of her life away from Julia. Given her literary ambitions, as well as her ongoing feud with Chev, it was inevitable that she viewed her children and her role as their mother with ambivalence. Chev left the most time-consuming tasks of childcare to her, but he never gave her free rein with the children. Thus, in no area of her life could she escape his domination. The demands of motherhood would, in any case, have been taxing; but discovering motherhood as yet another arena in which Chev asked her to subordinate her will to his meant that being a mother was at times maddening. It was no wonder that rage was ever the partner of love in Julia's relations with her family.

THE HAPPY HOME

What did the children think of all of this? There is no question that they noticed. They were conscious of their father's temper, and they could not help but discern their mother's depressions. They observed the ongoing battle of wills that marked their parents' relationship with each other. And they knew that caring for them took their mother away from the study time that she coveted. On some level, they must have sensed her resentment. Yet through it all, the children (at least publicly) declared that theirs had been the happiest of families.

As a group, the Howes were obsessed with documenting their family life. They saved letters, diaries, and other personal papers religiously, and were given to writing books about one another as well. Julia wrote a memoir of Chev at his death. Flossy wrote *Julia Ward Howe and the Woman Suffrage Movement*, and several narratives of Howe family life, including *Memories Grave and Gay* and *Flossy's Play Days*. Maud wrote *The Eleventh Hour in the Life of Julia Ward Howe* and numerous sketches of various persons and events in the Howe family, such as *Three Generations*, *This Was My Newport*, *Memoirs of the Civil War*, *Uncle Sam Ward and His Circle*, and *My Cousin F. Marion Crawford*. Laura wrote a biography of her father, edited his papers, wrote an account of his work with Laura Bridgman, edited Julia's religious musings into a volume entitled *The Walk with God*, wrote a joint biography of her parents entitled *Two Noble Lives*, penned her own autobiography, and produced a children's book about her life as a child entitled *When I Was Your Age*. Maud and Flossy wrote a book about Laura Bridgman together, and all three daughters (with Laura as the lead author) collaborated on a Pulitzer Prize-winning biography of their mother.[61]

The children's interpretation of Howe family life went like this: though Julia and Chev had their difficulties with one another, they were the most marvelous parents imaginable, full of creativity, and a sense of fun. The children enjoyed an Edenic childhood, packed with instrumental music, songs, dramas, outdoor frolics, and horseback riding. Though Julia and Chev were frequently at odds with one another, it was all for the best that Julia learned to submit to

Chev's will, because Chev was an apostle of humanity, and he prepared Julia to serve humanity as well. Admittedly, she had some difficult years during Chev's rule, but after his death, she was prepared to follow in his path, transforming herself from a sensitive poet into a tireless reformer.

Such an interpretation allowed the Howe children to account for the tensions in their parents' marriage by arguing that those very strains were necessary precursors to the career in benevolent reform that Julia fashioned for herself after Chev's death. As Laura put it, "[T]he marriage was like the wedding of the northwest wind and a mountain torrent." Like the prevailing winds, Chev was determined to have his way, and Julia "early learned to avoid, in times of stress, the full blast of the former. A stream works its way under or around an obstacle, as it can—as it must." As Laura insisted, Julia understood the necessity of submission. "She often said to us," Laura noted, "'There can be but one Captain to a ship; I shipped as First Mate!' and so it was."

Despite those tensions, Laura believed, her mother and father complemented and needed each other. Her father "could not be long without her (I have to have you! he would say)," and her mother depended on her father as well. "Through the long years of her widowhood," Laura asserted, "any sudden surprise or shock brought his name to her lips." Though Laura conceded that her parents occupied two very different worlds, she believed that their differences brought a richness to the marriage without which neither could have been the brilliant political reformers that they were. As she explained, "of their very essence neither could enter much into the other's special activities; but the full life of each enriched and sustained the other."[62]

Both Julia and Chev, according to their children, "labored unceasingly through life for the best and brightest as they saw it." This work came more easily for Chev; as a man, he was welcomed in and accustomed to the public sphere. For Julia, the work of social reform was not an instinct; by nature, she was a poet, not a reformer. Accustomed to the ethereal world of art, music, and literature, she found the drudgery of household duties required of her as a wife and mother extremely trying. But, her children argued, she was blessed to marry a man who revealed to her the noble work of humanitarian reform. Thus, even as she bewailed the fate that had consigned her to the kitchen and the nursery, "at her side was now one of the torch-bearers of humanity, a spirit burning with a clear flame of fervor and resolve, lighting the dark places of the earth." As a result, the children concluded, "her mind, under the stimulus of these influences, opened like a flower; she too became one of the seekers for light, and in her turn one of the light-bringers."[63]

By understanding their parents' anger at one another as part of a process that enabled their mother to become a public figure in benevolent causes, the Howe children were free (at least in retrospect) to isolate themselves from the unsettling emotions that had swept through their household. By presenting their parents' quarrels in a positive light, they could remove themselves from those tensions. When parents argue, children often blame themselves. They may worry that they have done something to upset their parents' happiness, or they may fear that simply by being present in the home they have created misery for their parents. It is also not unusual, when parents bicker, for children to side with one parent against the other, seeing one as a villain and the other as a victim.

It is likely that the Howe children experienced all of those feelings at one time or another as they matured. As adults, however, the Howes sought to explain their family's dynamics in a way that freed everyone from blame. The children did not wish to condemn themselves for their parents' problems, nor did they wish to censure either parent. Julia and Chev argued, the Howe children conceded, but even the bitterest confrontations concerned their parents' relationship to each other, not their feelings toward their children. As a result, the children concluded that marriage, not parenting, was the source of their parents' difficulties. If anything, parenting had been for Julia and Chev a saving grace, giving them an abiding joy that relieved the stresses of their relationship. The partnership of marriage came hard for Julia and Chev, but parenting came intuitively. "In both of them," as Laura put it, "parenthood was a deep, passionate and abiding instinct."[64]

Because their parenting was effortless, it was free, Laura asserted, from the power struggles that marked Julia's relationship with Chev. "In the garden," Laura explained, "he reigned alone; in the house there were two sovereigns. They were the king and queen of playfellows; 'Mamma' at the piano, singing or playing for us to dance; 'Papa' joining in the revels, frolicking till he developed 'a bone in his leg,' an ailment whose reality we never questioned." The children looked forward to pre-breakfast jaunts with their father, who taught them how to sit a horse. "The delight of these early morning rides," Laura remembered, "is not to be forgotten; the stealing downstairs in the cool dewy morning, springing into the saddle, the little black mare dancing with impatience; then the canter through the sleepy streets and out into the green blossoming country."[65]

There were other pleasures to be pursued outdoors. The Howe children declared that they enjoyed "perhaps the most wonderful childhood that ever children had. Spite of the occasional winters spent in town our memories center round Green Peace—there Paradise bloomed for us. Climbing the cherry trees, picnicking on the terrace behind the house, playing in the bowling-alley, tumbling into the fish pond,—we see ourselves here and there, always merry, always vigorous and robust." They loved to tag along at Chev's heels as he worked in the yard.

Inside the house, other opportunities unfolded. Julia's talents as a musician delighted her children. The children would gather around the grand piano and dance "to our mother's playing—wonderful dances, invented by Flossy, who was always *premiere danseuse,* and whose 'Lady MacBeth' dagger dance was a thing to remember." On other occasions, the children "clustered round the piano while our mother sang to us; songs of all nations, from the Polish drink-ing-songs that Uncle Sam had learned in his student days in Germany, down to the Negro melodies which were very near to our hearts." They loved to make up their own songs, and would shout out animals for Julia to invent verses about as she played the piano.[66]

But best of all were the escapades that Julia and Chev arranged jointly. Dramatic entertainment held a special place in the children's affections. "Among the plays given at Green Peace," the Howe daughters remembered, "were the 'Three Bears,' the Doctor appearing as the Great Big Huge Bear; and the 'Rose and the Ring,' in which he played Kutasoff Hedsoff and our mother Countess Gruffanuff, while John A. Andrew, not yet Governor, made an unfor-gettable Prince Bulbo." Occasionally, Julia and Chev would throw a party for their children, "such a party," their daughters declared, "as no other children ever had. What wonder, when both parents turned the full current of their power into this channel?"[67]

When they were little, the children assumed that such parental attentions were to be expected. "It was a matter of course to us children," they explained, "that 'Papa and Mamma' should play with us, sing to us, tell us stories, bathe our bumps and accompany us to the dentist; these were things that papas and mammas did!" In their adult years, however, the children recognized that their parents had had incredibly busy schedules, and they came to understand the sacrifices that Julia and Chev must have made in lavishing such care upon them. Rather than wonder if their parents, particularly their mother, had ever resented her children's demands on her time, the children concluded that Julia and Chev were such remarkable individuals that they could undertake amounts of work that might have defeated less exceptional people. "Looking back now, with some realization of all the other things they did," the children noted, "we wonder how they managed it. For one thing, both were rapid work-ers; for another, both had the power of leading and inspiring others to work; for a fourth, neither ever reached the point where there was not some other task ahead, to be begun as soon as might be."[68]

Moreover, as Laura pointed out, the children were not the only ones who came to Julia and Chev for attention and care. "Every day and all day," she said, "people of all kinds and all nations were coming to my father and mother for help, or comfort, or pleasure; but the happy home was always there for children."[69] Since the demands of outsiders did not ruin the "happy home," the children, at least as adults, came to believe that their demands did not impinge on their parents' happiness either, even though the children knew that Julia and Chev were at times pushed to the limit.

The children knew, for example, that they saw much more of their mother than they did of their father. Chev was often away on business, and, as Laura conceded, in the Rhode Island summers the family enjoyed, "'Papa' was a week-end vision, descending in a benevolent whirlwind."[70] Julia's "Rero, rero, riddlety rad / This morning my baby caught sight of her Dad" complained of an absentee father who all too often let his work as a humanitarian overshadow his duties as a father. Nevertheless, Laura's memory was that Chev was always present to love and comfort his children. "Most men," she explained, "absorbed in such high works . . . would have found scant leisure for family life and communion; but no finger-ache of our father's smallest child ever escaped his loving care, no childish thought or wish ever failed to win his sympathy."[71]

The children also recognized that Chev had quite a temper; they could hardly have denied it, since his fiery spirit was part of his public reputation. Still, Laura argued, "I do not remember his ever being irritable with any of us children; yet he was not a patient man. He did not suffer fools gladly; he rent them in pieces and went on over their trampled bodies. When he presided at a meeting, if a speaker exceeded the time, he pulled his coattails. If the beef were tough, he was capable of swearing at it. My mother was the better carver, having more patience."[72]

It is not hard to imagine that Chev might occasionally have lost his temper with the children as well as with the beef, but the children insisted that Chev had treated them with decorum and kindness, never showing anger. Such a memory was perhaps selective. Similarly, the children acknowledged that Julia had endured misery while struggling to be a good wife and mother. Although Julia later told the children that those had been the happiest days of her life, her daughters knew "she was often unhappy, sometimes suffering. Humanity, her husband's faithful taskmistress, had not yet set her to work, and the long hours of his service left her lonely, and—the babies once in bed—at a loss." Her daughters knew, moreover, that Julia blamed much of her suffering on the demands the children made on her. In going through her papers to prepare her biography, they read the letters cited in this chapter, in which she despaired that the children were draining her lifeblood. They also quoted from those letters in their biography. One citation came from a letter to her sister Annie, in which Julia declared, "I don't know how I keep alive. The five children seem always waiting, morally, to pick my bones, and are always quarreling over their savage feast. . . . Were it not for beer, I were little better than a dead woman."[73]

The children knew something else as well, or at least Laura did. In 1886, she wrote to Julia's sister Annie, indicating her desire to be made guardian of her sister Julia Romana's correspondence. Laura knew, from having visited her Aunt Louisa in Rome, what those letters might reveal (and what we will examine in later chapters): that Julia and Chev had separated after Laura's birth (the real reason for Julia's long visit to Rome in 1850–51); that in the 1850s Chev had repeatedly asked for a divorce, provided he could keep his two favorite children (Julia Romana and Harry); and that Chev had had affairs with other women. "But what of all that now?" Laura asked. "Against it, I have now the blessed memory of those last years, when the two great, noble hearts came together to perfect sympathy and peace when, perhaps for the first time, they fully understood each other." Laura knew the worst about her parents, but she continued to think the best. Reconciliation late in life made up for all the former pain. "Those brief years," she explained, "outweigh, to my mind, all the long, sad times of misunderstanding, clashing, the constant friction which seemed so long inevitable."[74]

It would appear that for Julia and Chev, the strains of parenting were inseparable from the tensions of marriage, but the children did not reconstruct their family history in that light. They were a bit in awe of the achievements of both their parents and searched for an explanation that would blame neither Julia, Chev, nor the children themselves for the displays of temper and depression that had periodically disrupted their parents' good humors. By creating a family myth that envisioned their parents as such efficient workers that they could handle tasks before which the average person might have wilted, the Howe children freed themselves from responsibility for their parents' emotional difficulties. They knew that their parents threw themselves eagerly into the work of benevolence. They knew that outsiders demanded time from them as Julia and Chev went about that work. If outsiders could make demands, then, surely, so could their children.

Thus, although the children knew that resentment was often in the air, they credited the tension in their household to the strains their parents encountered in their marriage, not to the pressures of parenting. And they asserted that the limitations of woman's sphere that confined Julia to the home gave way after Chev's death, so that she could continue the noble work that he had begun. Successfully surviving both his temper and his desire to dominate her, she had not succumbed to the fate of those fools whose bodies he had trampled. Rather, she had learned from him and then gone on to enjoy her own triumphs. In the end, the happy home became, in the Howe family mythology, the birthplace of brilliant careers as well as of much loved children. No one said it better than Laura: "I wish all childhood might be as bright, as happy, as free from care or sorrow, as was ours."[75]

Chapter Three

Conditions were often at fever pitch in the Howes' marriage. Crises abounded, emotions ran high, and both Chev and Julia often wondered just how much more they could take. But no events proved more pivotal than those occurring from 1847 to 1860. Between 1847 and 1853, Julia wrote a shocking novel, separated from Chev, left her two oldest children and moved to Rome, formed a powerful relationship with another man, returned to Boston, and published a book of poetry. She followed that book with a play and another volume of verse. The shock of it all was hard for Chev to endure, particularly as Julia's published works in this period were—to eyes that could see—terribly self-revelatory. Chev bitterly resented the ways in which she characterized him in her writings. Moreover, as his own involvement in abolitionism increased and the political climate became more volatile, Chev faced other pressures. His participation in the John Brown conspiracy caused him to fear for his own life once Brown was arrested and sentenced to death. To protect himself, in November 1859, Chev fled to Canada. Finally, as if all that were not enough, following the birth of Laura in 1850, Chev and Julia had two more children and Chev took a lover.

These were heady times indeed. But things were changing in the Howe family. Slowly, Julia was coming into her own, finding ways to assert her autonomy in spite of Chev's fierce resistance. In this period, Julia's literary work was a constant source of tension in her marriage, not only because her writing raised Chev's ire and gave her a sense of independence from him, but also because her work revealed painful themes in their relationship. Yet the children proved remarkably adaptive and flourished in the midst of the ongoing parental rumblings. If the children could not (or would not) admit the implications of their mother's literary work, however, their father found himself tortured by them. Ultimately, Julia's writing did more than help her establish an authorial voice of authority; it also spoke volumes about her opinion of Chev.

Nevertheless, behind all Julia's negative images of Chev—and some were quite brutal—lay a vision of harmonious gender unity that Julia was slowly developing. Dramatically portrayed in her novel, this ideal of man and woman moving beyond separate spheres into romantic and ethical partnerships that transformed each of them offered Julia a vision of a social order that would cherish her gifts rather than stifle them. By 1860, she was not sure exactly how to achieve this vision, nor did she know if it was available to all women or only to the exceptional few. But she was finding the courage to tell the world what she thought of domestic tyrants like Chev at the same time that she was dreaming fervently of the ecstatic communion accessible to sympathetic lovers.

QUITE A LITTLE ROMANCE

These themes of love, union, and the transformation of gender roles found vivid expression in a work of fiction. Sometime in the late 1840s, Julia began writing a remarkable novel, so sensational in its subject matter that it could never be made public. She never completely finished it. The manuscript consists of at least two different story lines, held together by a character named Laurence (or, occasionally, Laurent). To explain what made Laurence a most remarkable character is to demonstrate why Julia could not have dreamed of making her novel public: her protagonist was a hermaphrodite so sexually desirable as to ignite the lust of both men and women. The manuscript includes vivid scenes of attempted seduction and rape. A topic and a style more alien to Victorian respectability would be hard to imagine—but it made for compelling reading and also, presumably, writing.[1]

Despite its piquant subject matter, there were precedents for Julia's manuscript. By the 1840s the genre of the Gothic novel had long been established, and in her manuscript Julia made use of standard Gothic plot devices such as statues coming to life and the presence of abnormal and frightening human "monsters" as key characters. She also had access to French authors who were exploring themes related to gender confusion. In the mid-1830s, both Balzac and Theophile Gautier had published novels featuring hermaphrodites, and the novelist George Sand had achieved notoriety not only for her lascivious novels but also for her cross-dressing. As Gary Williams has observed, Sand had fascinated Julia's brother Sam during his stay on the Continent. In 1839, Sam encouraged Longfellow to meet Sand, crediting Sand with a "genius for writing" and dubbing her an enchanting "kind of moral hermaphrodite." Williams has also observed that Julia commented in her *Reminiscences* that after Sam's return from Europe in 1835, she began reading Sand and Balzac. As a young unmarried woman, Julia found Sand's work exhilarating, as she recalled in an 1861 article, describing the thrill of reading Sand secretly, knowing her father would not approve, all the while finding in Sand's novels a wondrous new world in which "a true human company, a living sympathy crept near us."[2]

Julia had, moreover, as early as her 1836 review of Lamartine's *Jocelyn,* carefully examined a work that highlighted gender confusion and sexual attraction. Lamartine's plot revolved around a young refugee named Jocelyn who inadvertently became the caretaker for an orphaned boy named Lawrence. Over time, Jocelyn became both spiritually and physically attracted to Lawrence, only to learn, to his surprise and sorrow, that Lawrence was not male, but female. Many of those narrative themes would find their way into Julia's own Lawrence manuscript.[3]

Unfortunately, much about this novel is difficult to reconstruct. The manuscript itself consists of several different strands, with no clear indication of how the parts fit together. There are also missing sections—sometimes only a page, but at other times, entire chunks. It is likewise hard to know exactly when Julia worked on the composition. A letter to her sister Louisa in May 1847 included a poem about two lovers named Eva and Rafael; that poem and those lovers also figured prominently in the novel. In her letter, Julia told Louisa that she had written "quite a little romance" about Eva and Rafael, but had chosen not to show her work to Chev or his friends. The last thing she wanted, Julia said, was to suffer the inevitable comparisons to Longfellow (or "Longodingdongo," as she called him).[4] It is not clear if Julia continued to work on the text while she was in Rome in the winter of 1850–51 or after she returned to Boston.[5]

In Julia's 1847 poem, Rafael was Eva's deceased lover, enshrined in full view in a crystal tomb, his body motionless as a statue. In her grief, Eva was visited by several angels. The first, the angel of despair, reminded her that death was irrevocable; her love was utterly lost. "The arms of the cross," said the angel, "reach wherever thou turnest . . . Thou'rt bound on it, nailed to it, / Born to it, wedded to it. / Persuade the wood to tenderness, / Caress the iron to softness, / Then only shall fate take pity on thee. . . . " The next heavenly counselor, the angel of the living world, urged Eva to turn her back on Rafael. "Beauty and love are not dead with him," the angel argued. "Seek them, and thou shall find them in other forms." A third angel chided Eva that her love for Rafael had been "partly sensual and partly selfish." Since Rafael was dead, the angel concluded, "thy sorrow is at the present useless and unreasonable, wherefore I bid thee go forth and do good works."[6]

Finally, the dead Rafael sent an angel of consolation to Eva. This angel promised Eva that if she remained utterly devoted to Rafael, a golden seed would take root in his bosom. When it bloomed, Eva would be transported to Rafael in heaven. Ignoring suitors and detractors, Eva remained at the tomb, receiving sustenance from a dove that brought her honey. When the seed finally bloomed, Eva was transfigured and reunited with Rafael, who gave thanks to God that Eva's "eye was single" throughout her trials. As Eva reconsidered her earthly life, she realized how much she owed to God, who had placed within her own breast a gentle teacher that enabled her to love steadfastly, seeking spiritual rather than material rewards. Locked in a fervent embrace, the lovers heard a heavenly voice proclaiming "one God, one faith, one baptism." And then a celestial light encompassed them, making them one forever.[7]

The romance of Eva and Rafael would provide a central motif for the entire Laurence novel: the theme of unwavering devotion rewarded, after much suffering, by ecstatic union. Related to this romance was the principal figure of the novel: a hermaphrodite named Laurence. His parents chose to raise Laurence as a boy, believing that as a male their child would have more autonomy in the world. While Laurence was attending college, he, like the other boys, found a twenty-eight year old widow named Emma far more attractive than the "tame and crude" maidens of college age. Emma fell deeply in love with Laurence. Because of his anomalous gender identity, however, Laurence could not encourage Emma as he would have liked; indeed, he feared "the hidden strength of her nature." Nevertheless, Emma crept into his room one night. In an unusually pointed conversation, Emma informed Laurence that she knew he would not marry her, but that her longing for him was so great that she would gladly trade her honor and her soul for one night of passion. "You cannot misinterpret this," she implored him. "Give me but this one night, but this one hour. . . . I can die tomorrow. I shall die happy."[8]

Laurence replied that he could offer her only "relations independent of sex," and for the first time Emma saw him as he truly was: "She saw the bearded lip and earnest brow, but she saw also the falling shoulders, slender neck, and rounded bosom. Then with a look like that of the Medusa and a hoarse utterance, she murmured: 'monster!'" Laurence could only reply: "I am as God made me, Emma." This consolation was of little use to Emma, who fell to the ground in a frothing convulsion. A student named Wilhelm helped Laurence carry Emma to her own room, and then Laurence steeled himself to endure "that most painful crucifixion"—an honest explanation of what had happened. Wilhelm swore "by the bloody agony of Christ" to keep Laurence's secret, and Laurence set out to return to his father's house. Emma subsequently died.[9]

Nothing good was waiting for Laurence at home. He quarreled with his father, who disowned him. Laurence then set out to wander alone, ultimately taking up residence in a secluded hermitage established by a count who had since died. There, Laurence subsisted on bread and water, read books of theology and metaphysics, and slipped into spiritual trances. A boy of sixteen named Ronald discovered him, unconscious. Laurence's hair had grown so long that Ronald assumed Laurence was a woman. Laurence insisted that he was a man. Ronald's father agreed to hire Laurence as his son's tutor, so Laurence went to live with Ronald. Not wishing to repeat the episode with Emma, Laurence was adamant about avoiding the company of women. Laurence devoted himself to Ronald, delighting in the boy's goodness and innocence, but the inevitable happened: Ronald came to love and desire Laurence.[10]

This attraction came to a predictably disastrous conclusion. Ronald dreamed that Laurence was a woman, found the prospect "glorious," and told Laurence so. Laurence was horrified. Laurence then examined a thesis Ronald had written, only to read a story of a pilgrim who so passionately worshiped at the marble statue of a saint that the saint came to life. Laurence found the prose beautiful, but cautioned Ronald not to ignore its lesson "that when we seek to wring the impossible from Heaven, we pray for our own destruction."[11] Eventually, Ronald's arm was wounded in a fight with a student who mocked Laurence as effeminate. His innocence lost, his shoulder bleeding, Ronald then accosted Laurence, saying, "You can change my torment to raptures of heaven. You shall be a man to all the world, if you will, but a woman, a sweet, warm, living woman to me—you must love me, Laurence."

There was more. "I am weary of seeing you thus encased, thus imprisoned," Ronald declared. "Do off, do off these hated garments which wrong your heavenly grace and beauty—float before me swan-like, in loose, light robes." And still more: "Throw off the narrow bondage of that vest—let your heart beat freely, let your bosom heave high, heave wildly, till the very remembrance of my sorrow be buried beneath it's [sic] white waves." At that, Laurence reached desperately for the pistols he kept on a shelf, intending to end his own life, but to no avail. Ronald had thought ahead and unloaded them. Ronald's entreaties continued: "Do not struggle—it is all in vain. I fear no curse but that of losing you. . . . I bear in my bosom a wondrous fire, a strange alchemy, that can turn marble itself to molten flame. You are mine by fate, mine by the power of my will, and my first crime is also your's [sic], for it is born of the union of your soul and mine." At the critical moment, when Ronald stood over him with a dagger and Laurence could resist no longer,

Ronald's wounded arm became paralyzed, and the drugged wine Laurence had in desperation given him earlier took effect. Ronald fell into a deep sleep, and Laurence's virtue, such as it was, was intact.[12] This section of the manuscript ends with Laurence fleeing into the night.

Julia continued the story of Laurence in another manuscript fragment, showing Laurence in Rome, studying Hebrew with a man named Berto. The text follows Laurence and Berto through a number of adventures, including an interlude in which Laurence dressed as a woman and passed time with Berto's three sisters. Laurence learned that Berto's uncle had endowed the hermitage where he had stayed before meeting Ronald. Berto then told Laurence of a sacred manuscript left by his uncle. This section of the manuscript then proceeds to more scenes of gender confusion. In once instance, people listening to Laurence sing assumed he was a castrato. In another scene, Laurence had an arousing dream of Ronald, who "almost made a woman of me."[13]

The remainder of the manuscript is even more chaotic, but a number of important scenes occur. First, the sacred manuscript of Berto's uncle was read—and turned out to be the romance of Eva and Rafael.[14] This story, as the manuscript has been catalogued in the Houghton archives, was actually the first scene of the novel.[15] Even if that ordering was unintentional, and Julia did not plan to begin the novel with that romance, the story nevertheless functioned as an overarching theme, since the motif of bringing statues to life (or cold marble to warmth) crops up repeatedly throughout Laurence's narrative. The manuscript also records scenes in which Berto and his sisters debated whether Laurence was male or female. Ronald resurfaced and told Laurence that he had found some relief from the desire that tormented him, but that even with the passage of time, Ronald could trust himself to be with Laurence "by day, perhaps again, but by night, never, never!" Engulfed in shame and agony, Ronald and Laurence held each other fast, in a mute appeal to heaven that received no answer. So Ronald departed, leaving "the beautiful monster" forlorn, as "mute and dead" as the stones on which he sat.[16]

The next day, Laurence felt "the last spark of life frozen out of me" and slipped into a kind of coma. Berto summoned a doctor, who opined that Laurence was neither man nor women, but instead was "rather both than neither." Berto's sister Briseida concluded that Laurence was an "integral soul" of the sort that Swedenborg had discussed in his mystical writings. In time, the physician treating him declared Laurence dead. Unable to move, Laurence nevertheless retained consciousness, and was touched to see that Berto and his sisters had not given up hope—they stayed with his body, praying that he might yet revive. Laurence then had a vision of a woman and a young man fighting over him, so that "my bowels were utterly torn asunder by the love I bare [bore?] to both of them." Then Laurence realized that "I was stretched upon a cross, and it was said in my ears: 'a cross is not formed otherwise than of two loves or two desires which cross each other or conflict.'" At last, Laurence was placed in his casket, ready to be entombed, only to hear well-known steps (presumably Ronald's). Desperate to hear Ronald's voice, wishing he himself could move . . . the manuscript ends in mid-sentence, surely one of the crueler cliff-hangers in American literature.[17]

What on earth did Julia mean by such an extraordinary story? Unlike typical Gothic literature, which presented readers with a subversion of domestic order and then, after an experience of terror, restored it, Julia's novel did not resolve the tensions it introduced.[18] Rather, Julia's "little romance" dismantled the ideology of separate spheres, offering in its place the gendered fluidity of the hermaphrodite Lawrence and of the transfigured lovers Eva and Rafael.

Undoubtedly the narrative of Laurence had many levels of significance. The most obvious was that this story gave Julia an opportunity to critique her culture's presuppositions about gender. Laurence's parents decided to consider Laurence male because that "would at least permit me to choose my own terms in associating with the world, and secure to me an independence of position."[19] In short, men had more autonomy, so life was easier for them. When Laurence masqueraded as a woman, he could see all the more clearly the desirability of life as a man: "it is a world of reality in exchange for a world of dreams—it is dealing with facts instead of forms, with flesh and blood, instead of satin and laces." Laurence's adventures in female masquerade also allowed Julia to ridicule the confining clothing worn by women in the Victorian age. For Laurence, they were garments of torture. Finally, the dispute between Berto and his sisters as to Laurence's gender—Berto insisting Laurence was male because he was intellectual and attentive to duty, with his sisters countering that Laurence was female because he was modest, tender, and pure of heart—allowed Julia to point to the arbitrariness of the traits assigned to women and men by nineteenth-century gender conventions.[20]

But what else? Julia did not have to construct elaborate scenes of attempted seduction and rape merely to poke fun at Victorian gender roles. On a theological level, the novel functioned to explain, in part, the suffering she endured in her marriage. Images of the crucifixion emerged repeatedly. Laurence learned, by the end of his tale, that a cross was the conflict of two loves. A simple definition, however, did not imply an easy solution; the war in his soul was so fierce he felt it was tearing him apart. Perhaps Julia was describing her own conflict with Chev. The image of the cross gave dignity to her struggles to find satisfaction in being a wife and a mother yet retain an identity apart from those roles.

In another discussion of crucifixion, the angel of despair told Eva that she was born and wedded to the cross and ought to embrace it, because only in doing so was relief possible. A second angel disagreed, rebuking Eva for bringing unreasonable suffering upon herself by mourning Rafael excessively. But Eva answered that Jesus, through his suffering, had brought redemption. Ultimately, of course, it was Eva's singleness of devotion, her unswerving dedication to Rafael, that brought about her transfiguration. All of these scenes suggested the path of single-minded devotion as the road to redemption. Perhaps Julia was justifying the necessity of clinging to her deepest understanding of herself as a person of important literary abilities. To turn away from suffering, to reconcile too easily the pull she felt between family on the one hand and autonomy and self-expression on the other, would be to lose forever the possibility of integrating both loves. Eva and Rafael were indissolubly united only after Eva's trial, not before.

Or perhaps Julia was suggesting, through the shocking image of the hermaphrodite, that Victorian culture was too entrenched in its prejudices to ask the right questions about gender. Throughout Laurence's story, people tried to assign him one gender identity or another. At times they chose ridiculous ways of judging him. Berto, for example, credited Laurence with a sense of duty and therefore assumed Laurence was male, since women, in his mind, lacked the innate respect for duty that characterized men. Surely the story of Eva disproved that notion. On other occasions, people judged Laurence according to his physical attributes. That invariably showed that he was never what they assumed. Ronald initially thought Laurence was a woman because he had long hair and a rounded figure; Emma thought Laurence was male because he had a beard. Dressed as a woman with Berto's sisters, Laurence was an oddity at six feet tall. Dressed in male attire, he had a high singing voice that sounded like a castrated man. One of the ongoing features of this story was that the reader (and the characters) could not get over their curiosity. Was Laurence male or female? The point, which neither the reader nor the characters wanted to accept, was that hermaphrodites were ambiguously sexed.

Julia may have used the story of Laurence to dramatize her own attempts to achieve autonomy. She dressed like a woman, but she wrote and thought like a man—with independence and conviction. In the end, it was the doctor who settled the debate: Laurence was neither a woman nor a man, but both. He was, as Berto's sister Briseida said, an integrated soul, capable of incarnating masculine and feminine attributes. In his sexual appetites, Laurence hungered both for Emma and for Ronald. He despised himself for his attraction to each of them; he felt worthy of neither of them; and yet the undeniable power of the two conflicting desires threatened to tear him in two. Perhaps Julia's point was that inner peace was possible only when Laurence accepted all that he was. Briseida and the doctor were able to do that and to see him as complete in himself, an exceptional being "presenting a beautiful physical development, and combining in the spiritual nature all that is most attractive in either sex." The doctor professed his astonishment, in fact, that Laurence differed so much from other "anomalous" cases he had seen, which were generally marked by "low organization" and "feeble and uncertain impulse."[21] If anything, Lawrence was an improvement on the norm: he combined qualities that others thought could not exist in a single individual. When people ceased trying to categorize Laurence according to their presuppositions about gender, they could appreciate him for the wonder that he was.

Or maybe not. Berto pointed out that Laurence was "the poetic dream of the ancient sculptor, more beautiful, though less of the human, than either man or woman." Briseida described him as a "heavenly, superhuman mystery . . . needing not to seek on earth it's [sic] other moiety, needing only to adore the God above it, and to labour for it's [sic] brethren around it."[22] Laurence, by this accounting, was complete in himself, but not truly human. Emma had another word for him: "monster!" The story of Laurence may have given voice not to Julia's assurance that the answer to her problems was to be true to herself, but to her deepest fears that Chev was right. Maybe there was something unnatural, even perverse, about her desire to achieve autonomy and exercise her voice independent of his. As Laurence's singing gave him away as unsexed, so Julia's desire to write might give her away as not fully a woman. Maybe something was fundamentally depraved about her and, like Laurence, she could only confess with shame: "I am as God made me."[23]

While the novel was saturated with ambivalence toward Lawrence, Julia depicted Eva as unambiguously heroic. Yet the romance of Eva and Rafael produced a being quite similar to Laurence—an individual in whom male and female were united. Perhaps Laurence represented for Julia the exceptional, and abnormal, individual who could combine attributes of both genders into one person. Laurence was a dangerous figure, a misfit, an outcast, a threat to the existing social order. Eve and Rafael, on the other hand, were not ominous characters, because they represented the height of romantic love.

Chev had, in a courtship letter to Julia, emphasized the delights of earthly life and had promised to clip off Julia's wings to keep her as a mortal imprisoned in his arms. Only after husband and wife had lived a full physical life together, each in his or her appropriate sphere, did Chev imagine them sprouting wings and flying to the spiritual realm. The image of lovers flying to heaven as Julia construed it in the romance of Rafael and Eva, however, was remarkably subversive of Chev's vision. In the first place, Eva was rewarded for rejecting earthly life in favor of absolute spiritual devotion; she concentrated, as Chev would put it, on growing her wings, not on earthly duties and responsibilities. Secondly, when Eva and Rafael ascended into the heavens, they did not remain separate individuals, but merged in an ecstatic transfiguration that disrupted the carefully defined gender spheres of the Victorian age.[24] If Chev's vision stressed the husband's power to restrict the wife to the marital realm, Julia's answer was to depict true romance as a transformative spirituality that freed lovers from the bonds of earthly roles and metamorphosed them into a radical new being.

In the 1860s, Julia would say that earlier in life she had assumed that only exceptional women would break the bonds of domesticity that confined women to the private realm. By the time she was involved in the woman suffrage movement, however, Julia came to believe that a better model of progress was available. Not simply the exceptional woman, but all women, in partnership with men, could learn and grow from one another. It was possible to talk about the expansion of women's rights as part of the wider evolution of the human race. In the late 1840s, however, Julia had not yet made that transition in her thinking. Those women who escaped the constraints of separate spheres would be those who were exceptional enough to do so on their own.

It is possible to read the story of Laurence as Julia's way of representing the choice between the doctrine of the exceptional woman and the doctrine of man and woman sharing in partnership the attributes of the other. Laurence could function as a model of the exceptional "woman" who dared to take as her own certain attributes of men. Eva and Rafael modeled the partnership of man and woman, joining together to achieve greater heights for humanity. Both models were subversive of Victorian gender roles, since both models presented gender as a dynamic experience, subject to change and growth, rather than as a static essence. In each instance, a single individual manifested gender attributes of both male and female. But the model of the transfigured and united lovers, appealing to popular romantic notions, clearly did not produce in Julia the same misgivings that she found in the figure of Laurence. Eva and Rafael, united before God, did not seem to Julia to be a "monster!" Given Julia's relationship with Chev in the late 1840s, however, Julia was hardly in a position to imagine working in loving partnership with men as the path to achieving her own autonomy. For the time being, she would continue on her own, the exceptional woman isolated from other women and from men sympathetic to women's rights. Like Laurence, she would be a wonder and a marvel, prodigious in her talents, but insecure about her place in society.

The implications of a manuscript as complex (not to mention unfinished) as the Laurence narrative cannot be exhausted in a few pages of commentary. The text is astonishing in its subject matter, in the emotional extravagance of its tone, and in the wracking sense of pain that it evokes. The story is haunted by Laurence's self-hatred and loneliness as well as by the recurring images of Eva and Rafael, the lovers who became one through Eva's unremitting devotion. Pain, anger, desire, and alienation formed Laurence's lot; ecstasy and union were the promise of the romance of Eva and Rafael. Both cases represented the integration of two natures, but that integration lay beyond this world and the merely human; it was metaphysical and spiritual, not earthly, as "normal" gender differentiation was earthly. In any case, the Laurence manuscript would have struck proper Bostonians as a succession of erotic scenes connected by interludes of loneliness and madness. It is worth noting that whatever else this manuscript meant to Julia, she testified that the process of writing it had offered her a "golden tide" of creativity and the heady experience of entering, truly, into "the strange history of a strange being."

ROMAN HOLIDAY

If the story of Laurence was a private way of expressing herself in the midst of a marriage gone awry, Julia also needed to find other sorts of accommodation. She was having a bit of luck with her poetry. In 1848, nine of her poems gained inclusion in anthologies of women's poetry assembled by Rufus Griswold and Thomas Buchanan Read.[25] Julia complained to Louisa, however, that she could not even afford to buy the books and could only hope to receive free copies in return for the poems she contributed.[26] In any case, contributions to anthologies did not satisfy her literary ambitions, and they offered no assistance with her domestic trials. Julia's problems with Chev were at their peak, and the new pregnancies had taken their toll as well.

Harry was born in March 1848, and Laura in February 1850. By then, Julia's sister Louisa had married a sculptor named Thomas Crawford and was living in Rome. Sister Annie had married Adolphe Mailliard, a descendent of Napoleon Bonaparte, and a family reunion at Annie's home in New Jersey after Laura's birth prompted the three sisters to propose a Roman sojourn. For Julia, the prospect offered an opportunity to escape her life in Boston, and Chev agreed to take a six-month leave to accompany her to the Continent. Taking Harry and Laura, and leaving behind Julia Romana and Flossy in the care of a family named Jarvis, Chev and Julia joined the Mailliards, Louisa, and her children on a trip to Europe, meeting Thomas Crawford in Paris. When Chev's leave expired, he returned to Boston, and the rest of the group moved on toward Rome. Crawford had rented a large estate, and the Mailliards moved in with Louisa. Julia rented an apartment near the Crawfords for herself, Harry, and Laura, and set about the task of finding out what life without Chev and the constant possibility of pregnancy might be like.[27]

This Roman sojourn signaled a crisis in Julia's marriage—it was, after all, a lengthy separation from Chev—and many of its details remain shrouded in mystery. Since Julia was living near her sisters, there was no need to write them. Thus, there are no letters to reveal what was on her mind during these months. She did exchange letters with Chev, but apparently they were so revealing and painful that at his death he asked her to burn them.[28] The three communications that did survive indicate that both Julia and Chev were under stress. Part of a letter remains from the early days of Julia's stay, in which she scolded Chev for not having written her recently: "It is a week since we parted, dear Chevie, and with all the uncertainties of life in my mind, you may imagine that your silence causes me great uneasiness."[29] Also extant is Chev's letter to Julia describing his return to Boston. When he went to Concord to retrieve Julia Romana and Flossy from their lodgings with the Jarvis family, he found the girls wild to see him. "As fast as two stout legs could carry her, came rushing along a stout little girl, with out-stretched arms and streaming hair,— crying out—Papa! Papa!" he reported. "She was in my arms in a moment, and soon Julia was there also, and my heart took its feast of affection, and I wept for joy as freely as ever I have wept for sorrow."

Chev spared no details of his older daughters' delight in him. "I could not have believed that at their tender age they could feel and manifest such warm and continued tenderness and affection for a parent," he marveled. "I have been with them four days, and yet they hang round me all the time,—they kiss me every moment, and seem willing to give up any play to come and love me. I have no power to express the joy and gratification I feel in the possession of such treasure of the heart." As joyous as Chev was to receive the love of his older daughters, however, he was terribly anxious about his wife and his treasured son Harry. "I will not trust myself to write or think of you—or of Harry—it makes me wretched to do so," he confessed. "I will only hope—my heart prays though my lips do not move—God bless you and keep you! Kind love to the Girls and Adieu-adieu."[30]

If Chev was worrying about Harry, Julia was anxious about her older girls. In November 1851, she sent a letter saying that she missed them and that Harry and Laura were doing well. Julia urged Flossy and Julia Romana to make their father happy, and then confessed, "Mother is often sad to think that she cannot see your dear faces. Sometimes she dreams of you at night, and then when she wakes up, she is grieved to find out how far away you are, and that she cannot hope to see you for many long days."[31] Julia Romana would never forget this letter; it told her that Julia was drifting away from her and Flossy. One result was a permanent breach in family loyalties. From this period on, Flossy and Julia Romana would feel closer to Chev than to Julia and would take his side in domestic disputes. The formative experiences in the nursery in Rome also solidified the relationship between Harry and Laura; they remained best of friends for life.[32]

If this was a time of strained relationships in the Howe family, it was also a period of tension between Julia and Louisa. There is no way to know exactly what went wrong, but letters written after Julia's return to the United States offer some clues. In October 1851, Julia wrote to Louisa, indicating that she knew Louisa hesitated to write to her. Julia apologized for her "faults of temper, want of consideration, etc." and asked Louisa to forgive the "eccentric habits of life" she had exhibited in Rome. "Try to remember," Julia pleaded, "how much there had been to unsettle my mind, how utterly I seemed to have been cast adrift, and given up to the caprices of life." Julia admitted she had not been the easiest companion and promised to do better. "I felt sometimes the pleasure of a naughty child in being bad. I had been tormented. I liked perhaps to torment others. But that sad ruthlessness is over now."[33]

Receiving no reply, Julia wrote Louisa again in April 1852, remarking on Louisa's silence once more. In an August letter, Louisa explained that she had quit writing because she had felt alienated from Julia. During the winter Julia had spent with her in Rome, Louisa confessed, she had despaired that she had lost the way to Julia's heart. But, Louisa concluded, all of that was immaterial now; the thing to do was not to blame one another, but to renew their love.[34]

Vague as Louisa's comments were, it is not hard to imagine that her ire may have been stirred by Julia's social life during her Italian sojourn. For one part of Julia's life that did go well in Rome was the marvelous feeling of liberation she enjoyed. She had had four children in seven years and had endured domestic strife; now, suddenly, she was on holiday in Rome. Years later, Julia wrote Maud that she had felt "absolutely intoxicated" that winter in Rome and had danced across Louisa's parlor singing "Liberty! Liberty!"[35] She enjoyed another wonderful experience in renewing her friendship with Horace Binney Wallace, an old acquaintance whom she met again at a Roman Christmas party. In her *Reminiscences,* Julia described Wallace as an "exhilarating companion," a rosso (redhead) like herself who delighted in discovering other redheads.[36] Wallace brought her flowers, took her for trips around the city, and encouraged her study of philosophy, especially of Auguste Comte. He delighted in her poetry and was happy to critique it. Julia later told Louisa that Wallace was "so precious, so full of help and comfort," that together they "were very sympathetic to each other." She had finally found a soul mate, Julia believed, someone who could appreciate and improve her poetry. "He helped me to my best thoughts," she explained, "and knew which were my best."[37]

Just how close were Julia and Horace Binney Wallace? Clearly she considered him her best friend,[38] and certainly he made her happy in ways that Chev did not. Was Wallace more to her than a friend? Like so much of Julia's Roman holiday, insufficient evidence exists to answer this question. Not surprisingly, neither her autobiography nor any of her daughters' works address the issue. According to the various Howe written sources, Julia was alone in Rome simply because Chev could get only a six-month leave. One thing we do know about that winter is that eventually word got back to Boston that Julia was giving parties and making her mark on Roman society. The news occasioned gossip.[39] Mary H. Grant has argued that Julia fell in love with Wallace in Rome, that Chev knew it, that his letters confronted Julia with his knowledge, and that his demands for Julia's return were the impetus for her leaving Rome in the summer of 1851.[40]

Such a scenario is unlikely. The surviving correspondence suggests that Chev did not order Julia to come home and may actually have forbidden her to return. A letter from Annie to Chev in April 1851 depicted Julia as thoroughly miserable because Chev would not permit her to come home to him. Warning "dearest Chevie" that Julia looked poorly and that the uncertainty of her relationship with Chev was wearing her down, Annie begged Chev to invite Julia back to Boston. "Julia is only anxious to do your bidding, and I am sure that a little word from you, added to our entreaties, would bring pleasure to you both," Annie opined. "We all feel," she added, "that it would be difficult for her to pass another [winter] . . . so entirely alone and unprotected." Between Louisa's growing family and the limited number of rooms in her home, Annie was certain that Rome offered Julia no long-term comfort. She needed to return to the United States.

If Chev refused to ask Julia home, then Annie saw no other alternative than to invite Julia into her own house, although Annie blanched at "how much it would grieve me to leave her in such a position." Still, the sadness Annie perceived in Julia's face when she played piano for the children's evening dances gave Annie no other choice. On Christmas, Annie confided, Julia had "cried bitterly, as she helped us to arrange their tree, and thought of the one that she had made last year for her own children." Annie urged Chev to reply by the end of May. If he did not, she concluded, she would do all that she could to convince Julia to go home, and would console herself with the thought that she was "fulfilling, although unbidden, your wishes."[41]

Gary Williams points out that Horace Binney Wallace left Rome in April 1851 to visit Comte in Paris. He suggests that when Wallace departed, Julia also began to think of leaving. Perhaps, too, Annie's letter to Chev indicated that Chev had threatened to turn Julia out, and that Julia had panicked; the disgrace would have overwhelming.[42] In the end, there is no way to determine the extent of Julia's involvement with Wallace. It is hard to imagine that she would have risked her Roman "freedom!" to pursue a physical relationship with him. She did not need to do so to account for Chev's ire. It was enough that her heart was close to Wallace, enough that her days were relatively carefree, enough that she was making her mark in society. As far as Chev was concerned, the Roman sojourn had bombed.

Julia faced the homeward trip with trepidation. She later said that on this visit Rome did not seem medieval, as it had in 1844. Instead, it had become the one place where she was truly alive. "I enjoyed many pleasures, both of study and friendship," she explained, "and in a stay of some eight months, learned to love the city so that it seemed like death to leave it."[43] Julia suggested that the difference was the changed political climate—that the revolutions of 1848 had modernized Rome—but the real issue was personal, not political, freedom. In her Reminiscences, she contended that upon returning to Boston she was in anguish that she might never see Rome again. The fear of losing the autonomy she had enjoyed in Rome or the anxiety of not seeing Wallace, however, were more likely sources of her distress. In any case, as she anticipated her return to Boston, Julia could only confess, "I left Rome after those days, with entire determination, but with infinite reluctance. America seemed the place of exile, Rome the home of sympathy and comfort."[44] She turned her face toward home, but not with joy. The only consolation was the anticipation of seeing Julia Romana and Flossy again. As she wrote Louisa of the journey across the Atlantic: "[I]t was all pleasant, save the direction, but that too assumed an interest when we approached the place where my children were."[45]

Her reunion with the older girls did not carry the sense of absolute satisfaction that Chev had recorded the previous autumn. Upon her arrival at Green Peace, Julia reported, "two children whom I sh[oul]d not have recognized as mine ran out to meet me, and after some little show of shyness, hugged me heartily." Cautiously noting that the house seemed to be in good order and Chev welcoming, she could not help but feel frustrated at the sight of her older girls. "They seem to me," she told Annie,

> very petulant, and a little coarse mannered, I mean, given to loud and quick talking, contradicting each other, etc. They are in good health, but constant exposure to the sun has injured the beauty of their complexions. Julia is freckled, and Flossy badly tanned. I cannot help a feeling of disappointment at finding them so, they were so fair when I left them—their voices too have a harshness of tone, most unpleasant to me, who esteem so highly grace of speech in a woman. Still, there will be ample time to reform all these things, if their father is willing.[46]

Warily settling in, Julia assured her sisters that she was calmer than in the old days and that life with Chev was less worrisome. "Chev knows that I don't pretend to meddle with anything," she told Annie. "I get no scoldings, and am in great peace."[47] In an April 1852 letter, she informed Louisa: "My principal occupations are my own studies and teaching the children, which devolved entirely upon me. I have a housekeeper, but otherwise live very much as when you were with me, and with no great alteration in any way, save that I am calmer and more self-sustained." In June, Julia wrote Louisa again:

> I get on quietly, and better than of old. I acquired a little firmness and inde-pendence during my year of freedom, and no longer quiver at a cold look, or weep at a sharp word. Books are much to me, writing somewhat much to me, though remotely, is the thought of that blessed land which received me before, in my extremest misery, and which would again, in case of necessity, unfold its maternal arms to take me in. Do not think from this that I have any thought of returning to Rome—in all probability, I never shall. Only, I think you can imagine that to one who has been an exile, it is blessed to remember that there is such a refuge.[48]

AN IRREPARABLE LOSS

But the peace could not last forever. In time, as Julia put it, she lost the "elastic-ity produced by my pleasant Roman life," and she and Chev were at it again. She told Annie in November 1852 of the latest disaster at Green Peace. She had given a dinner party, and Chev had not only offered her no assistance, but had actually managed to ruin the entire evening by banning wine. That was it, Julia declared: no more company. Later, she said, "Chev gave me (unasked) permission . . . to invite half a dozen of my friends every week to tea and whist! that I might not, he said, have all my gaiety abroad." Julia was not impressed with the offer. "What an ass he must take me for!" she fumed. "Do you think that Giant Despair ever gave tea-parties?"[49]

One thing that did interest Julia in these months was her correspondence with Horace Binney Wallace. They were apparently able to see each other once,[50] but Julia's hopes of a continued close relationship suffered when Wallace returned to Europe in the autumn of 1852. In January 1853, Julia wrote him: "I have been made happy by hearing that you are miserable in Paris." He could not possibly be as disconsolate as she felt, Julia insisted. She had looked forward to meeting him in New York for "endless talks and happy communion," but instead she faced an ocean-wide gulf. "I miss you so much, and life is so short, and friendship so precious—ah me!" Julia sighed. She confided that she had continued to work on her poetry, and complained that his unavailability to offer criticism was an "irreparable loss." She had even considered publishing the poems in *Putnam's New Monthly*, "but I still keep them all to myself, waiting for your advice."

Even greater than her need for Wallace's editorial assistance, Julia claimed, was "my need for you as a friend. I have been leading a very lonely and unsympathetic life," she explained, and she had counted on his support. Yet Wallace had not written from England, as he had promised, and might not write from Paris either. "You shall or shall not write me from Paris, just as shall please you best, but you must not forget me," Julia pleaded. "I am too lonely, too helpless, too orphaned to be deserted by you, my dear brother." Life, she concluded, "brings us too little occupation for the heart—we must prize and make the most of any dear relation it brings us."[51]

Devastating news was to follow. Julia learned just after completing her letter that Wallace had committed suicide in December 1852. The trusted friend was gone forever, and Julia took it hard. She wrote Louisa that she was living in her books and in her writing. "Of course, you exclaim: what madness!" Julia conceded. "But indeed, I should have a worse madness if I did not cram myself with books—the bareness and emptiness of life [is] more than insupportable, and that distant but terrible vision of insanity which has haunted my life, would become reality." Julia was convinced, she said, that Wallace must himself have been insane to take his life. The loss was grievous—the worst she had suffered since her brother Harry's death.[52] Even Chev, she claimed, was trying to help: "Chev has been much kinder to me since the event—he seems to know how much I have lost. I go often to see [Wallace's] poor mother, who is much broken—we sit and are sad together—his beautiful portrait hanging in the room."[53]

In her sorrow, Julia would focus her energies as never before; before 1853 had ended, she would publish the book of poems she had so long dreamed of writing—without Chev's permission or knowledge. With the success of *Passion-Flowers* she acquired, finally, a literary reputation, at the same time that she drove Chev to the brink of madness. Predictably, he came close to taking her down with him. The fallout would be significant: more discussions of separation and divorce, continuing struggles over sexual intimacy and additional children, suspicions of unfaithfulness, and, not least of all, more publications. Julia did not win all the battles, but once she found a public voice, there was no turning back. Chev often prevailed at home, but he could not silence her pen. The balance of power was shifting.

PASSION-FLOWERS

With Horace Binney Wallace irrevocably gone, Julia took steps to see that the poetry he helped inspire during Julia's days in Rome found public expression. She received advice from a German named Emmanuel Vitalis Scherb as well as from Henry Wadsworth Longfellow.[54] As she prepared her manuscript for publication, she said nothing to Chev, but privately wavered about allowing her name to appear on the book's title page.[55] In a letter to Annie in December 1853, Julia told Annie that Longfellow had advised against using her name and that so far Chev still knew nothing of the project. Julia was excited by the book's imminent publication. "If I succeed," she assured Annie, "I feel that I shall be humbled by my happiness, devoutly thankful to God."[56] Writing a week after the book was issued in late December 1853, Julia had much good news to share. "Hundreds of copies have already been sold, and everyone likes it," she exulted. "Fields foretells a second edition—it's sure to pay for itself. It has done more for me, in point of consideration here, than a future of a hundred thousand dollars." Indeed, she declared, Theodore Parker had even "quoted seven of my verses in his Xmas [sic] sermon, and this I considered as the greatest of honours. I sat here and heard them, glowing all over." Only one "bitter drop" threatened her happiness: "Chev took it *very* hard." Still, she thought he would come around: "He is now consoled by its' [sic] success, and behaves very well indeed. The authorship is, of course, no secret now."[57]

The question of thwarting Chev's will aside, the content of the poetry would have been enough to infuriate him. Readers bought *Passion-Flowers* because they had never seen anything like it—at least not by a woman, particularly a prominent woman.[58] As had been her style in the works she had written for her eyes alone, Julia had composed *Passion-Flowers* so that the text spoke on at least two different levels. The poems drew readers not only into the surface images depicting Rome, motherhood, abolitionism, and European democratic movements, but also into the mysterious background, where there were enticing hints of autobiographical disclosures. Sometimes the personal revelations were obvious; at other times they were muted, unclear, and incomplete. Julia did not tell everything, but she told enough, and she suggested more. The book was spectacular because it was tantalizing.[59]

Passion-Flowers opened with a "Salutatory" that called upon "brother and sister poets dear" to comfort Julia "as a child of Art" by listening to her verse. Any reader who knew her would have been able to see Julia's domestic troubles played out in the poems. The book's second poem, "Rome," might as well have been written to answer this question: Did she have fun in Italy without Chev? "Rome" began:

I knew a day of glad surprise in Rome,
Free to the childish joy of wandering,
Without a 'wherefore' or 'to what end?'
By querulous voice propounded, or a thought
Of punctual Duty, waiting at the door
Of home, with weapons duly poised to slay
Delight, ere it across the threshold bound.

Finding the opportunity to move to a "free cadence of mine own wild singing," Julia rejoiced at a grace "more than maternal." She celebrated the glorious freedom her time in Rome had offered:

The winter, like a college boy's vacation,
Seemed endless to anticipate, and lay
Stretched in a boundless glittering before me,
Unfathomable in its free delight.[60]

In other poems, Julia considered the topic of maternity. In "Mother Mind," she proclaimed that writing poetry was for her a matter of necessity and inspiration, not conceit or whimsy.

⁓

I never made a poem, dear friend—
I never sat me down, and said,
This cunning brain and patient hand
Shall fashion something to be read . . .

But not a word I breathe is mine
To sing in praise of man or God;
My Master calls at noon or night;
I know his whisper and his nod. . . .

⁓

In lines reminiscent of Eva's utter devotion to Rafael while awaiting the maturation of the golden seed within him, Julia explained the patient concentration and suffering required to give birth to poems she described as "children of my soul":

⁓

'Tis thus—through weary length of days,
I bear a thought within my breast
That greatens from my growth of soul,
And waits, and will not be expressed.

It greatens till its hour has come;
Not without pain it sees the light;
'Twixt smiles and tears I view it o'er,
And dare not deem it perfect, quite.[61]

⁓

Other poems referred obliquely to lost love—intended, perhaps, to evoke images of the dead Horace Binney Wallace. In "Thoughts," a poem inspired by a visit to the graves of the star-crossed lovers Heloise and Abelard, Julia asked the forsaken Heloise how she had endured the pain of losing her beloved. "When the first force of agony went from thee, / And left thee stunned and swooning, faint and dull, / How did thy garb of holiness become thee? / Was it ennobling? was it weariful?"[62] In "The Royal Guest," Julia spoke of an unidentified visitor for whom she would clothe her heart with "holiest purpose, as for God himself."[63] "My Sea-Ward Window" depicted Julia looking at the moon, thinking of the "ship that bore my friend from me" and tracking the silvery splendor where "our two souls met" and made "vows of earnest import." Puzzled, her children asked why she gazed at the window; Julia replied: "'I kneel to bless my parting friend, / And even ye forgotten are.'"[64] In "The Fellow Pilgrim," Julia claimed that she could still feel the power of a departed friend whenever she read the lines she had written when they were together. Indeed, she celebrated that pilgrim:

The mind that laid its grasp on me,
A friendly grasp, but firm and strong,
First from my errors shook me free,
Then led me, brother-like, along. . . .
There seemed a glory in thy smile,
A lesson in thy lightest word.[65]

In addition to these images that established the writing of poetry as a kind of giving birth and celebrated the attraction of a distant or dead love as more compelling than that of marriage or motherhood, *Passion-Flowers* employed images of sexual desire. "Coquette et Froide" spoke of rending the bosom of a maiden rose with kissing and crushing; "Coquette et Tendre" alluded to smoth-ered sighs and caressing hands.[66] And "Handsome Harry" sang the praises of a gorgeous sailor with "manly shoulders," a "rounded throat," an "azure eye," and "golden curls." Declaring Harry nothing less than a "glowing Mercury," Julia left no doubt she found him desirable. "Were I the vessel he commands," she claimed, "I should obey with pleasure."[67]

Finally, two poems unambiguously poked fun at the Howe marriage. "Mind Versus Mill-Stream" depicted the problem of a Miller who chose a rush-ing stream rather than a quiet brook upon which to build his mill wheel. The stream resisted all the Miller's efforts to tame it, leading the poet to conclude in a section entitled "Moral" that those who wished to marry "on the shady side of life" should choose a "placid tempered wife." Men who desired peaceful lives but married brilliant wives could expect to be challenged:

For men will woo the tempest,
And wed it, to their cost,
Then swear they took it for summer dew,
And ah! their peace is lost![68]

"Philosoph-Master and Poet-Aster" was even more direct. Here, Julia depicted her ongoing struggles with "Theologus," a figure clearly intended to represent Chev. Describing herself as one "whose domain is poetical-quizzical," and Theologus as one "who affects the concrete metaphysical," Julia posed the question: "When I and Theologus cannot agree / Should I give up the point, pray you, or he? / Shall I out-hector him, stubborn and horrid, / Growing brick-scarlet from bosom to forehead?" There was more. Julia poked fun at Chev's beloved work as a social reformer: "Saving the perilous soul of the nation, / By holiest, wholesomest vituperation— / He is a Vulcan, concede me that prithee, / Forging old ploughshares to swords in his smithy." When he was angry at her, Theologus settled matters by crying out: "'Acknowledge your Master!'" No clearer illustration of just how horrifying a Howe dinner party gone awry could be was ever penned:

⌒⌯⌒

If I venture to call for the sparkling Sillery,
He serves me a salvo of heavy artillery;
Or offer some sweet thing: 'I made it myself'—
He pushes the rubbish, and smashes the delf—
My terrified guests sit in silence around,
Their eyes wide with wonder, or fixed on the ground;
They leave at the earliest signal, that day,
The Thund'rer has frightened the Muses away.[69]

⌒⌯⌒

Given all this, it should have come as no surprise that *Passion-Flowers* mortified Chev. Bad enough that Julia had published a book against his will; even worse, she had published a book that held him up to ridicule. Julia wrote to Annie, "[W]e have been very unhappy. The Book, you know, was a blow to him, and some foolish and impertinent people have hinted to him that the Miller was meant for himself—this has made him almost crazy. . . . He has been in a very dangerous state, I think, very near insanity."[70] In another letter Julia complained of a "weary, dreary" winter of "loneliness, desolation, much fault finding," remarking, "these things go far to counterbalance any pleasure that my Book has given me." A letter in the spring of 1854 lamented a fever that produced in Julia a terrifying "spasmodic hysteria."[71]

Chev's ire must have been fearsome indeed, as the second and third editions of *Passion-Flowers* suggested. Following the original publication in

December 1853, a second edition appeared in February 1854, and a third edition a month later.[72] In both the second and third editions, the title of "Mind Versus Mill-Stream" was changed to "The Mill-Stream," and the section entitled "Moral" disappeared altogether.[73] Julia must have been frantic about keeping peace in the family to have modified "Mind Versus Mill-Stream" in such a decisive way. Nevertheless, Chev remained unhappy with the book. After the appearance of the third edition, he took Julia to task over another issue that pained him. "There are things in the book which made my cheeks tingle a little with a blush, " Chev complained. "They border on the erotic . . . [and] have been privately & publicly pronounced such as a pure minded & sensitive lady should not write." At least, Chev thought, Julia could omit such passages in future editions, for the sake of the children if not for him. "Julia, when our girls grow a little older," he remonstrated, "I shall be pained by their reading anything their mother wrote & blushing when they read,—but I shall be more pained if they do read without blushing." Chev promised to forgive and forget only if she would alter the book. "For the effect which the book had upon me, for the injury it does my reputation—I care little if any, now;—the thought of it shall not come as a shadow between us;—but for you,—you whom I would have the world, & more especially my children, regard as pure—pure in heart as an angel—for you & their sakes I would have every expression,—every allusion bordering upon the erotic erased & forgotten."[74]

A fourth edition of *Passion-Flowers* never appeared. Still, home life was hellish. To salvage her marriage, Julia agreed to resume sexual relations with Chev. In June 1854, Julia told Annie the worst: not only was she pregnant once again, but "Chev is as cold and indifferent to me as a man can be. I sometimes suspect him of having relations with other women, and regret more bitterly than ever the sacrifice which entails upon me these months of fatigue and suffering. God will help me through, I hope. But it all looks very dark before me." Julia reported suffering fits of "raving hysterics" in which she "was perfectly mad, and rushed from room to room like a wild creature."[75]

In July 1854, Julia wrote to Louisa that Chev's displeasure was so overwhelming that Julia "only kept body and soul together by a long and intense effort . . . I really thought at one time that he would have driven me to insanity, so horribly did he behave . . . when he is angry, he has no control over his own feelings, and no considerations for those of others. Indeed, dear Wevie, you may believe all that Annie tells you of my trials on this score—they are sometimes such that I would not endure them for a day, but for my children's sake."[76]

A continuation of that letter to Louisa in November revealed further information: the stir produced by *Passion-Flowers* could hardly have come at a
worse time. For three years, Julia explained, Chev had been proposing a
divorce, demanding that she give him custody of his two favorite children, Julia
Romana and Harry. The prospect, she claimed, was "so favorite a project" with
Chev that "he would bring it up even in our quietest hours, when there was
nothing whatever to suggest it." His dream, she revealed, "was to marry again—
some young girl who would love him supremely." Julia confessed that she had
run out of options; she had had no choice but to attempt a reconciliation.
"Before God, dear Louisa, I thought it my real duty to give up every thing that
was dear and sacred to me, rather than be forced to leave two of my children,
and those the two dearest, Julia & Harry. In this view, I made the greatest sacrifice I can ever be called upon to make."[77]

Marital reconciliations in the Victorian age came at a high cost to wives. By
now, Julia was facing confinement again. "I can scarcely trust myself to speak of
it, so bitter and horrible a distress has it been to me," she agonized to Louisa.
The old fears of childbirth held no terrors compared to this pain, a mental suffering so dreadful that Julia declared, "I cannot be afraid of any bodily torture,
however great. Neither does the future show me a single gleam of light. I shall
not drag this weary weight about with me, it is true, but I can not feel that my
heart will be any lighter." Certain she would hate her child, Julia could only
hope that the sacrifices she had made for the sake of family unity would serve
as expiation for the errors of her life. "I can suffer & die with my children," she
sighed, "but I cannot leave them, until God calls me from them." Such thoughts
provided little consolation. "Burn this," she instructed Louisa. "I shall never
speak of these things again."[78]

A letter written in December after the birth of baby Maud showed Julia
continuing to chaff at her inability to study and write. Still, she asked, "Why
should I add another chapter to the complaining of Job?" She could not help
but point out, however, that life was "weary" and "tasteless," without "hope,
love, or courage to help one." On the other hand, when Chev had refused to
read the newspapers to Julia in a punctual manner, she had managed to prevail
upon Flossy to do so. "I now perceive," Julia noted wryly, "the use of having
one's children taught to read."[79]

All in all, it had been an amazing twelve months: a new book, a new baby,
a new resolve to work on her marriage. In some ways, Chev had won; Julia had
agreed to resume sexual relations and had given birth to yet another child. She
was trying to be meek, or at least meeker, at home. For the moment, Chev had
(more or less) what he wanted. Yet Julia had also won something, something

that she had wanted since she could remember: a literary reputation. She was an author; her book had earned money; she had been recognized as a talent. As Deborah Clifford has remarked, "By 1854 Julia Ward Howe was no longer simply the wife of a great hero and reformer but a woman with a reputation of her own."[80] Nothing could have made her happier.

I Spoke in Fables

Once she embarked on a literary career, Julia was determined to press forward. The year 1857 saw the publication of *Words for the Hour,* another book of poetry.[81] In March 1857, her first play, *Leonora, Or The World's Own,* was performed in New York City. More works would follow.

Although several of its poems concerned political issues of the day—slavery, the Crimean War—*Words for the Hour,* even more than *Passion-Flowers,* echoed domestic affairs in the Howe home.[82] Three poems got to the bottom of Julia's feelings about Florence Nightingale. In "Florence Nightingale and Her Praisers," the second of two poems about the famed nurse of the Crimea, Julia complained that too many people debased women in general in order to praise and elevate Florence Nightingale. For Julia, Florence Nightingale was exceptional not in her compassion and generosity, but in her opportunities. "She had freedom," Julia explained, whereas other women akin to her were "held as springs shut up, as fountains sealed." It was time, Julia thought, to recognize the valor of the great mass of women who patiently accepted life's burdens, since "the sublime of Nature's excellence / Lies in enduring, as achieving Fate." In "Furthermore," the poem immediately following, Julia made certain that her readers would not be left to wonder what it was that women suffered at the hands of men; the poem's opening stanzas read like an indictment of her own marriage:

⌒

We, that are held of you in narrow chains,
Sought for our beauty, thro' our folly raised
One moment to a barren eminence,
To drop in dreary nothingness, amazed:

We, dwarfed to suit the measure of your pride
Thwarted in all our pleasures and our powers,
Have yet a sad, majestic recompense,
The dignity of suffering is ours. . . .

We wait upon your fancies, watch your will,
Study your pleasure, oft with trembling heart,—
Of the success and glory of your lives
Ye think it grace to yield the meanest part.[83]

∽

Julia had a special word for another exceptional woman, the universally derided Fanny Kemble. Kemble was an author who had ceded custody of her children in order to obtain a divorce from her husband. For Victorian society, Fanny Kemble was the quintessential woman who did not know her place; she prized personal ambition above the bonds of domesticity. Julia knew only too well why a wife and mother might give up her family to regain her independence, and she contrasted her children, cooing in her lap, to Fanny Kemble's motherless daughter. In "Fanny Kemble's Child," Julia mourned for Kemble, even as she criticized her:

∽

Oh! many-passioned Woman—fervid soul!
Thou, rich in all save Meekness—strong in all
Save that strong Patience which outwearies Fate,
And makes Gods quail before thy constancy.
Which was forgotten in thy gifts of birth?
Of all the powers the greatest only—Love.

∽

But Julia knew that all was not serene with her own children. She, unlike Kemble, knew how to be patient in the face of suffering, but as she acknowledged in "The Nursery," there were times when she could not shield her babes from "all the secret sorrow" of her life. In those moments, surrounded by her children, Julia was "no mother then," nor "sister, helpmeet, daughter," but simply an "agonizing creature / That looked to God in tears." Only the bewildered and panicked faces of her children, Julia claimed, strengthened her to throw aside her pain and present a merry face.[84]

Julia's repeated emphasis on the virtue of patient suffering in these poems echoed her celebration of the wondrously faithful Eva, whose fortitude had created a transfigured life of glory for herself and Rafael. In "The Shadow That Is Born with Us," Julia told of enduring an unremitting grief, "Constant as Fate, inalienate as life." She had tried in the past, she said, to put her torment into words, but "I spoke in fables—deeper lay the truth." In the end, grief was destined to be her constant companion, but she had learned to use the artistic skill God had given her to respond to her anguish. "I mould an angel from the sombre mass," she concluded. Faced with a marriage that thwarted her and a culture that insufficiently valued her gifts, Julia could only proclaim that ambition and love would not be unrequited forever.[85]

But not all was fables and allusions in *Words for the Hour.* Where *Passion-Flowers* had sung the praises of an unnamed friend, in *Words for the Hour* a poem called "Via Felice" celebrated Horace Binney Wallace by name, dwelling lovingly on the treasured companion who in Rome had brought Julia "morning violets" and happily discussed poetry.[86] A poem entitled "Maud" referred to her new baby's "unwonted coming," but argued that the infant's glory was so bright it revealed God's light. "Love in Exile," however, backed off that conciliatory note to proclaim the "utterness of sorrow" that Julia had endured since a character that could only be Chev had "banished Beauty from my soul." She warned: "In this divorce from Beauty lies a wrong. ... My mortal frame is welded to her might, / And my soul worships, as a captive does, / Who murmurs holy words 'mid heathen foes, / While cruel hands forbid the happy rite."[87]

Words for the Hour also contained a poem about Chev entitled "The Rough Sketch." Julia's daughters would find the poem heroic;[88] certainly, its first two stanzas conveyed Chev's energy and absolute mastery:

❧

A great grieved heart, an iron will,
As fearless blood as ever ran;
A form elate with nervous strength
And fibrous vigor,—all a man.

A gallant rein, a restless spur,
The hand to wield a biting scourge;
Small patience for the tasks of Time,
Unmeasured power to speed and urge.

❧

The imagery *was* romantic, but Julia did not fail to note her mate's self-absorption and impatience. "Did he smile but once a year," she observed wryly, it "were a Christmas recompense." Moreover, she described him as relatively harmless around children, but hard on wives.

⌒∾

I thank a poet for his name,
The "Down of Darkness," this should be;
A child, who knows no risk it runs,
Might stroke its roughness harmlessly.
One helpful gift the Gods forgot,
Due to the man of lion-mood;
A woman's soul, to match with his
In high resolve and hardihood.[89]

⌒∾

Certainly Chev would have preferred to see himself in "The Rough Sketch" than in "Philosoph-Master and Poet-Aster" or "The Mill-Stream" from *Passion-Flowers,* but even "The Rough Sketch" was profoundly ambivalent. He was dashing and forceful, in Julia's words, but unsmiling, strong-headed, and not a little dangerous as well. And of course Chev suffered by comparison to the cherished Horace of "Via Felice," who offered emblems of "love divinely wise," and whose "generous learning" and "reconciling Art" consoled Julia during a time of uncertainty, creating in her a "tower of Beauty lifted / From ruins widely strewn."[90] In the end, Chev was the one who banished Beauty from Julia's life, while Horace Binney Wallace restored it.

Words for the Hour did not enjoy as much acclaim as *Passion-Flowers* had garnered, and *Leonora, Or The World's Own,* Julia's first play, dismayed audiences with its grim tone. *The World's Own* seemed an odd work for a woman who delighted in beauty and humor. In light of Julia's troubles with Chev, the plot was in some respects humorous: an innocent girl named Leonora fell in love with a man named Lothair. Leonora eagerly accepted his offer of marriage ("becom'st my gentle thrall, / Bounden to follow where thy master bids"), declaring that to call Lothair "Master seems the crowning name of all." Unfortunately, Lothair was already married and interested principally in seducing Leonora. Eventually he deserted her, but she refused to believe him unfaithful. After much suffering, Leonora finally conceded the truth about Lothair and vowed revenge.[91]

Endearing herself to the local prince, Leonora informed him that Lothair was a traitor. When the prince demurred, noting that Lothair treated women badly but was hardly a traitor, Leonora answered: "A man that can betray a woman's love / Avoids no crime for its enormity." Convinced that Lothair intended him harm, the prince signed Lothair's death warrant. The play's conclusion was deliciously vengeful: Lothair's wife was arrested, his child kidnapped by Leonora, and he himself delivered to death—with Leonora present to urge on the guards. The final scene showed Leonora in her bedroom, with Lothair's child asleep in the bed. Leonora mused at the ways in which Lothair, the idol of her girlhood dreams ("O, what a god he seemed! He stood on clouds") had fallen from grace, only to be confronted by a masked man (a former suitor who had vainly sought to persuade her to forget Lothair and begin life anew). The masked man showed Leonora a picture of herself—innocent, pure—as she had been before she devoted herself to ruining Lothair and his wife. Seeing that she had degenerated from the glories of her youth, and hearing the masked man describe her as a fiend too "proud to bear the fortune of her sex; / Wronged ever more than wronging, save this one," Leonora seized a dagger and killed herself.[92]

The play ran for over a week in New York and later played in Boston as well.[93] People who knew Julia well—and who knew the agonies revealed in her letters—might have recognized in *The World's Own* the dark moods with which she struggled. People who knew her only as a clever poet and witty conversationalist, however, were confused and dismayed by the play's grim vision. The exuberant Mrs. Howe had produced an unusual play indeed, a play that in its dark and vengeful tone seemed most unladylike. Not only had Leonora given in to blood lust, but the play made it clear that she was condemned only for her vengeful spirit, not for having been seduced by Lothair in the first place. Longfellow's wife Fanny speculated that poor Chev "must feel it painfully" that Julia's play was so shocking that he could not allow his daughters to read it.[94] Oliver Wendell Holmes expressed surprise that "so quiet a blend as yourself should have such tropical flashes of passion running through your veins."[95]

Julia's brother Sam was quick to rise to her defense. "All women should stand up for the author of 'The World's Own,'" he wrote. "Men have an object in abusing it. . . . Could women be the critics how different would have been the tune! But beastly men, knowing how true a picture you have drawn of the debasing customs of their sex, take up the cudgels to frown down the adoption of revenge instead of paying the damages." Following up on his point, Sam revealed that he, like the critics, read the play as an argument for woman's rights; he simply happened to agree with that cause:

> To defend anything else, skill of plot, distinction, etc., is useless. . . . They
> have endeavoured to pique you, and silence your freedom, and drive back
> so stern and fearless an advocate of women's rights and contemner of man's
> dirtiness, and faithlessness, into the ranks of the propriety army of dumb
> and conventional forbearance. To be candid I think all the critiques I have
> seen save the first one in the *Herald* and parts of White, are asinine.

Indeed, he concluded, the only clever review to emerge was in the *New Yorker:* 'in view of the frequent allusions to his Satanic majesty's headquarter's 'The World's Own' should be called 'The Devil's Own.'"[96]

In the late 1860s, Julia would embrace the campaign for woman suffrage, but in 1856, she had enough problems already. The Howes could withstand criticism for Chev's abolitionism, but the women's rights movement was beyond the pale. Therefore, feminist readings of Julia's play stung—though such interpretations were not unfair. Just as Julia's poems, in more enigmatic and occasionally lighthearted ways, often did, *The World's Own* depicted the world as a place in which men betrayed women and treated them like servants. Sentiments of anger and betrayal that the poems could counterbalance through rhyme and humor (or the obscurity of their references) were starkly portrayed in the play, as was Leonora's desire for revenge. *The World's Own* presented a vision of suffering and vengeance that did not resolve in a happy ending like the saucy conclusion of "The Mill-Stream" in *Passion-Flowers*. The play, in short, made audiences uncomfortable.

As were Julia and Chev. The birth of Maud had failed to reconcile them to one another. In October 1857, Julia wrote Annie that she had just returned from Newport, where she had spent the summer getting healthy. She had felt encouraged at feeling "stronger than I have been for quite some time, when down comes Chev upon me again with his fall madness of separation," thereby undoing all the summer's gain. "The ground this time," she explained to Annie, "is that there is no unkindness between us, and that therefore the present is the best time for such a division." Julia was furious. "I will rather die, now," she fumed, "than have this infamous farce repeated, every autumn, to the utter disturbance of all family feeling, and individual peace."[97]

This particular chapter of the family saga had one more tale to unfold. In February 1859, Julia and Chev took a trip to Cuba for Chev's health. Julia would produce two offspring from this undertaking: a travel book about her Cuban adventures and a son. Predictably, for a couple never quite in harmony with one another, Julia's pregnancy came at the most trying of times. In October 1859, John Brown staged his famous raid on Harper's Ferry, and in November Chev fled to Canada after being exposed as one of Brown's supporters. Just weeks away from delivery, Julia had suffered more pain than usual in this last pregnancy and was worried—as ever—that childbirth might kill her. She begged Chev to ease her mind. He, as usual, was unperturbed at her anxieties. "Dear child, do not be hypochondriacal—like me; you have no cause for it," he counseled from Montreal. "Look! You inherited a sound & vigorous constitution: you did not marry until it was fully matured." Warming to his subject,

Chev advised, "Child-bearing when the number does not exceed eight, or about that number & is not too frequent, & if the system is healthy, tends to prolong, not to shorten the duration of life." As for her fear that she might die in childbirth while he was hiding in Canada, Chev assured Julia that "I will be with you some how or other, only do not say any thing about it . . . you would suffer more if I were taken away to Virginia, & there maltreated, than if I were absent, & here in safety." All things considered, Chev concluded, Julia should "cheer up and look at the bright side: the chances are nine hundred & ninety nine out of a thousand of your getting through your confinement well, & being happier & better for it."[98]

Cheered or not, Julia survived her most difficult pregnancy. Chev returned safely from Canada, and treated her with relative kindness.[99] Both of them came to adore little Sammy. Still, Julia did not forget the many days of despair she had endured since the publication of *Passion-Flowers.* In an unpublished poem called "Maidenhood," written around 1860, Julia celebrated the unmarried woman who was "not made to cringe in fear" or to "soothe some ruffled Tyrant's ear" with a "submissive tune." Remembering Chev's repeated outbursts of temper, in a companion poem called "Matronhood," she seethed:

⁓

Think of thy children that number and grow for his pride
More than thy cheer;
Beautiful gifts fondly brought and put coldly aside,
Year after year.

⁓

Julia remembered, too, Chev's words "that are murders, and looks that transfix me like steel," and proclaimed the fear she experienced at Chev's fireside as "sterner than death-battle din" or the "hangman's call." Noting that slaves were "as wretched in well-fashioned garments" as in chains, Julia ended in prayer:

⁓

So, give us measure to think our poor narrowness out,
Live our frail lives,
And let magnificent men, that talk greatly about,
Pity their wives.[100]

⁓

Some things never seemed to change.

THE CHILDREN

And, yet, there was more to Howe family life than the antagonism between Julia and Chev. Somehow, in the midst of marital separations, infidelities, and acrimony, Julia and Chev were nurturing an exceptional group of children. It is hard to know, exactly, how all of the strife affected the children, since as adults they publicly pretended that none of it had ever happened. Julia's *Reminiscences* and her daughters' biography of her shared a common feature: they utterly ignored the marital dissension engendered by the publication of *Passion-Flowers*. In their biography, Julia's daughters began the chapter entitled "Passion-Flowers" by reproducing glowing reviews from Whittier, Emerson, and Holmes. They moved on to consider *Words for the Hour* and *The World's Own* and then gave loving accounts of elaborate parties that their parents had given them.[101] The reader is left to muse that *Passion-Flowers* somehow laid the groundwork for gala family celebrations.

One hint of a worrisome family dynamic that emerged from this period concerned Julia Romana. Scattered comments in letters from Chev and Julia indicated that their oldest daughter was undergoing considerable stress. Chev wrote Sumner in August 1852 that Julia Romana was frantic with grief, "in a continual state of self-reproachment, & at times almost in agony at the recollection of the merest trifles."[102] In July 1859, Chev informed Sumner that he had "been in great alarm & distress about my dear & beautiful daughter Julia breaking down under her course of study." The signs, Chev asserted, had been frightening. "For a few days," he confided, "there was danger of aberration of mind, but happily all the . . . symptoms have passed away, & she is doing well." In the future, Chev resolved, he would insist that Julia Romana follow a reduced schedule of academic studies. Julia Romana's mother reported further difficulties in December of that same year. Writing to Chev, she commented that Julia Romana was "relieved and more tranquil today, but believe me, the trouble is in the *other* organ, not the brain, and should be cured. . . . She is perfectly well and happy, only sometimes too extravagant in her spirits."[103]

Whatever might have been going on with Julia Romana or with any of her siblings failed to emerge in the writings the Howes published about their childhood. In their accounts, the magic of childhood was heightened by the incredible stimulation offered by their parents. The principle anxiety the children recorded was simply the challenge of living up to their parents' genius. Flossy would later say that it had been a "great privilege and happiness to live, not under the shadow, but in the light of two honored names."[104] Maud would acknowledge a greater burden: "Looking back upon the first six or seven years of my life, I find myself in a dim enchanted land, which I have come to think of as 'The Twilight of the Gods,' for the figures that peopled it were, indeed, heroes and demigods." At times, she conceded, a "kind of impatient despair often seized me. Was I never to get out of the shadow of these two monumental persons, who, between them, had brought me into the world?"[105]

Laura resolved the issue in a different way. She had grown up, she said, cradled in poetry, romance, and philanthropy. Of her mother, it would be impossible to say too much; and her father was, quite simply, "an angel."[106] Harry may have been the most sanguine of all the children. Looking back on his own distinguished career as a metallurgist, he admitted, "in accomplishment we cannot compare with him [Chev], yet I believe that we have accomplished as much as we were given strength for ... on the whole, we could look our parents in the face unembarassed [sic]."[107]

Whether the children experienced the Howe name as oppressive or inspiring, the astonishing creativity and energy they poured into daily activities was undeniable. Julia Romana was the quietest of the children, and the most literary. At age five, she informed her mother that she had written a poem and set it to music; by age ten, she had produced a book of novels and plays. To the delight of her younger siblings, Julia Romana led them on daily morning walks, telling stories, revealing opera plots, and singing songs.[108] She also edited (with her mother's help) a weekly paper called *The Listener,* which described family and school events.[109] She and Flossy invented a language they called Patagonian, filling it, at Julia Romana's insistence, with numerous irregular verbs. Patagonian gave the children a way to talk to each other while ignoring the adult guests who frequently dined with them. On occasion they got so carried away that their mother imposed silence. The children were also fluent in a language called Sdrawkcab ("Backwards"), which turned Uncle Joseph into Uncle Hpesoj (with the "H" silent, as in "hour").[110]

If Julia Romana was quiet, Flossy was a hellion. Her clothes were perpetually grass-stained, her knees were scraped, and, given the opportunity, her boots were muddy. She invented "Yeller's Day," which the children observed annually, climbing to the top of a hill near their Newport summer home to scream their lungs out. Flossy was also keen on devising dances for the children's nightly revels. With their mother on the piano, and Flossy leading the dance, anything could happen: sword fights (with kindling wood for swords) as they enacted Flossy's Julius Caesar dance, knife fights (kindling wood again) for the hunting scene in her "Four Seasons" dance, or the near decapitation of a member of the audience when Flossy got carried away with her Lady Macbeth dagger dance. Flossy regaled the younger children with the saga of Patty, a fairy who lived in a pearl palace under the sea and threw a ball every night, which Flossy always attended. Sometimes Flossy promised to take the younger children with her, with the understanding that upon waking they would be unable to recall their adventures until Flossy refreshed their memories.[111]

Flossy also invented a curious ritual involving a footstool she dubbed "Pistachio," which she imagined to be sickly. Harry, Laura, and Maud were never certain they fully understood the significance of the ritual, but in the mornings they eagerly helped transport Pistachio to a nearby brook. In utter solemnity, with one child holding a parasol over Pistachio, two pushing his carriage, and two more running ahead to clear the way, they would advance to the brook, where Flossy would set Pistachio on a flat stone. Each leg would be dipped in the water and then dried with a towel, after which the children would walk him around, give him a rubdown (in the hopes of improving his circulation), then return him to his carriage and soberly return to the house.[112] It is hard to imagine what the neighbors thought.

Harry, like his father had been in his youth, was a practical joker and a daredevil. He pulled dogs' tails, slid down the long banisters at the Perkins Institute, and dropped wet sponges on people's heads in the entrance hall. He took delight in sitting in the upper gallery of theaters and dropping oysters on bald men seated below. When put into the closet for bad behavior, he occupied himself by cutting the pockets off the dresses hanging there. All the Howes were nervous—deservedly so—when Harry paid an extended visit to relatives. One day he stole his young cousin's rocking horse and set it on top of the chimney; another day, he tossed the family's shoes down the chimney. In his relatives' closets, he tacked shoes to the floor and mutilated the clothes. Also like his father, Harry had definite views about women. At age six, he proposed marriage to his nurse, under the condition that she quit her job in the nursery, since he thought it improper for his wife to work for a living. Harry was, in short, a handful, and the family breathed a collective sigh of relief when he avoided expulsion and graduated from Harvard in 1869. He would go on to make his reputation as a scientist.[113]

Laura was two years younger than Harry and devoted to him and to poetry. She and Harry loved to sit in the wine cooler in the dining room at Green Peace; she was also willing, when provoked, to shoulder a wooden log and march around the dining room table, shouting dire threats to their teacher: "We'll kill old Feaster! We'll kill old Feaster!" Maud was several years younger than Laura, but she did not lack flair. After her first visit to the Institute, she poked out her doll's eyes and tied a green ribbon over the holes so that her doll would be like the blind children she had met. The summer when she was seven, having borrowed a green parasol from her mother, Maud decided to elope with a boy who lived near the Howes' Rhode Island home. The two were gone for hours, trudging down the railroad tracks, exploring Portsmouth Grove, and failing to board a steamer for Providence only because they could not afford tickets. A soldier finally ordered the children home, where, walking hand in hand, they ran into a frantic Julia, who was scouring the roads for them in her carriage.

As a group, the Howe children were feisty. They loved to swim at the Rhode Island shore and treasured as one of their great adventures the night that high tide stranded them on their favorite beach. While their nurse blanched at the prospect of spending a night outdoors, the Howes turned the evening into high drama. Already they could imagine the romantic tales they could write later: "The Deserted Children!" or "Alone on a Sandbank!" or "The Watchers of the Tide!" As the sun set, the children sang German student-songs their mother had taught them, and then sister Julia Romana told them a story. All was going beautifully until a boat pulled up to rescue them—an unfortunate ending to what all except their nurse agreed would have been an extraordinary night.[114]

The children credited much of their sense of fun to their mother. Her laughing mood, they said, formed the background of family life. And, while there were many children, Julia could make each one feel special. She composed a lullaby for each of them and welcomed their company when she went for walks. The children knew that Julia experienced "red despairs" as well as jubilation in the 1850s.[115] Yet if Julia were depressed, her children preferred, at least publicly, to remember her otherwise. As Laura put it: "Through all and round all, like a laughing river, flowed the current of her wit and fun. No child could be sad in her company. If we were cold, there was a merry bout of 'fisticuffs' to warm us; if we were too warm, there was a song or story while we sat still and 'cooled off.' We all had nicknames, our own names being often too sober to suit her laughing mood. We were 'Petotty,' 'Jehu,' 'Wolly,' and 'Bunks of Bunktown.'"[116]

Julia loved parties, giving them, as Maud noted, at the slightest provocation. The adults' gatherings could be boring (the children dismissed Julia's literary friends as the Owls, and their father's guests as the Fashionables), but the parties Julia gave for the children were fabulous. She would write a script, Chev would build a theater, and the children and their friends would be the delighted audience as the adults performed Julia's play. For one party, Julia invited eighty of the children's friends. A donkey carriage, swing, and bowling alley provided outdoor entertainment, followed by a theatrical presentation of

"Bluebeard" on a stage complete with curtains and real footlights. The adults had a grand time putting on the show, and the children enjoyed both the play and the ice cream, cake, blancmange, oranges, and sugarplums that followed.[117]

It was a grand affair that few parents would have had the courage or energy to attempt—particularly at a time when they were overburdened with work and estranged from each other. But the Howe children were accustomed to the unusual: Lord Byron's helmet was a treasured relic that hung on their wall, and, after Theodore Parker's death, his brain resided in a jar at the Institute. To the Howe children, both objects made sense; they lived in an extraordinary world of fantastically accomplished people. Their mother wrote books, their father brought sight to the blind, and their parents' friends were famous authors and reformers. In time, the Howe children would be celebrated for their own achievements in literature, art, and science. If their parents' marriage was tumultuous, the children nonetheless flourished. Undoubtedly there was a cost to it all, but that side of the story they kept to themselves.

Chapter Four

In the 1860s, Julia at last achieved the desire of a lifetime: public renown. In writing the "Battle Hymn of the Republic," she created an enduring legacy for herself. Originally conceived as a rallying cry for the crusade against slavery, the "Battle Hymn" became, after the Civil War, an anthem celebrated throughout the entire nation. For the rest of her life, wherever she traveled, Julia was greeted with choral renditions of her masterpiece. From Memphis in the deep South to Salt Lake City in the far West, people were eager to serenade her.

Julia's "Battle Hymn" provided additional benefits. By establishing her as a celebrity, the "Battle Hymn" gave her leverage in her struggles with Chev. Between 1860 and 1876, Julia explored woman suffrage reform, gave lectures on philosophical topics, and traveled to London to organize an international conference on peace. Chev did not find these developments encouraging. He and the children derided Julia for her support of woman suffrage, complained that she was too frequently absent from the home, and poked fun at her devotion to philosophy. She continued undeterred, convinced that she had at last found her niche. Julia's philosophical and theological reflections in these years were critical in helping her reformulate her understanding of what it meant to be a woman or a man. She had chaffed at the restrictions of woman's sphere her entire life; now she had found a way to overthrow them. No longer would Julia labor alone as the anomalous exceptional woman invading the prerogatives of man's world. Rather, she would unite with other social reformers so that men and women could learn from one another, imparting their own particular strengths to aid the progress of the race. And Julia would also come to see that rather than being static, gender identity was necessarily fluid, because it was only through mutual sharing and growth that men and women together could create the new humanity.

WAR WORK

Julia converted to abolitionism later than her husband did, but by the time of the Civil War, both Julia and Chev opposed slavery. The children were proud to be teased by their schoolmates for being abolitionists, reasoning that suffering on behalf of the cause of humanity was a way to share in their father's work.[1] For a brief period in the early 1850s, Julia and Chev had worked together on an antislavery paper called the *Commonwealth*.[2] Being antislavery did not necessarily mean regarding African Americans as social or intellectual equals. Julia observed in 1859 that African slaves in Cuba were notably inferior to free African Americans in New England, lamenting that the Cuban slaves had not enjoyed the heady tonic of exposure to Anglo-Saxon culture. She also suggested that, given what she saw as the laziness of Cuban blacks, slavery was in some ways a benefit to them, allowing them to overcome their natural indolence.[3] As a descendant of Francis Marion, the South Carolina "Swamp Fox" of Revolutionary War fame, Julia had Southern slave-holding relatives whom she respected. Abolitionism did not come easy to her, and she never questioned the superiority of her own race. By 1861, however, having experienced the trauma of John Brown's trial and execution, as well as the secession of the Confederate states, Julia firmly supported the antislavery cause.[4]

The Howes had solid antislavery connections. Chev's friend Charles Sumner became one of the most famous abolitionists in the nation through his work in the United States Senate.[5] Chev's labors on behalf of abolitionism became particularly well known after John Brown's raid on Harper's Ferry in 1859. When war finally came in 1861, Chev was happy to accept a position with the Sanitary Commission. The commission was charged with establishing healthful conditions in the Union army and with caring for the wounded. In November 1861, Chev and Julia journeyed to the nation's capital to inspect the condition of the troops. They were accompanied by William Andrew, the governor of Massachusetts, and by their pastor, James Freeman Clarke.

That visit later assumed legendary proportions. The Howes joined some Union soldiers in singing one of the army's favorite songs: "John Brown's Body." Clarke, according to Howe family lore, then told Julia that she should write lyrics that would better fit the song's stirring melody. When Julia went to sleep at the Willard Hotel that evening, she did not realize that the hours ahead would change her life forever. Roused from sleep in the early morning by a sudden gush of inspiration, she rushed to gather pencil and paper so that she could record the stanzas of the poem that was running through her head. Upon completing the poem, she returned to bed.[6]

Julia later credited the inspiration for the "Battle Hymn" in part to her inability to do anything else to help the Union cause. She could not join the army herself, nor could the men in her family—Chev was too old, and her son Harry was too young. A voice inside her lamented, "You would be glad to serve, but you cannot help any one; you have nothing to give, and there is nothing for you to do." Nevertheless, Julia concluded, "because of my sincere desire, a word was given me to say which did strengthen the hearts of those who fought in the field and of those who languished in prison."[7] That word would win her world-wide acclaim.

Julia's "Battle Hymn" was first published, anonymously, in the *Atlantic Monthly* in February 1862. From there, numerous newspapers and songbooks picked it up. The song's popularity among Union troops became legendary. Its salutary effect upon its author was immeasurable. As Julia's daughter Florence explained, "It brought its author name and fame throughout the civilized world, in addition to the love of her countrymen. As she grew older and the spiritual beauty of her life and thought shone out more and more clearly, the affection in which she was held deepened into something akin to veneration."[8]

Julia claimed that after writing the "Battle Hymn," she said to herself, "I like this better than most things that I have written."[9] Her poetry had often evidenced an overly dramatic quality, and she had frequently used archaic terms like "methinks." In the "Battle Hymn," the fervency of the language matched the ardor of the hour, and antiquated phrases like "mine eyes" or "builded him an altar" carried with them biblical overtones that saturated the entire poem. Julia's "Battle Hymn" repeatedly invoked apocalyptic images from the book of Revelation, where, preparatory to the dawn of the millennium, the Son of Man gathered the grapes of unrighteousness and crushed them in the great winepress of God's wrath.[10]

One line of the hymn, however, puzzled listeners: the beginning of the fifth stanza that claimed, "In the beauty of the lilies Christ was born across the sea." As a historical reference, the line made no sense, and Florence later wrote that numerous people had asked her to explain it. The best she could postulate was that the allusion was "to the lilies carried by the angel, in pictures of the annunciation to the Virgin, these flowers being the emblem of purity."[11] Given the content of the stanza's second line ("With a glory in his bosom that transfigures you and me"), one wonders whether Julia was not, consciously or unconsciously, calling upon imagery from Rafael and Eva. The dead Rafael had had a seed planted within his breast that produced a blossom, and when Eva touched it, she was transfigured in light. Perhaps Julia had the dramatic union and transformation of the lovers in mind when she imagined Union supporters, at one with the crucified Jesus, offering their lives on behalf of those in bondage. She urged the friends of freedom not only to be absolutely steadfast in their devotion to their cause, but also to find in it spiritual transfiguration and personal communion with the God of hosts, because God, too, was marching on.

While we may never know all that Julia intended to imply in the fifth stanza, the stirring qualities of her words would inspire generations of Americans, who would find in her "Battle Hymn" a call to action like no other. Even in the next millennium, while mourning the destruction of the World Trade Center, Americans would gather at the National Cathedral in Washington to hear the hymn that beyond any other could enkindle their hearts and make sense of their suffering. Never more so in American history than in Julia's "Battle Hymn" have high moral purpose and an impassioned declaration of the divine will united more perfectly with an author's poetic voice. Julia captured the Union's grim certainty that the unfolding events were portents of universal consequence. The struggle was not simply that of nations, but of more primordial elements. Unswerving judgment, ardent commitment, willing self-sacrifice: these were the tools by which God was bringing about the divine will. And Julia at last commanded the authority to speak on behalf of the multitudes that sought to answer God's call.

Clearly, Julia had come into her own. She later wrote that when the war finally ended, "a whole new testament of work and service" opened up to her. She would see, then, that the war had not merely freed a race of slaves; it also beckoned to women. This new impulse of freedom, she said, invited women to "Come up higher. Extend your work more broadly."[12] Julia's "Battle Hymn of the Republic" was the last poem she would write that would widely engage the public's interest. Her poetry never sold well after 1861.[13] She would find other forms of expression—lectures, essays, and articles—that would bring her a new life as a social reformer. Though she would continue to write poems for ceremonial public occasions, politics, not poetry, would become her primary medium of expression.

THE BEAUTIFUL BOY

Before she gave herself over to the public career that would mark the later years of her life, however, Julia faced another trial as a mother. In May 1863, her young son Sammy contracted diphtheria and died within a few days. The Howes were devastated. To the siblings who survived him, Sammy represented the child of their parents' maturity, the child given to them after their parents' marriage had survived innumerable spats and serious separations. To lose

Sammy was to lose hope; as Laura later noted, Sammy was their "Beautiful Boy." In time, the children learned to see his death as providential. As Laura put it, "the Beautiful Boy was taken home to heaven while he was still very little; and it was good for the rest of us to know that there was always one to wait for and welcome us in the Place of Light to which we should go some day."[14]

For Julia, grief was not so easily managed. She called Sammy her "dear angel" and dreamed repeatedly of him. Chev was so distraught he could not ride in the carriage with the body for the funeral. Julia did ride with Sammy, taking a last opportunity to "kiss him & talk to him all I can." Nevertheless, in the days after his death she found herself "almost strangled with grief," frequently seeking comfort by retiring to Sammy's room to read the New Testament.[15] As the weeks passed, Julia continued to struggle with her pain, seeking relief in prayer. Simply hearing a pipe organ at church was enough to send her into tears, as the organ made her think of Sammy praising God in heaven. She continued to visit Sammy's grave and his bedroom regularly.[16] Even in their grief, Chev and Julia could offer each other little consolation. Julia took comfort in thinking of Sammy, going so far as to write a lengthy letter to him, awash in details of his happy life and sad final days. To Chev, the constant revisiting of their loss was torture. "We take a different course about dear Sammy," he told Julia. "You seem to cherish his memory,—I strive to let him go,—but he comes back constantly."[17]

Ultimately, her studies led Julia through her grief. She had become interested in philosophy and theology and had planned, even before Sammy's death, to give a series of lectures on various philosophical and metaphysical topics. After Sammy died, nothing calmed her mind more than her philosophical explorations. Bearing abstruse titles like "Proteus," "Duality of Character," "Moral Trigonometry," and "Doubt and Belief," Julia's essays were hardly the stuff of controversy, but they raised difficulties in her relationship with Chev. He was not pleased with her insistence on reading her papers to audiences, even to small groups invited to their home. Julia complained bitterly in October 1863: "Last night, Chev declared that I must read my lectures without compensation; I think he is mistaken, but cannot disregard his wishes in this." She noted with contentment on November 16: "My first reading—a success, as people said—to me, what is more, a satisfaction."

Five more readings in the home followed, and then in May 1864, Julia traveled to Washington to deliver her lectures there. Chev's opposition was a matter of course, but even Charles Sumner campaigned against her journey, arguing that no one in Washington wanted to hear her. Julia hoped to prove Sumner wrong. "I go," she noted, "in obedience to a deep and strong impulse wh[ich] I do not understand nor explain, but whose bidding I cannot neglect. The satisfaction of having at last obeyed this interior guide is all that keeps me up, for no one, so far as I know, altogether approves my going." On May 27, 1864, her forty-fifth birthday, Julia observed that the year had begun in "intolerable distress" with Sammy's death, but had become "the most valuable one of my life. I soon found my only refuge from grief in increased activity, after my kind." Her writing was a solace. It was also a source of self-identity; no longer was she simply a poet. Rather, she was a philosopher who served humanity by sharing her insights publicly.[18]

That comfort did her no good at home. Chev was so angry on her return from Washington that Julia felt "seized" by anxiety. Chev's face, she said, "has the power of emptying my brain of all vitality, so that I scarcely know what I am about. It feels like a violent electric shock, & is irresistible." She attempted to ameliorate the situation by relating details of her trip, but he was having none of it. "His comment," she complained, "was that he was glad I had been gratified, but that all of them here had been much pained. I went to bed with a horrible oppression, the fruit of my disturbed day."[19] In November 1864, she accepted an invitation to read a poem at the New York Century Club for the celebration of poet William Cullen Bryant's seventieth birthday. The experience was a heady one—she sat with Oliver Wendell Holmes on the train, was met at the station by George Bancroft, and delivered her poem after Ralph Waldo Emerson's address. "I was full of it, and read well," she exulted; yet the price was high. "This required a painful effort," she conceded, "as Chev was much opposed to my going." And so no one in the family celebrated what Julia considered "the greatest public honor of my life," prompting her to note in her diary that she could at least record the event for her grandchildren.[20] Presumably, they would be more enlightened. Julia would later devote four pages of her autobiography, quoting freely from her diaries, to a description of her experience at the Bryant celebration. Her daughters would also highlight the event in their biography of Julia. None of them would mention Chev's opposition or Julia's misery; in the official family history, only the public triumph would remain.[21]

Nevertheless, Julia's public endeavors had caused the family considerable pain. Chev was convinced that Julia's persistence reflected a desire for self-aggrandizement; Julia believed that her work was a moral calling. She was long accustomed to Chev's animosity, and she was now absolutely confident that she had crucial contributions to make to her society. "I feel more than ever impelled to make some great effort to realize the value of my mental capacities and acquisitions," she wrote in her diary in April 1866. Later that year, she defied Chev by reading at the Lexington Lyceum against his will. "Chev was much displeased, for which I was deeply sorry," she commented. "But his displeasure does not, in my eyes, absolve me from the duties of exercising my talents. A husband's authority is relative and contingent—that of conscience is absolute." In the end, she would do what was necessary to fulfill her vocation. As she declared in another diary entry, "I have so dreamed of high use that I cannot decline to a life of amusement, or of small occupation."[22] Like the trumpet in her "Battle Hymn," she refused to sound retreat. Nor would her equally persistent spouse.

THE SAME OLD SONG AND DANCE

As Julia and Chev wrangled, their arguments took on a familiar tone. Neither could do anything right in the other's eyes. This time around, however, the children were old enough to be more actively involved in their parents' disputes. The two older girls, Julia Romana and Flossy, often defended their father. Flossy in particular expressed resentment that Julia's activities outside the home were detrimental to the family's welfare. So Julia antagonized her daughters as well as her husband, as everyone in the household continued the dance of anger so familiar to them. To get a sense of life in the Howe family, a look at Julia's diary for the year 1865 is instructive. A day did not pass without tension, as Chev and Julia maneuvered for control.[23]

On February 7, 1865, Julia noted in her diary that she "had planned a modest dinner for today, which Chev made me put off, because [he] had a headache yesterday." As she reluctantly told her guests that dinner was canceled, she found herself in tears. Nothing but the soothing balm of philosophy could console her: "It took a full hour of Kant to quiet my mind."[24] Some days, even that comfort was denied her. She observed on February 11 that she had been "much tormented by interruptions. . . . Everybody torments me with every smallest errand. And I am trying to study philosophy!"[25]

On March 12, Julia Romana celebrated her twenty-first birthday. Her mother was unsure what to make of it. "Twenty-one years old, and almost a stranger to me," she mused. "I suffered much when this child was born—suffered in utter ignorance of pain and how to endure it. I would suffer a thousand times more to know that this child is to lead a good and happy life, to know that the life I gave her was a boon, not a bane." Julia was not confident that her daughter was wise enough to learn from her mother's experience. "She does not know her own value," Julia fretted. "I did not know mine at her age, nor for many years." Unfortunately, Julia concluded, she had no way of convincing

Julia Romana to learn from her. "She is not teachable, and will experience good & ill for herself, & take her knowledge of life at first hand. I cannot rehearse her with this. . . . Whether it is the best way, God knows."[26]

By March 17, more trouble was afoot. When Julia informed Chev that she would be reading a lecture that night, it "was like pulling the string of the shower bath." He was furious, yet she was unwilling to cancel her talk.[27] The next morning, Chev left for Newport with Julia Romana, abandoning his wife to the terrors of an angry Flossy. "Flossy came down in the morning, very cold & ungracious—the lecture being the cause," Julia noted. "I bore this as well as I could, knowing that such a result was inevitable, and will be, until I am able, if ever, to establish my point and read when and where I like." The only way to restore harmony was to sacrifice her study time. "To propitiate dear Flossy," Julia sighed, "I strolled into shops with her, to look at spring goods, and so wasted the precious morning."[28]

A day later, Julia was still trying to make sense of it all, puzzling over "Chev's insistence on the supremacy of his will as authority in the household." Acts of will, Julia concluded, must be judged by reason. Those who asserted their wills irrationally "may be a tyrant, but cannot be a master."[29] In mulishly depriving Julia of opportunities to exercise her God-given gifts, Chev could rule by might, but never by right. As she had observed a year earlier, "modesty is as much shown in our judgments of others as in our judgments of ourselves. It is in connection with S. G. H. that I have thought out and formulated this. Did he not suppose him self [sic] exempt from human errors, he could never berate me as he does."[30]

The study of philosophy offered Julia distinct consolations even in these verbal battles. After a conversation with Chev and Martin Conway on March 24, Julia noted with pleasure that she had "found my late training of great use in withstanding the assumptions of the former [Chev], who has great practical force, but is utterly lacking in philosophical culture." As Julia continued to ruminate on her most recent disputes with Chev, she concluded that she had no choice but to soldier on. "I determine that I can only be good in fulfilling my highest function—all else implies waste of power, leading to demoralization."[31]

That resolve was soon put to the test, as more squabbling erupted in April, on Julia and Chev's anniversary. Julia had made plans to attend church, dine, and then do a reading for the women incarcerated at a nearby prison.[32] Before she left, she said, "Flossy first attacked me—not unkindly, but from her usual point of view, and spoke of the pain my project gave her father, who soon came to speak for himself. He attacked me with the utmost vehemence and temper, called my undertaking a mere display, a mere courting of publicity, would not argue, nor hear me at all." Chev then "threatened to shape the whole government of the family according to his wishes, which," Julia observed wryly, "he has always done as far as he could. I said little, and suffered much. Could not promise anything . . . I feel utterly paralyzed."

As Julia reflected further on the incident, she mused, "I should be sorry to stand to any human being in the light in wh[ich] Chev stands to me in this thing. I feel utterly paralyzed and brought to a stand-still.—know not how to live and work any further." The more she thought about it, the more it seemed that the incident typified her life with Chev. She noted:

> I have been married twenty two years today. In the course of this time I have never known my husband to approve any act of mine. . . . Books— poems—plays—everything has been contemptible or contra band in his eyes, because it was not his way of doing things. Perhaps when I die, with half my work undone, he will be sorry that he did not try to be more magnanimous. As it is, I feel that today makes a great difference in my feeling towards him. I never knew him to be so small and unjust before, though I have known him to be both.

Unswayed by Chev's objections, Julia stuck to her plans for the day: she went to the prison. "God help me," she prayed, "for I am much grieved and disconcerted."[33]

The fireworks continued the next day. Chev read her diary entry for the previous day and, Julia seethed, left a note "coolly desiring me to destroy it all, which I shall not do." She remembered his remark of the previous day, when he had claimed that even if he had been engaged to Florence Nightingale and deeply in love with her, he would have nonetheless have given her up as soon as she began her career as a public woman. It was an argument that Julia had heard many times before: married women belonged at home. "This phrase needs no comment," she groused to herself.[34]

Yet all was not gloom and doom. She had a good talk with Chev on May 4, after a policeman visited to inquire if their son Harry had been throwing pie buckets out of fourth-story windows. As was usually the case when mischief was involved, Harry was indeed the instigator. The policeman did not press charges, and Julia and Chev talked amiably for a good while. Julia wrote that she went to bed happier about her relationship with Chev than she had been in a long time.[35] She commented a few weeks later that she had received "a surprisingly kind note from Chev. It so amazes me when he shows any sort of liking to me," she commented, that she wondered if their presumed mutual antipathy was simply "an illusion resulting from our want of active sympathy."[36]

More reflections followed. Her participation in a performance of *The Messiah* in late May led Julia to ponder her old musical ambitions. Perhaps it was best she had abandoned them for a different life with Chev. "If I had kept up my music as I intended, in my early youth, I should never have done what I have done—should never have studied philosophy, nor written what I have written. My life would have been more natural and passionate," Julia concluded, "but I think less valuable."[37] Two days later, she was thinking, as she had so often during her marriage, about her need for autonomy. "I feel," she wrote, "that a woman's whole moral responsibility is lowered by the fact that she must never obey a transcendent command of conscience. Man can give her nothing to take the place of this. It is the divine right of the human soul."[38] Weeks later, in August, she returned to this theme, noting that a year earlier she had been excited about the prospect of giving lectures on philosophy, anticipating the opening of "a vista of usefulness to me, and . . . to others." Unfortunately, she concluded, "the opposition of my family has made it almost impossible for me to make the use intended of them."[39]

Diary entries in November and December 1865 give further insight into the squabbles that marked the Howes' domestic lives. Their lease on their Chesnut Street house—where Sammy had been born and died—had expired, and Julia noted with sadness her last day in the house on November 3. By November 4, she was already unhappy with Chev's behavior in their new residence at 19 Boylston. Her diary noted that she "was very angry with Chev, who is carrying out his plan of putting a hearth & grate in the parlour, entirely against my wishes."[40] This was a prelude to the battle of the furnace that would transpire in December.

On December 18, Julia observed in her diary, "I complained to Chev this morning of the severe cold of the parlour, last evening, with no unkind intention." Chev was not sympathetic. "He retorted furiously, saying that it was all my fault, the result of my want of system. I told him that these repeated chills w[oul]d shorten my life." Chev answered that the dirt in the house would shorten his life. Julia had had enough. "I said, 'it does not seem to.' He left, and Maud cried, and Flossy attacked me most severely."

It was all very upsetting. "What was the truth?" Julia fumed. "I had complained, not improperly, of a dangerous discomfort, from wh[ich] I still suffer, & the only result was to excite Chev's passion, & through these, those of the children against me. I now must resolve to have nothing further to say." Of course she did not have to be silent in her diary, reporting that an inspection subsequently revealed that the "trouble with the furnace was that the cold air flue was shut; & not my fault in any way." She was still depressed, even if exonerated in her own mind. Julia's diary December 19 recorded that she was "very melancholy on account of yesterday's disagreement."[41]

OPPOSITION

The philosophical essays Julia was writing reflected this energetic family bickering. One of the most striking characteristics of Julia's lectures from the 1860s was her fascination with polarities—she was drawn, over and over again, to a consideration of opposing elements. The titles of her lectures— "Doubt and Belief," "Duality," "Polarity," "Polarity II," "Limitation," "Equality," and "Third Party"—illustrated her efforts to align competing forces. Julia was fully aware of the connection of her philosophical interest in opposition to the stormy dynamics of her relationship with Chev. She wrote in her diary: "Chev is one of the characters based upon opposition. While I always seem to work for an unseen friend, he always sees an armed adversary and nerves himself accordingly. So all our lives turn on what I may call moral or personal fiction, which are to us what mathematical and legal fictions are to the operations of their respective sciences."[42]

The fascination of the topic of opposition, of course, lay in finding a solution. Somehow, Julia was convinced, in a world in which people invariably clashed, there must be a way of understanding the essence of natural conflict; it must be possible, even amidst dualities, to find resources for coexistence and cooperation.[43] Her 1867 essay aptly entitled "Opposition" stated the premise of this worldview, arguing that the existence of opposites was a "divine necessity." Indeed, Julia asserted, "the oppositions of sex, of fortune, and of position may be viewed . . . as among the fundamental conditions of human consciousness. Man demands his opposite in woman; woman demands her's [sic] in man. Neither could exist as much without the opposition of the other . . . both dwindle in proportion to their isolation from each other."[44]

Few of her listeners would have disagreed; the entire convention of separate spheres depended on such reasoning. Julia, however, wanted to rethink just what that polarity might mean. This puzzle of gender identity over which she had agonized for years—most painfully in her battles with Chev and most dramatically in her Laurence manuscript—at last found its resolution in her philosophical essays. Her conclusions were far reaching. Indeed, in reconsidering the philosophical implications of what it meant to be gendered, Julia laid the groundwork for her future career as a women's rights activist. In time, she would turn the convention of separate spheres on its head, arguing for the elasticity of gender roles. Male and female, she insisted, were not rigidly divided into separate gender spheres except by social conditioning, and that social conditioning interfered with the development of the human race. Ideally, God intended for male and female to live in mutual sympathy, learning from one another, so that each gender aspired to acquire the best characteristics of the other. In this way, civilization truly advanced.

The easiest way to see how radical these arguments were for Julia is to compare them to an earlier document in which she had also considered the issue of woman's relation to man. Except for a few poems in *Words for the Hour,* Julia had, up to this point in her work, sought autonomy for herself, but she had not advocated equality for women in general. She had based her own desire for autonomy on her private sense of herself as an exceptional woman of unusual talents. "In my own youth," she later explained, "the doctrine of the superior woman prevailed. I was taught, as others were, that here and there some lovely Marcia, towering above her sex, attained the heights of human intelligence."[45] "The Woman's Rights Question"—a speech that must have caused her exquisite embarrassment in later years—is the oldest surviving essay in which Julia formally addressed the rights of women. It is undated; given its tone and content, the essay must have been written before the Civil War.[46] The document reads like a parody of Julia's later suffrage writings, and the reader can only imagine what mood of self-loathing or contrition prompted her to write it.[47]

"The Woman's Rights Question" began by setting out the proper roles of man and woman. "To him," Julia contended, "belongs the functions of the outer world—War, Commerce, in a degree, Government and Public Instruction. To her belong the functions of the inner world of home—the bearing and rearing of children, domestic economy, and elementary instruction." This was separate-spheres doctrine at its purest. Julia proceeded to consider the problem of the woman who was dissatisfied with a purely domestic role and longed to pastor churches, teach in colleges, or speak at political meetings. Such a woman ought to be pitied, she said. In her proper sphere, woman was the equivalent of man. "But that woman, taken out of her sphere, melted over and recast as it were in the social mould of man," at best functioned at the level of a third-rate man. Certainly, Julia conceded, she herself might wish to speak in a pulpit; fortunately, however, she knew better. "I should only dwarf myself," she explained, if she spoke in Theodore Parker's place. "The wide echoes of the Music Hall would laugh my high toned treble to scorn." Better, far better, to know one's place and keep to it. "It shall content me playfully to cross swords with him in a parlour fight—but it contents me to hear his great words, and to feel that through study and earnest attention, I understood him."[48]

Women who acted like men, Julia concluded, were "unsexed." Truly great women, such as Florence Nightingale, achieved renown "through an intensification of womanliness, rather than through any exhibition of masculine traits of character." The womanly woman would not presume to usurp man's prerogatives any more than a well-trained cook would dream of dining with her employers. The true wife would respect her husband's authority, being careful to avoid "publicly insulting his manhood and marital office" by conspiring to "fling him a bank-note, wherewith to pay her fare" when they traveled together. Woman's greatest glory and duty, Julia concluded, lay in raising children, for in "our children we are immortal." Ultimately, women could be happy only if they accepted the domestic discipline that was their lot. "If we can see that the thing has a deep, a philosophical, and abiding necessity," she urged, "we shall be conscious of the true dignity of our position, and our minds will rest in it."[49]

The initial philosophical lectures that Julia delivered in 1863–64 did little to revise this rigid separation of man and woman. She was able, at times, to provide pointed critiques of marriage, but those comments did not undermine the notion of separate spheres upon which domestic discipline depended. Still, she did get off a few good shots. In "Proteus," an address first delivered in December 1863,[50] she castigated "self-love" as the bitterest enemy of all social harmonies and the source of many marital disappointments. "People who love themselves supremely never did love any thing but themselves," she observed. A marriage ruled by one partner's self-love was liable to prove "irksome and dangerous," leaving the unfortunate mate no choice but stoicism. Nevertheless, "no accident of marriage can undo a pure, noble, disinterested nature," she insisted. "Suffering will but fashion it with a sharp and enduring sculpture. Humiliation will but prepare the way for future exaltation."[51] Julia's listeners (had they but had the advantage of reading the Eva and Rafael romance) would have recognized a familiar litany in her insistence that suffering engendered nobility. But in "Proteus," Julia did not conclude that patient suffering could transfigure husband and wife so that, like Eva and Rafael, they might be joined in an inseparable union of male and female. Rather, she asserted that the "power of man is to be a man"—not a beast that degraded humanity, but a man who elevated it. The power of a woman, conversely, was "to be greatly a woman, and not a man at all. To bear children, rear and love them" constituted woman's duty.[52]

In an 1864 lecture titled "Limitation," Julia returned to this theme of separation of spheres, here discussing what she called the "division of offices" in human experience. Her thesis was that limitation was both necessary and inevitable. The infinite was the source of human existence (a theme that formed the focus of another essay called "Polarity"), but all life in the tangible world was subject to limitation by virtue of its finitude. Julia advised her listeners not to bewail limitation, since it allowed for variety—some people preached sermons, some sewed garments; the tropics supported elephant life, while the arctic regions produced polar bears. Because limitation was inevitable, she warned, people erred when they expected any one person to incarnate the entire range of human possibilities. If, for example, "your wife is pleasing and affectionate," it would be folly to "make it the unhappiness of her life and of your's [sic] that she has a want of skill here, and of wisdom there." Instead, Julia asserted, people should find their particular niche and fill it. Ultimately, society was organic, and each person had a place in it; any attempt to leave that position was doomed to fail. "The great fundamental equality," Julia counseled, "is after all the equality of necessity. We are all essential to the maintenance of society, not in our persons indeed, but in our place and function." In the end, "the whole race may be lifted on the wing of progress and inspiration, but I do not believe it will ever be lifted out of its' [sic] present order, in which higher compels lower, and richer poorer."[53]

Nothing in these lectures necessitated an end to the status quo of separate spheres. But the roots of such a critique were emerging. In her 1864 lecture, "Polarity," Julia had argued that God was the source of all life. Male and female emanated from God, forming two poles of the divine expression. Neither pole was superior to the other, since both had their source in God. In an argument that would come to be crucial to her eventual dismissal of separate-spheres rhetoric, Julia maintained that both men and women (as poles of the divine) had equal capacities; if women deemed themselves men's inferiors in American culture, that understanding was the product of social custom and conditioning, not a reflection of innate qualities.[54] In "Polarity II," written in 1865, Julia noted the dire consequences of denying to women their God-given right to develop their potential: "Interdict your daughter the sphere of social sympathy . . . and she will cherish mono-maniac loves or fancies which may destroy her. Restrict your wife from the legitimate exercise of her talents, and she will develop a folly, or a vice." Sounding as if she knew quite well what she was talking about, Julia warned that the ultimate consequence of restricting woman to an impoverished sphere was the annihilation of her self: "the vital powers unavoidably deteriorate, and the results of life cease to be accomplished," she insisted. "So, in the midst of life, death may overtake us," and the wife who might have refreshed her husband's world with "social, domestic, or aesthetic inspiration, may, if confined in a mean and narrow tyranny, become a sot, a debaucher, an unbeliever."[55]

In her 1867 essay entitled "Opposition," Julia returned to the theme of gender polarity. There she conceded that it was not only the case that "man demands his opposite in woman, and woman demands her's [sic] in man." It was also true that anyone contrasting men and women would conclude that woman was "poor and unequal, based on her weakness and his will." To the casual observer, men appeared superior to women. But, Julia continued, that inequality was not inherent in women. Rather, a careful examination of the relations of men and women showed that the "opposition" of the sexes was not static. Man could influence woman, and woman could influence man; and together both could grow toward new realities. In short, both could learn from and acquire the virtues of the other. Gender—and the presumed character traits that adhered to masculinity and femininity—was fluid; people could and did change.[56]

Other lectures from 1867 and 1869 indicated that Julia was increasingly willing to consider expanded roles for women in the public sphere. Her studies in philosophy had prompted her to think in broad terms—she was considering the relationship of the finite and the infinite, of male and female as emanations of the divine. These reflections were pushing her toward a position that she knew would destroy any semblance of family harmony in her home. Her husband would protest and her daughters would accuse her of ruining their father's happiness, but Julia was well on the way to embracing women's rights to political and social equality.

Julia's advocacy of women's rights was clear in a lecture she gave on "Representation and How to Get It" in 1867. There she conceded that the true interests of men and women were the same, just as, in theory, the interests of masters and servants were the same. "But," she cautioned, "it is not safe to allow the master to represent the servant, or the servant to represent the master, because the one . . . has special interests to which he may sacrifice the rights of the other." In short, men could not be trusted to represent women's interests. "Is it for woman's interest that the children of her pain and of her love should belong to one who knows no such bond as motherhood, to be taken away from her at his pleasure?" she asked. "Is it for a woman's interest that dignity, power and authority" should be wrested from her and reside in the opposite sex alone? The answer was obvious, and the conclusion was clear: "[W]oman's husband cannot represent her." American culture, in depriving women of political rights, subjected women to tyranny. "There is no America for us women," Julia charged. "It is America to you [men], it is Russia to us . . . absolutism and despotism."[57]

Julia reiterated that point in an essay entitled the "Position of Women." That position was, she argued, "devoid of human rights and features, deprived of efficient will, of property and of representation."[58] In an 1869 sermon, Julia addressed directly the issue that had haunted the women's rights movement: If women gained the rights and privileges of men, would they not become unfeminine, coarse, and manly? How, in short, could women really be women if they acted like men? Julia conceded that some people thought the emancipation of women would "destroy the sacred types of the wife and of the mother" and replace true womanhood with a "half male monster." They need not fear, she answered. "I see in the new Womanhood only an extended & glorified motherhood," a motherhood that did not confine nurture to the child in the cradle, but followed that child out of the home into the world to spread the civilizing influences of motherhood to the public sphere. In her youth, Julia confessed, she used to "dream of a miraculous woman who should be to women all that Christ was to men." Now she knew such a dream to be unnecessary. "Every true woman has the mother in her and this grand spiritual motherhood, exerting it's [sic] direct influence and watchfulness in all the walks of life, will give every woman a noble part to perform."[59]

In her Laurence manuscript, Julia had put the word "monster!" in the mouth of the rejected lover Emma upon her realization that Laurence was a hermaphrodite. The fear of being a monster herself was an anxiety with which Julia had long struggled; her own desires to enter the male world of writing and lecturing were suspect in an age that assumed woman's natural place was in the home. The essay that Julia had earlier written on the "Woman's Rights Question" revealed just how powerful Julia's desire to appear respectable was. In that work, Julia had mocked herself, implying that she would never dream of preaching from a pulpit, that simply understanding the words of a great man like Theodore Parker was more than enough to satisfy her. By 1869, however, she was preaching from pulpits, and she was looking directly at one of her deepest fears and renouncing it. The emancipated woman, who dared to ask for rights and privileges reserved for men, was not a monster; rather, she was a glorified mother who sought to advance the entire human race. The well-being of man depended on his ability to absorb woman's nature and lessons into his own character. In the end, Eva and Rafael were prophetic figures for Julia; as their story revealed, the union of male and female represented the hope for all human progress.

Julia was thus well on the way to disproving what she had once called the philosophical and abiding necessity of the subordination of women. Her lectures had given her a theoretical springboard from which to deconstruct the necessity of separate spheres. Her increasing involvement in political and social reform would provide opportunities for active engagement in the public world of men. Both in thought and in deed, she would labor to prove that the newly autonomous woman was not only respectable but also a political force of no mean ability.

GIVING PEACE A CHANCE

Nothing made as big a difference in Julia's life as her decision to join the women's movement. She became active in the cause of woman suffrage in 1868, and also threw herself into the newly developing woman's club movement. Soon she was president of the New England Woman's Club and president of the New England Woman Suffrage Association as well. One of the grand consequences was that, for the first time in her life, she was surrounded by other talented women committed to social reform. She spoke with gratitude in her *Reminiscences* of what joining with other women had meant to her, recalling "the relief which it afforded me from the sense of isolation and eccentricity."[60] But Julia was not a separatist. The New England Woman's Club, over which she would preside for decades, did not exclude men. Neither did the suffrage organization (American Woman Suffrage Association) that she joined. While she embraced causes that were unpopular, she did so in a way that was moderate, refusing to cut herself off from men who were also sympathetic of women's rights. In the political struggles that were to come, she would always appear respectable, not overtly revolutionary.

Belonging to a woman's club that held weekly meetings and making herself available as a lecturer meant that Julia was increasingly absent from home. Other duties also demanded her attention—she was devoting time and energy to the *Woman's Journal,* a weekly suffrage paper of which she was one of the founding editors. Knowing she would be called away from home frequently, Julia did not always inform Chev in advance of her excursions; he would only fuss. Besides, Flossy was old enough to manage the home in her absence (no one even suggested that Julia Romana take charge, since she was hopeless at domestic tasks). Laura's fiancé, Harry Richards, found the whole family rather odd. "It was a strange household," he remembered, "with Grandmother Howe slipping off to lectures and conventions, while Polish and Greek refugees flocked to Grandfather Howe, hoping for employment." Harry wondered how Julia and Chev ever got anything done; they pulled so hard in such different directions.[61] It is hard not to sympathize with him. Chev was moving the family (from Green Peace, to the Institute, to rented houses in town) so often in those years that Harry had trouble keeping up. He said goodbye to Laura one evening, only to find on his return the next day that the family had moved. He had no idea where.[62]

Julia Romana, Flossy, and Laura married within twelve months of each other in 1870–71. Their departures left Julia all the more free to attend meetings and give lectures. Chev suspected that Julia left on unexpected trips simply to escape him, and probably to annoy him as well. When Julia was home, he said, the stream of visitors was unending, and she was always the center of heady conversation. When she left, it was without warning. "Imagine your awakening your Harry from a sound sleep at 5 o'clock some morning," he wrote Laura after her marriage, "& astounding him by announcing that you are going away immediately, for all that day & the next! that[,] however[,] is nothing here. I expect that some morning early my chamber door will be opened & Mama will appear with bonnet & shawl on & announce that she is going off immediately for some place west . . . to be absent any[?] number of days or weeks!" Such, Chev concluded, were the fruits "of the promise made thirty odd years ago at No. 32 Bond St.!!"[63]

It was not just Julia's frequent absences that grated. Chev simply could not reconcile himself to Julia's absorption in woman suffrage. He grumbled to Laura that the "first act in the new Gospel" of woman suffrage would be "husbands obey your wives," and suggested that part of the lure of Julia's "organizing all sorts" of clubs and associations "under the guise of human progress" was the opportunity to enjoy elegant teas, lobster salads, and clam bakes.[64] To George Finlay, he was even more disgruntled:

> Mrs. Howe grows more and more absorbed in the public work of obtaining
> women's suffrage; and, like most of her co-workers, shows more zeal than
> discretion; and, in my opinion, does more harm by subordinating domestic
> duties to supposed public ones. Surely women have the right of suffrage;
> and will obtain it soon; but zeal in pursuit of it, does not justify neglect of
> domestic relations and occupations; nor attempts to abolish those deficien-
> cies in our political and social sphere and duties, which spring out of the
> difference in the very organization of the sexes. The leaders of this reform
> already show by the unwisdom of their publical objects and the overzeal in
> their action, that they are actuated, however unconsciously, by that devil's
> doctrine of justification of means by the end.[65]

Oddly, the Franco-Prussian War brought a measure of peace to the household. Hoping to distract Julia, Chev urged her to turn her attention to protesting the war, assuming that peace activism would prove a more benign occupation than suffrage. Julia, however, found in the cause of peace a perfect opportunity to reflect further upon the philosophical and theological topics to which she had devoted her public lectures. Thinking about war and peace meant thinking about human nature. Analyzing human nature meant pursuing the essential core of what it meant to be male and female. Thinking about gender led Julia to a rationale for public involvement that freed her forever from the prison of domesticity. In continuing to develop her earlier theories about the bipolarity of human nature, she would come to believe that true womanhood was not static, but dynamic. To progress, man and woman would have to absorb the vital characteristics of the other. The true woman (or man) was a mixed being, but decidedly *not* a monster.

As Julia commenced her considerations of war and peace, she posed this question: Why did men persist in settling political disagreements violently? She also wondered what she, a woman lacking the right to vote, could do about it. Feeling both politically marginal and morally outraged, she began to reimagine—once again—what it meant to be a woman. "During the first two thirds of my life," she later explained,

> I looked to the masculine ideal of character as the only true one. I sought
> its inspiration, and referred my merits and demerits to its judicial verdict.
> In an unexpected hour a new light came to me, showing me a world of
> thought and of character quite beyond the limits within which I had hith-
> erto been content to abide. The new domain now made clear to me was
> that of true womanhood—woman no longer in her ancillary relation to
> her opposite, man, but in her direct relation to the divine plan and purpose,
> as a free agent, fully sharing with man every human right and every human
> responsibility. . . . Oh, had I earlier known the power, the nobility, the intelli-
> gence which lie within the range of true womanhood, I had surely lived
> more wisely and to better purpose.[66]

Julia was not alone in her thinking; many others would use similar arguments to defend women's rights. Though she did not invent the rhetoric, Julia discovered that it served her purposes extremely well. As she further considered the role of the true woman, Julia concluded that the moral sublimity of motherhood reached beyond the confines of the home. Echoing earlier advocates of peace, she argued that mothers were naturally inclined toward peace, since they, knowing the cost and pain of childbirth, were innately disinclined to send their sons to die on the battlefield. But in considering the full implications of motherhood, she suggested, as no prominent peace reformer before her had, that the maternal instinct was fundamental to the nature of God. God, she contended, was both mother and father, and in a very real sense the maternal side of the divine was superior to the paternal side.[67]

Borrowing from the evolutionary language popular in her time, Julia proposed that human development consisted of three stages. The first stage was that of primitive animal nature, in which individual men rose to power by brute force. The next stage was that of organized power, in which the "war-ideal, with its rules of loyalty and honor" surpassed the "savagery of primitive man." Thus, she claimed, "the savage individual gives way to the father-ideal, just and noble." Nevertheless, the age of the father-ideal celebrated masculine violence, and needed itself to give way to divine love. "Now where," Julia asked, "do we find provided in Nature a counter-influence, a passion and power which shall be as conservative of human life as masculine influence is destructive of it?" The answer, of course, was in motherhood, "an organization," she explained, "which gives ... life through months of weariness, through hours of anguish and through years of labor—an organization in which suffering is the parent of love, and all that is endured receives its final crown in the life and love of something other than itself." In short, she contended, "The womanly power is that which links the divine to the human soul. God is born of a woman."[68]

In thus positing the divine nature as comprising both the father-ideal and the mother-ideal, Julia suggested that woman's nature was akin to that which was highest and best in God. For her, men represented justice, but women represented mercy and love. "In woman's ideal of the divine parentage," she explained, "love is paramount even to justice. ... The soul which can resist the onslaught of well-merited reproach must finally yield to the invitation of divine mercy; and God becomes father and mother at once, awful in judgment, but untiring in forgiveness."[69] There was thus hope that peace could replace war, but only if women were free to lead the human race up the evolutionary ladder to its sublime destiny. Men were unable to accomplish this task in their present state. "I think ... that the pacific ideal will never be established and perpetuated without the direct intervention of Woman in the administration of the human estate," Julia concluded. "Hers is that opposite organization which is constrained to hold life sacred, knowing its bitter cost, which is impelled to patience, to disinterested endurance and affection, by every instinct, whose opposite renders man violent and self asserting."[70]

In an 1875 lecture called "The Halfness of Nature," Julia spelled out the full implications of the bipolarity of human nature that she had begun to explore in 1863. "The halfness of the individual," she explained, "is literally shown in the division of sex." But the human spirit is dissatisfied with this halfness; it longs for union—for enduring union. "The other half of sex is not to be found in a succession or simultaneity of mates, easily taken, and as easily discarded," Julia asserted. "This great value of a perfected life is only to be had through an abiding and complete investment." The ideal union was marriage, "one of the most difficult and delicate achievements of society." If either partner sought to dwarf the other, Julia insisted, the marriage could not elevate either partner. But a marriage of equals was transformative. "The relations of sex, lifted up to the communion of the divine, unified by the good faith of a life time, enriched by a true sharing of experience," made possible what Julia called a "mystic self-hood" that was the consummation of human nature. "The ideal human being," she averred, "is man and woman united in the ideal plane."[71]

Once again, Julia's rhetoric was reminiscent of her descriptions of Eva and Rafael, the lovers transfigured in a glorious union that was itself a reflection of the divine. Earnest devotion, loving kindness, and rigorous humility before one's mate offered the possibility of transformation into the divine image. Once Julia posited God as female as well as male and concluded that the goal of human experience was to incarnate the divine as fully as possible, the romance of Eva and Rafael could serve as a model for civilization's progress. Faithful lovers triumphed over the limitations of separate spheres and led the human race on to the full expression of the divine nature it was created to reflect.

Rhetoric aside, Julia's achievements in the cause of peace were noteworthy. In 1870, she called for mothers around the world to organize a crusade on behalf of peace. Hoping to establish what she called "a mighty and august Congress of Mothers, which should constitute a new point of departure for the regeneration of society," she held two well-attended meetings in New York City to publicize the cause. In 1872, she traveled to England, where she organized the first women's peace congress. In 1873, she established the tradition of observing a Mothers' Day of Peace in early June. The first Mothers' Day was celebrated in eighteen American cities, as well as in Rome and Constantinople, and friends of peace in Philadelphia continued to observe her mothers' day for over fifty years, even forming a Julia Ward Howe Peace Band.[72] Ultimately, her influence in the suffrage and woman's club movements helped promote enthusiasm for peace among hundreds of thousands of women. By World War I, legions of women in groups such as the Federation of Women's Clubs, the Council of Mothers, and the National Council of Women were all committed to promoting peace.

But even if Julia had never organized a single public activity related to peace reform, sustained reflection about pacifism would have remained critical to her intellectual development. Analyzing issues of peace and war allowed Julia to bring to fruition the theoretical notions about gender that she had begun exploring in her philosophical lectures. Through her investigation of the roots of peace, Julia discovered that God was a mother as well as a father and concluded that without the uplifting influence of women, human civilization could not pull itself out of savagery. The only path for human progress lay in the ability of men and women to come together and learn from one another—to unite, like Eva and Rafael, in union before the divine.

In her peace work, as well as in her club work and her woman suffrage activities, Julia enjoyed the exhilarating tonic of joining with like-minded persons committed to social reform. For the first time in her life, she belonged to a sympathetic community of talented women, united in their dedication to work for the common good. While Julia emerged as a leader, she was no longer the exceptional woman estranged from her less accomplished sisters. In the work of political reform, she had found her place and her voice; nothing less than a public stage could have been equal to her task.

THE FINAL CURTAIN

In October 1866, Chev had written Julia's sister Louisa that Julia was "in the maturity of her talent and power." And so she was. These were heady days for her. As Julia looked back on it all in 1874, she told her sister Annie, "these last years have brought a great unfolding of possibilities. One begins to see the part women are to have in the world's redemption." Her only regret, Julia added, was that it had taken her so long to understand her own capacities. "I knew not," she mourned, "that women could take hold of these things."[73] Once she took hold she did not let go. When Dr. Edward Clark of Harvard read a paper against coeducation at the New England Woman's Club, Julia groused that his argument was "based entirely upon the monthly indisposition, as it may be called, of women,"[74] and launched a counterattack. Women's reproductive organs were not topics that readily lent themselves to elegant public discourse, but Julia pulled it off, both in speeches and in an edited volume that she published in 1874.[75] Her reputation was not sullied by her foray against Dr. Clark. One reporter lauded her as "ladylike to an exceptional degree," even "when treating of such topics as 'pre-natal influences.'" There was, the reporter marveled, "a refinement and exquisiteness, and yet an intensity" about the remarkable Mrs. Howe.[76]

Chev's vitality, on the other hand, was beginning to fade. There were some rousing moments left to him—a triumphant return to Greece in 1867, the excitement of seeing his three older daughters married, and pleasant trips to Santo Domingo in 1872 and 1874. Chev also had the privilege of standing by his daughter Laura when she delivered her first child in 1872. Laura's husband commented that Dr. Howe's presence was a comfort to both of them, since he took labor and delivery in stride. "He told," Harry Richards remembered, "a story of an Irish couple, living in a farmhouse; the wife went out to the shed to get kindling wood, and soon her husband heard her calling, 'Mike, Mike come fetch the kindlings, and I will bring in the che-ild.'"[77] Apparently Chev never ran out of childbirth anecdotes.

Nor did he come easily to the end of his sexual vigor, managing to maintain a mistress until at least 1866.[78] Exactly how Chev justified his philandering to himself is hard to say, but it is clear that he did not condone infidelity in other men. In 1869, his friend Conway consulted him about his desire to divorce his wife and marry, as Chev put it, "a lady more to your taste, and with fortune enough to gratify your ambition." Chev conceded that he was in "entire agreement" with Conway "on the subject of the slavery of ill assorted marriages," but he professed shock that Conway proposed to make his wife a "party to the act" and require her "to aid and assist in bringing about a divorce and making her children fatherless." To a gentleman, Chev told Conway, "his promise—his word of honor, deliberately given, is a bond forever." Only one course of action was possible, Chev concluded. "You took a young, attractive girl— you solemnly swore [to] love & cherish her for life; she has been faithful to you; she has borne to you many children—she is now worn—feeble—distasteful— You may not be able to love—but you can cherish her, & be faithful to your vow until death do you part."[79]

Easier said than done, obviously. In any case, by the 1870s, Chev was clearly in decline. Long convinced that he was on the verge of death—his letters to Sumner had been predicting it for decades—Chev developed a number of physical problems. Trips to the tropics were of some help, but returning to Boston would prompt relapses. Illness exacerbated his temper, and the final years of his marriage were even more tumultuous than usual.

Julia's diary told a tale of woe occasionally relieved by humor. In October 1872, Chev had one of his fits of hypochondria and became convinced in the middle of the night that he had a heart condition. Rousing everyone out of bed by 5:20 a.m., he insisted that Julia accompany him on the 7:20 train so that he could rush into town to consult his physician. "His ailment turned out to be nothing serious," Julia reported. Moreover, by the time they had boarded the train to return home, Chev's mind was on other things. "He soon forgot it in the cars," Julia noted wryly, "when people congratulated him on his good looks."[80]

Other stories were more pathetic. As they traveled by boat to Santo Domingo in March 1874, Julia agonized over Chev's now frequent swearing. "I will say here in great privacy that Chev swore all the time he was dining, while I piteously prayed thru' my toilet. . . . I certainly meant more by my praying than Chev did by his swearing."[81] By April, she was in despair. "The object of this journal is not to tell how good I am & how bad other people are," she insisted. "But poor Chev's excitability & restlessness make it hard to live with him. The passion for absolute control of every thing, without reference to what any one else may think or wish grows by constant indulgence. The least reluctance or complaint perfectly maddens him. He swears terribly, & wastes time & money as if they were water."[82]

By Thanksgiving, the family feared that Chev was on his last legs. "It seems," Julia said, "as if the pale messenger were hovering near us, waiting for some one," making the dinner seem "weird & and a little ghostly."[83] By the end of the year, however, she and Chev were back at the furnace wars. This time he was burning her up, and she complained of being "nearly crazed with furnace heat," claiming that Chev kept it at a sort of "hell-point."[84] Two days before Christmas, Julia confided to her diary, "This day I feel that if I do not soon have an interval of entire freedom from care & responsibility of any kind, the thin cord of sanity will snap, & let me down. It is the perpetual effort to make ends meet, not so much in money as in time & action, which seems latterly to distress my head so much. Add to this the intense heat wh[ich] we often suffer in this house."[85]

Conditions did not improve. On January 16, 1875, she remarked, "This morning I cried aloud to God: why do you not help me? There is my husband, grown to be almost a selfish animal, making the house a perfect hell of heating suffocation, abuse, and ill-humor. You have made it my duty to be faithful and kind to him. He is destroying my health and that of my children. Can't you, won't you do something to make it better for me?" Later in the day, Julia managed to persuade Chev that "everyone in the house—not just me—felt the atmosphere of the house." Chev then opened the cold air flue, and Julia declared, "the house became comfortable at once."[86]

Julia was devoting a good deal of time to Chev's care, but she did not give up her public activities. She continued to attend numerous meetings and indicated in July 1875 that, after several days of nursing Chev, she had slipped out of the house to listen to an evening lecture. He was furious. "Chev was very unkind to me on my return," she observed. He "would not let me help him to undress, & told me to go to hell. I was rather angry, in consequence, but saw that he was very feeble."[87] In August, Julia recorded another depressing incident: "Chev got quite furious because I wanted to rub him instead of letting Julia [Romana] do so. I went into his room & told her to leave it, my desire being that she should not see him expose . . . his body as he does whenever he is to be rubbed. He shook me violently, from head to foot, threatened to jump out of the window." Julia felt sad and angry the entire day as a result, although she did add that at bedtime Chev asked her to forgive his ill humor.[88]

Despite the family's fears, Chev lived to see another Thanksgiving. He and Julia had conversations in November and December 1875 that profoundly shocked her. Julia had long suspected that Chev had been unfaithful to her, and now, finally, he confessed his philandering. Julia remarked on November 23, "I have had some sad revelations from dear Chev of things about some of my own sex which greatly astonish me. . . . I learn that women are not only sensual and lustful, & that men are attracted, rather than shocked by this trait. The privacy of offices, or at least their remoteness from domestic visitation, is eagerly made available by these women for the vilest purposes."[89] Julia found it hard to forgive Chev his infidelity, but finally, on December 8, they came to an understanding. "I have solemnly sworn to him never to allude to any thing in the past which, coming up lately, has given us both harm," she wrote. "Gloria in Excelsis Deo! I have reached the bottom of these years of estrangement, in wh[ich] there has been fault & wrong on both sides, & we shall begin to rebuild our life in common. My double bed is to be moved into his room, in order that we may have the comfort of being near each in the dark and silent hours. God has granted me my prayer."[90]

As early as the next evening, however, Julia found herself assaulted by anger and pain over Chev's revelations. She recorded in her diary that she had been in agony before going to bed that night. She had imagined a conversation with Chev's mistress "to discuss her 'shameful conduct' and wrongs to me. I wished to see her ghost more than I ever dreaded to see one. I remembered with joy that she died by inches a painful death, in poverty alleviated by the care of friends. When I felt how devilish these thoughts were, I prayed, & so slept." Julia reproached herself for such thoughts, only to fall into a mood of dark self-recrimination. The morning after her imaginary conversation with Chev's mistress, she wrote, "at waking, the spirit seemed to show me my own faults, and it seemed a great comfort to have the burden of offence laid on my shoulders. Strange as it may seem, it was comparatively delightful to me to accuse myself, & to make my own sins point out the hypocrisy & unkindness of which I have had so long an experience, without in the least understanding the facts, as they were. . . . 'Pray without ceasing' was now the word for me."[91]

As Julia struggled to reconcile herself to Chev's revelations, Chev continued to decline physically. On January 4, 1876, Julia wrote that she was preparing for a lecture trip when Chev called her in the middle of the night to help him, but that she left him to the care of Paddock, his attendant. In the morning, Julia rubbed Chev's feet and then she and Paddock took him for a walk. He went into convulsions afterward and was taken to his bed. There was little hope. On January 8, Julia chastised herself for years of selfishness, feeling remorse for the attention she had so often "given to other things & taken from him." The next day, January 9, Chev died.[92] Julia recounted on January 10 that she had awakened about four in the morning to experience "the chastening hand of God," for "every shortcoming, every offence rises grimly up against me. I would have been glad," she declared, "to see dear Chev's ghost, to have it reproach me. The silence is so painful." In the end, she sadly observed, "in place of my dear husband I have now my foolish papers. Yet I have often left him for them."[93]

The funeral was on January 13. It featured mythic figures from the life of the Chevalier. Laura Bridgman cried upon the coffin; James Freeman Clarke read "The Hero," John Greenleaf Whittier's poem of tribute to Chev. On February 8, Boston celebrated a memorial service at Music Hall. Julia then went on to publish a memoir honoring Chev's accomplishments. She was generous in her praise, commenting that all "that is most sterling in American character may be said to have found its embodiment in Dr. Howe." Julia even put aside the rhetoric of motherhood that had become so significant to her to note the importance of recognizing that "there is also a fatherhood of human society, a vigilance and forethought of benevolence recognized in individuals who devote their best energies to the interests of mankind."[94]

Julia had done her best by Chev, but already her reputation was eclipsing his. One editorial noted that much of Chev's success "was due to his fortunate domestic relations . . . and beautiful home life, by which he was cheered during his active manhood." Indeed, the editorial asserted, Chev's marriage was so crucial to his success that it stood as proof of the old adage "two heads are better than one." Chev's distinguished wife had "given her husband's name a renown all its own," the editorial concluded. "It was the crowning success of his remarkable life to have proved that the happiness of marriage is enhanced by the fullest individuality of both the parties in that relation."[95]

Julia well knew that her marriage had fallen short of bliss and that any autonomy she had enjoyed had been won in spite of Chev. If she had ever doubted it, she soon had opportunities to relive the bitterness and pain. Chev was generous to the children in his will, but left Julia so little that she and Maud would be forced to take up residence in a boarding house. Julia would not own a home in Boston again until her brother Sam bought her one in the 1880s. Julia also faced the dreadful chore of going through Chev's personal papers.

Michael Anagnos, Chev's assistant at the Institute and Julia Romana's husband, worked with her on this task. Michael refused to let her read the letters relating to Chev's philandering, but she read enough of his papers to suffer intense pain. Michael burned the letters in front of Julia, so that no one would ever have access to this dark side of the Chevalier's character.[96] Certainly neither Julia nor her children would ever tell that part of the story. Their readers would know the Chevalier only as an angel of light.

Julia found great sorrow in Chev's absence, and prayed that she might truly repent the errors of her marriage.[97] When her father, the first male authority figure in her life, had died, Julia had retreated to the social and theological conservatism he had favored. When Chev, the overwhelming alter ego of her life, died, she experienced a great deal of guilt, acknowledging that her own shortcomings had contributed to the problems of her marriage. She fretted that she had not willingly made sacrifices for him.[98] But Julia did not revert to the domestic roles that Chev had enjoined upon her. Rather, Chev's death liberated her to devote herself to a public life of social reform. In the years to come, her daughters would marvel at her achievements. Who would ever have thought, they asked each other, that their mother would manage to overshadow the Chevalier?

When she married Chev, Julia had dreamed of becoming an important literary figure. She longed not to be a man, but to exercise the privileges that men enjoyed. Through her relationship with Chev, Julia came to value political action and social reform as well as poetry. She fretted at the cultural and familial restrictions that denied her a public life and searched for a way to reconcile her ambitions with her understanding of true womanhood. In the Laurence manuscript, particularly in the romance of Eva and Rafael, Julia explored ways of expanding woman's nature and of being faithful to the inner voice that drove her out of the confinement of her life as wife and mother. In the 1860s and early 1870s, Julia found the theoretical underpinning she needed to enter the public sphere. She now believed that man was not superior to woman, but that together man and woman formed opposite poles of the divine creativity. As men and women dedicated themselves to the unfolding of human possibilities, they would also see the necessity of wedding action with reflection. "Desk-dreamers end by being mental cripples," Julia warned in "The Halfness of Nature." In the end, life should be "a perpetual marriage of real and ideal, of endeavour and result."[99]

Most importantly, Julia had learned to trust herself. She had feared once that her ambition was unwomanly; now she knew that civilization depended on women's best efforts at self-development. Her release from seclusion and from feelings of eccentricity was profound as well as visible to others. As T. W. Higginson, one of her colleagues in reform, later noted, Julia had never fully been at home in Boston, because she moved there "at a time when all New Yorkers were regarded with a slight distrust; she bore and reared five children . . . she went into company, and was criticised [sic] by cliques which she did not applaud. Whatever she did, she might be in many eyes the object of prejudice." Moreover, Higginson added, "there was, I suspect, a slight uncertainly in her own mind that was reflected in her early poems." Higginson was convinced that aligning herself with colleagues in the suffrage movement had enabled Julia to find her true calling at last. "From the moment when she came forward in the Woman Suffrage Movement, however, there was a visible change; it gave a new brightness to her face, a new cordiality in her manner, made her calmer, firmer; she found herself among new friends and could disregard old critics."[100]

For her part, as Julia celebrated her newfound sense of purpose and belonging, she was enjoying a critical turning point in her life. "In my own youth," she later explained, "women were isolated from each other by the very intensity of their personal consciousness. I thought of myself and of other women in this way. We thought that superior women ought to have been born men. A blessed change is that which we have witnessed."[101] A blessed change, indeed; Julia was ready to enjoy a freer life than she had ever before known.

Julia Ward Howe, during her honey-moon *The Yellow House Papers: the Laura E. Richards Collection, Gardiner Library Association and Maine Historical Society, Coll. 2085, Record Group 10*

Samuel G. Howe *The Yellow House Papers: the Laura E. Richards Collection, Gardiner Library Association and Maine Historical Society, Coll. 2085, Record Group 10*

The Howe children, 1869. Harry is at the top with Laura on the reader's far right. Maud is in the plaid dress at the bottom, and Julia Romana and Flossy are in the middle *The Yellow House Papers: the Laura E. Richards Collection, Gardiner Library Association and Maine Historical Society, Coll. 2085, Record Group 34*

Samuel G. Howe with granddaughter Alice Richards *The Yellow House Papers: the Laura E. Richards Collection, Gardiner Library Association and Maine Historical Society, Coll. 2085, Record Group 34*

Flossy *The Yellow House Papers: the Laura E. Richards Collection, Gardiner Library Association and Maine Historical Society, Coll. 2085, Record Group 18*

Maud and Laura, 1885 *The Yellow House Papers: the Laura E. Richards Collection, Gardiner Library Association and Maine Historical Society, Coll. 2085, Record Group 10*

Julia Ward Howe lecturing
*The Yellow House Papers: the
Laura E. Richards Collection,
Gardiner Library Association
and Maine Historical Society,
Coll. 2085, Record Group 34*

**Laura and family canoeing. From rear: Henry "Skipper" Richards
(husband), Laura, and children: Rosalind Richards, Alice Richards,
Henry Howe Richards, and Julia Ward Richards** *The Yellow House
Papers: the Laura E. Richards Collection, Gardiner Library Association and
Maine Historical Society, Coll. 2085, Record Group 10*

Julia Ward Howe and children. From left: Laura, Julia, Maud, and Harry *The Yellow House Papers: the Laura E. Richards Collection, Gardiner Library Association and Maine Historical Society, Coll. 2085, Record Group 10*

Julia Ward Howe with great-granddaughter, 1903. Grandmother Flossy and the father, her son Henry Marion Hall, are on the left. *The Yellow House Papers: the Laura E. Richards Collection, Gardiner Library Association, Coll. 2085, Record Group 2; photo by Bill Nunn*

Rosalind Richards (Laura's daughter and family archivist) *The Yellow House Papers: the Laura E. Richards Collection, Gardiner Library Association and Maine Historical Society, Coll. 2085, Record Group 10*

Julia Ward Howe, writing in old age. *The Yellow House Papers: the Laura E. Richards Collection, Gardiner Library Association and Maine Historical Society, Coll. 2085, Record Group 34*

The final triumph: Julia in her doctoral gown from Smith College, 1910

The Yellow House Papers: the Laura E. Richards Collection, Gardiner Library Association, Coll. 2085, Record Group 2; photo by Bill Nunn

Maud in 1916, in the midst of campaigning through 32 states on behalf of presidential candidate Charles Evans Hughes

The Yellow House Papers: the Laura E. Richards Collection, Gardiner Library Association and Maine Historical Society, Coll. 2085, Record Group 15

Maud in 1926, returning Byron's helmet to the people of Greece on behalf of the Howe family *The Yellow House Papers: the Laura E. Richards Collection, Gardiner Library Association, Coll. 2085, Record Group 2; photo by Bill Nunn*

Helen Keller and Laura at the Yellow House, 1939. Behind them is a bust of Samuel Gridley Howe by Laura's husband, Henry Richards *The Yellow House Papers: the Laura E. Richards Collection, Gardiner Library Association, Coll. 2085, Record Group 2; photo by Bill Nunn*

Chapter Five

While Chev's passing marked the end of an era, Julia had long since begun to prepare herself for a career less focused on home life. From the time she joined the woman suffrage movement in 1868, she had been traveling and doing public speaking on behalf of suffrage reform. In her zeal for the cause of peace, she had journeyed to London. Yet for family members left behind, home life did not collapse; for years, Julia had been turning over management of the household to her daughters. The results were initially mixed. Flossy had a reputation for stinginess in her role as family treasurer, and her imagination in culinary matters was notoriously limited. At one point, she resolutely served stewed prunes and toast for supper daily until the family begged for relief.[1] Maud proved, at least at first, to be of dubious use in practical matters. She lacked the intellectual seriousness of her siblings, and she was such an accomplished flirt that her brother Harry once remarked, "Maud can make a human male say almost anything."[2] After her father's death, Maud unknowingly spent good money on a broken-down horse, and then was so gullible about real estate practices that she actually paid a realtor to let her buy a house—not realizing, as she put it, that sellers, not buyers, compensated realtors. In time, however, Maud would come to rule the roost, earning the nickname of "Boss" from her mother.[3]

Even if she had not yearned to travel, Julia faced the necessity of earning money. Her funds from the Ward inheritance at this point were fairly meager, although she continued to receive a modest annual income. Between business losses incurred when her father's firm under brother Sam's guidance had to be liquidated, and Chev's knack for selling her Ward real estate holdings for next to nothing, the estimable fortune that had once promised a comfortable living was no longer intact. Plus, Chev had left his (and her) estate to the children, figuring that Julia would always find a way to get by. The pressure of earning a living gave Julia a justification for her public work. By traveling and speaking, she would make her own way.

Thus, for the first time in her life, without undue hindrance or scandal, Julia could devote herself to the career for which she had long hungered. She had satisfied the demands of domesticity, seeing her husband through to the end of his life and raising her children to responsible adulthood. Julia still owed Maud attention, but even her youngest daughter was no longer a teenager. By now, moreover, Julia had learned to argue persuasively that social reform and domestic duties went hand in hand. As she asserted in the *Woman's Journal* in 1875, suffrage workers were quintessential Victorian women, steadfast both in their love of home and in their desire for freedom. "Remember that five years are just ended, in which we have stood and knocked, asking that the door of human right might be opened widely enough to allow us to pass through, bearing our babes, not leaving them, assisting our husbands, nor forsaking them," she said.[4] And so it was.

Nevertheless, none of the rich dynamics of conflict, accommodation, and pride that had routinely driven Howe family life disappeared. In the years ahead, Chev would not be there to chide Julia for doing too much outside the home, but her daughters would take up the call. Their mother was aging, and they were anxious about her hectic schedule. Fiercely protective, they (and their own daughters) would creative a supportive home environment that allowed Julia to do her work at the same time that they would hector her to do less of it. In 1886, Julia would face the death of her oldest daughter, and that loss would resurrect all the old insecurities about ambition and self-centeredness. But on the whole, Julia would increasingly emerge as a singularly confident social reformer. She would critique American culture with poise and assurance and become a national institution, deluged with requests for speaking engagements. Even her dreams would be considered newsworthy.[5]

When Julia died in 1910, she had achieved not only autonomy and respectability, but celebrity as well. The ambitions that drove her to find her own voice while maintaining her place in genteel society did not die with her. Her children and grandchildren were fiercely protective of her and were determined that the public would know only the best about their family. Even before Julia's death, her daughters had begun to publish volumes designed to depict Howe home life as idyllic. With Julia's death, a mad scramble ensued to write a definitive biography—a task that produced enormous sibling hostility, as Flossy, Laura, Maud, and Harry debated just how such a project should be done. The publication of the biography did not end their efforts to present the best side of the Howes to the public. There were additional concerns, particularly the dilemma of overseeing authors outside the family who were interested in writing about the Howes and the difficulty of managing the immense collection of letters and diaries that had accumulated over the decades.

In their marriage, Chev and Julia had labored to reconcile two contradictory impulses: a desire for control and a desire for freedom. Chev assumed his right to freedom and strove to control Julia; and Julia struggled for autonomy from Chev. After their father's death, the children attempted to balance two other impulses with regard to their mother: celebration and control. While Julia was alive, the children (with the possible exception of Julia Romana) marveled at her abilities at the same time that they tried to control what they regarded as her excessive activities. After Julia died, her children—especially her surviving daughters—dedicated themselves to celebrating her (and their father's) remarkable lives. But for the Howes, celebration meant whitewashing; they could not tell the whole truth in all its pain and complexity. So they told the parts that seemed to them respectable and did their best to see that no one else told the rest.

RAMBLING ROSSA

Even before Chev's death and her wholehearted turn toward a reform career, Julia had been traveling. When Julia went to England on her peace crusade in 1872, Laura had taken steps to ensure that her mother would remember her. Filling out pages of Julia's diary in advance, she announced for May 22: "Darling Mammy's birthday. God bless her, and send her many happy returns, and bring her safe home to her Wolly." Julia replied in print: "Not my birthday, dearest daughter. I cannot mistake your's [sic], but you may mine." Laura instructed Julia for June 13: "Perhaps Laura has smallpox. Write to inquire." For June 17, she wrote: "Wolly's wedding day. Have picture taken to please her." For July 4, she inserted: "Wolly wants to know when coming home. Write & tell her."

Julia Romana found her mother's trips less amusing. She wrote Laura at one point: "Our troubadour Ma, accompanied by the Empress Maud, are said by the voice of history to be in Philadelphia."[6] On the occasion of a visit from her mother before Chev's death, Julia Romana wrote with obvious hostility, "She came, we saw her, & I do not know whether we were conquered or not. She emerged up the staircase about an hour after tea. Her right hand was encumbered with a huge bunch of old fashioned sweet peas. Her right grasped a ruset

[sic] bag. . . . A pile of books [was] waiting for her here, which we put upon her head. Thus only her tongue was left free, & she conversed with it glibly."[7]

Julia endured it all, an old hand at absorbing (and ignoring) criticism. "Does you know you doesn't got no mamma?" she teased Laura in an 1871 letter. "She has took up now with the Public entire, and meant to left [sic] you lone [sic]. I s'pse you've thought so, to be so many days . . . and hear nothing from the Maternal Magistrate, Preacher, Poet, and Pudding consumer."[8] Underneath the teasing was a more serious message. Julia would not be swayed from her public work. There were times when she wondered if she had been wise to forsake her literary career for reform work,[9] but nothing slowed her down for long. To her children's dismay, she spent the first Christmas after Chev's death in Chicago as part of a Western lecture tour.

Julia tried to make it up to Maud after that, taking her on an extended trip to Europe at a time in her life when Julia not only was strained financially at such an undertaking, but also taxed emotionally. She had no real interest in Europe at this point; her life belonged on the lecture circuit in the United States. Maud, universally acknowledged by her family members as flirtatious and pleasure seeking, lacked the studious nature that her other siblings had inherited. In later years, Maud conceded, "the trip was made entirely for my sake, and that she [Julia] was loath to leave the many interests of her Boston life. President of the New England Woman's Club and the Association for the Advancement of Women, she held important positions in half a dozen other organizations for public service. She made the great sacrifice for my sake, and I, like other young people, accepted the maternal devotion as a matter of course!"[10] Maud eventually married a British painter named Jack Elliott, but she continued to spend much of her time living in (and directing) her mother's homes in Boston and Newport.

Once Julia returned from her trip abroad with Maud in July 1879, her continuing labors on behalf of reform produced both despair and admiration in her children. By then, Laura was living in Gardiner, Maine, and she fretted that Julia visited only twice a year.[11] Laura complained to Julia's sister Annie in 1885 that "Mother is 'out West' somewhere, 'gallivanting,' as Maud says, which means lecturing and attending suffrage conventions." Whereas Maud had earlier visited Laura for five "precious weeks," Julia was more sparing of her time. "The little blessed Mother I had but for two short days: she loves not this country-side," Laura grumbled.[12]

Eventually, even the grandchildren would be enlisted in efforts to slow Julia down. Laura wrote to Julia's sister Annie in 1890 with the news that Julia was "frisking about in her own wonderful way." Laura's information came from her daughter Rosalind, who had been dispatched to Boston to help run Julia's household. Rosalind also reported, "[D]ear Grandmamma went to Philadelphia today, but is coming back tomorrow." In mock frenzy, Laura cried, "Why, of course! just stepping across the street to Philadelphia: what could be more simple?" After all, Laura concluded, "I had her dear Blessedness here a month ago, for merely a week, and every moment was a jewel to be counted and treasured."[13] No one had great luck in toning down Julia's activities, though Laura reported in 1893 that the family had managed to dissuade her from a third visit to the World's Fair in Chicago. "Mamma would have gone a third time," Laura confessed, "if she weren't afraid of Maud."[14]

In 1891, Flossy became concerned about Julia's gallivanting and persuaded Laura to try to put a stop to it. The resulting scene was not pretty, as Julia made her position exceedingly clear. Her "gadding about," she informed Laura, was not useless; rather, it represented an "extension of my sphere of interest and sympathy" and was the result of years of hard work. "The past year, which is so much deplored by some of you," Julia wrote, "has been to me unusually rich in instruction and in satisfaction, and I cannot say that I find any occasion to regret any of its' [sic] outings." It was sad, Julia complained, that she could not devote herself to her work without "censure and lamentation" from her family. But "the price of liberty, even at my age, should be 'eternal vigilance,'" she concluded, adding, "Now you won't like this letter, and yet . . . I must make a stand for freedom to do the work which, humanly speaking, I cannot hope to do very much longer. I have said my word, and so, let us kiss and be friends, and say no more about it."[15]

Laura never forgot Julia's ire. Five years later, as she was cataloguing her mother's letters, she reread the missive. It had not softened with time. "I came across one most terrible wigging this morning, administered when I had remonstrated about her hoppings and leppings [sic]," she wrote to Maud. "Flossy had set me on to it, and I had made a modest but earnest plea. Wow! I never did it again, and never will. . . . Her life must be as she wants it, dear naughty angel." Too timid to try another frontal assault, Laura contented herself with occasional admonitions and sympathetic letters to family members. Describing one visit to Julia's home in 1897, Laura confided to Julia's sister Louisa that Laura had "had occasional glimpses of her. The 'Old Bird' has kept her wings flapping very actively this winter. The world holds up its hands in amazement, we, her own, sigh and tremble; yet there is no denying that she thrives on it."[16] In 1906, regretting an earlier letter in which she described her "Blessed Angel mother as 'ruthless,'" Laura enjoined Maud, "of course I only meant in her insisting upon the life which brings us such distress of mind! But oh! let us be glad, thankful, to be distressed, so she but live her own way and is happy. Destroy that letter!"[17]

Sometimes, in moments of doubt, Julia's daughters would wonder if they were too protective. Julia's will was so strong that she "shan't be balked or coerced by me or anybody else!" Maud conceded to Flossy. "My chief regret . . . is the fear that I have often influenced her too much—but in most cases I can honestly say I have considered what I thought her good, before my own."[18] Julia knew the answer to that one—she had long since told Flossy that the "chronic struggle" with Maud was "a drawback both to my health and to my happiness." Julia had lectures to give and trains to catch—"you know how easy the journey to Iowa is," she wrote Flossy, a month before turning seventy-five. "When I think that some of my children, through mistaken kindness, would have deprived me of this great profit and pleasure, I realise [sic] a little that 'a man[']s foes are that of his own household.' You are not to take this as if unkindly said."[19]

There was no question that the attention could be smothering, particularly with Maud making sure that all was done properly. In 1893, Maud sent Flossy a staggering list of instructions to follow when Julia came to visit her. In the morning and evening, a special oil mixture was to be heated and applied to Julia's knees and legs. Milk and cold water were to be supplied with each meal, plus a hot drink (with milk) before bed. A can of hot water at her door in the morning was essential to Julia's comfort. For breakfast, oatmeal (with cream and milk), eggs or hash, and toast would do. Soup or beef tea should be served at noon, and then the midday meal should include more soup or beef tea, minced meat of some sort, or fish, or poultry. Vegetables and stewed or fresh fruit should be available in generous quantities. If Flossy's cook were unskilled, then mushes throughout the day would be good, as well as oyster stews and clam stews. Only the finest quality butter was acceptable, and Flossy would need an extra quart of milk per day during Julia's visit. The windows in Julia's room should be open during the evening, but closed thirty minutes before bedtime. She should take at least one walk—two, if possible—during the day. If it rained, Flossy should join her in calisthenics and ball playing. And of course, Flossy should see that Julia took a nap each afternoon at five. All of which would lead, Maud promised, to a visit with "a perfect beautiful sunbeam," a mother who was "happy & sweet and angelic."[20] If, of course, Flossy had time to notice.

As trying as it all undoubtedly was, this family attention enabled Julia to avoid the burdens of running a household. Maud conceded that her mother "did escape the 'chores' of life more than any one I know."[21] Laura's daughter Rosalind, who spent nine years as Julia's housemate, agreed completely. "Housekeeping matters," Rosalind said, "were not in her picture in the least. . . . Darling, heavenly-minded creature, she never knew or for a moment thought about how food came to the table, or how the house was cleaned. The resident daughter or granddaughter, and the two good helpers, would see to it." No one saw the priorities that motivated Julia more clearly than Rosalind did. "The most living part of her life, the most significant," Rosalind explained, "was, as she has so often said to me, spent in the four walls of her room."[22] The intense moments of Julia's "P.T." devoted to study and to writing ultimately provided her with her deepest sense of herself. Everything else flowed from those hours of reflection and creativity.

The loving attentions of her family enabled Julia to define herself by her studies and by the public explications of her thoughts. Nevertheless, sometimes Julia felt squelched. A 1908 diary entry ruefully noted, "I have opposed my children and their dear father . . . [but] Rosalind has a way which is difficult to withstand."[23] The constant scrutiny of one's daughters and granddaughters could be infantilizing, an issue that Laura was not inclined to appreciate. She wrote Maud in 1907 that her daughter Julia was doing a wonderful job at keeping her grandmother in line. Daughter Julia "and Mammy have become extremely chummy, and she even exercises a little very gentle control at times," Laura reported. "She is allowed to do the Royal Hair at night, to take off the Royal Boots, etc. etc. And when things are really too bad, and Grandmamma looks at her and says 'I think I ought to go!' (to some Devil's Rinktum), Julia has learned that a firm 'No, you ought not!' is what is really wanted, and gives relief."[24]

At other times, however, the family felt powerless. "My dear, we cannot force her to have a companion," Harry counseled Flossy, admitting that Julia "loathed the idea" that her well-meaning children thought would serve her well in the 1890s.[25] Nothing was more exasperating to the children than the prospect of the public's exploiting Julia. "I do verily believe people of this sort would persist in their efforts if they knew that Mammy would be in her coffin the next day," Laura complained to Maud. "They would say, 'Oh, if that is the case, we must have her last appearance!'"[26] If Julia had to give public talks, Laura thought, at least she should insist on a decent honorarium. "Better, I think, to let her do the easy things as long as she can, provided she is well paid," Laura reasoned. "I think she should refuse all ten dollar Club lectures, much more the free ones she is constantly giving."[27] But there was no stopping Julia.

"Each month she says 'Next month I must make no engagements;' we know the result," Laura ruefully acknowledged.[28]

Other plans did work. When Julia's brother Sam offered to buy her a house in 1881, Julia did not have to waste a minute in house hunting. Sam financed the closing, Maud picked and decorated the house, and Julia moved in, sight unseen. When Julia went to New Orleans in 1883–84 to run the women's department of the Cotton Centennial, Maud went along to make sure that Julia did not kill herself with overwork.[29] When a bad knee proved to be a persistent problem over the years, Laura and Maud conspired to install an elevator in Julia's Boston home while Julia was summering in Newport.[30] And when Julia was ill in 1906, Laura surreptitiously formed the Howdy Club. "The members never meet," she explained, "but come to see Mammy each once a month; she not to know, of course, that it has been arranged." Laura was nothing if not thorough. The Howdy Club women gathered on Mondays; she arranged for still other women friends to visit Julia on Fridays, and for Sundays she was planning a "Men's Auxiliary."[31]

In the end, Julia was always zealous about guarding her freedom, and her children were equally determined to protect her from harm. Everyone compromised more than they wished, but even Laura conceded that Julia thrived when engaging the public. "These streams of adulation are fountains of life to her, bringing renewed youth and strength," Laura noted on Julia's eighty-eighth birthday. "If so, then we ought to welcome them, instead of hunching our old backs and spitting, like that cat on the wall yonder."[32] Her family never managed to be quite that sanguine, but one thing was clear: family ministrations freed Julia from the demands of domesticity and enabled her to travel the country in pursuit of the public life she relished.

LIKE MOTHER, LIKE DAUGHTER?

In fact, Julia's wanderings constituted a challenge to her daughters in more ways than one. While Chev was alive, it was easy for them to be uninterested in woman suffrage. As the years passed, however, and their mother became a suffrage celebrity, they had to come to terms with her legacy. They had always known how to follow in the footsteps of their father; that meant pressing onward in the face of adversity. The Chevalier's children, above all, should be brave and dutiful. As Harry put it, "The great note in Papa's character . . . was 'your duty once clearly seen, do it utterly regardless of consequences.'"[33] Should they also be, like their mother, devoted to the unfashionable cause of equal rights for women?

In later years, commentators could not imagine there were ever any doubts. In 1895, Margaret Field of *Munsey's Magazine* would simply assume that Julia's daughters had "seen her preside over suffrage societies all their lives," and that naturally "as they grew older they added their share."[34] But it was not that easy or simple. Early on, Maud found Julia's commitment to suffrage bewildering. As she wrote Laura in 1884: "The naughty mother is away. . . . I received the first news in a telegram sent yesterday to tell us that from Buffalo she was going to push on to Louisville, Kentucky, to some meeting of that most cursed and infernal association for the suffrage of the creatures who rule the world. Strange infatuation!"[35] Eventually Maud did become involved in suffrage work and was a founding member of the Progressive Party, whose 1912 presidential candidate (Theodore Roosevelt) was committed to woman suffrage.[36] Maud had a style all her own, one that marked her as far more fashionable and flighty than her siblings. Perhaps her inimitable demeanor was best revealed in an incident during World War II, when she was working to raise funds for the Allied war effort. On a visit to Newport, Admiral Nimitz asked to meet Maud, who then invited him and his staff to her home. As historian Danny Smith describes it, no one but Maud could have created such an electric effect:

> At the appointed hour, cocktails were readied, Rosa the maid opened the door, and [Maud's niece] Laura Wiggins received the Nimitz entourage. Maud as usual was waiting to stage a grand entrance. The young subalterns rigidly lined up to either side of Nimitz, "scared blue" as Laura Wiggins characterized them. She did her best to make everyone feel at ease but to no avail. When Maud finally did come down "properly naked in a cocktail dress," she paused at the landing in the staircase, the butler brought a cocktail tray to her and then passed cocktails to the others. Maud lifted the glass and offered the toast: ". . . as they say in the Navy, 'down the hatch!'" Tension broke, and the Maud Howe Elliott hospitality prevailed. FDR decorated Maud for her efforts in raising twelve million dollars for the allied cause.[37]

Leave it to Maud to transform war work into a cocktail party.

Julia Romana and Laura faced different challenges as they sought to come to terms with their mother's suffrage work. Julia Romana was so fiercely shy that it was inconceivable she would involve herself in suffrage activities. Laura, too, disliked crowds of strangers, and she had no inclination to lobby for political reform. Yet this she would occasionally do to honor her mother's legacy. As late as 1915, five years after Julia's death, Laura reported forlornly that she was "going up, a very unhappy woman, to the suffrage hearing in Augusta, to show myself and say my little word." The prospect promised nothing but misery. "Very much scared I am; it is not my line at all," she confessed. "I do it to please mother."[38] Laura did enjoy writing on behalf of public causes she supported; her war poetry during World War I was unabashedly sentimental and patriotic. But, given the choice, she would never have spent her mature years involved in public speaking for social reforms or, even worse, giving elegant cocktail parties for admirals. Only her mother—and her sister Maud—regarded such occasions as tonics.

Ironically, the daughter who most consciously claimed Julia's mantle as social reformer was the child who had, in her youth, most vigorously opposed woman suffrage: Flossy. The burgeoning of the woman's club movement in the late nineteenth century became for her, she said, a sign that "women of America had outgrown the old, narrow, often selfish life of utter absorption in the affairs of the individual home." In the work of the clubs, Flossy claimed, "we were attending a school of citizenship and learning that order which is part of the divine law." Although Flossy conceded that Laura and Maud did their part on behalf of social reform, she could not help but point out that "to neither of them have club work and club association been the real joy that they were to our mother and me."[39] Committed wholeheartedly to woman suffrage—and usually strapped for cash as well—Flossy was only too glad to lecture on behalf of a cause she deemed particularly her own.

There was a sense of rivalry among the siblings—a rivalry that the Howes went to considerable pains to conceal from the public. Just as the author daughters strove to present respectable portraits of their parents to the public, so they worked to give the impression of family harmony among themselves. In reality, of course, there were tensions, as in any family. Julia Romana and Flossy were closer to each other than to the others, Maud and Julia Romana had a series of spectacular spats,[40] and Harry always sided with Laura during family disputes. Laura was closest to their mother, and Chev had felt special ties to Julia Romana. In a family in which literary and intellectual accomplishments were assumed,[41] only Julia Romana followed her mother's interest in philosophy. Laura was the most successful author of all, eventually writing over eighty books. Her output included nonsense verse, children's stories, and serious biographies of both her parents. Maud wrote light novels, family memoirs, and newspaper articles dedicated to travel or the social scene. Flossy wrote books about the family and, when no one else took up the publisher's invitation, established herself as an authority in books of manners. Harry (now known in the family as Big Man Howe) stuck to science, becoming a leading expert in the properties of steel and serving as a professor at Columbia. He wrote technical works on metallurgy but never strayed emotionally from his family roots. He named his New York home "Green Peace," and, like his father, loved to work outdoors. Maud noted that Harry found "delight in every leaf & flower" on his property.[42]

Behind all this success, however, were darker currents. Everyone knew Maud was caught up in society; everyone also knew that Julia Romana was unable to function in it. Her public awkwardness was the stuff of family legend; what no one could figure out was how she could possibly have grown up with a mother renowned for her social brilliance. Everyone also knew that Flossy was poor and that her husband David Hall made little money. For years, Flossy managed to get her family to the seashore only by serving as Julia's housekeeper for Newport summers, and in 1898 her son Harry, unable to find a better summer position, worked as Julia's Newport "handy man."[43] Maud—of all people—became so incensed at nephew Harry's lack of initiative (or at Flossy's inability to rise out of genteel poverty) that she lashed out when Flossy asked for a loan so that Harry might enjoy the "usual perquisites" of his senior year at Harvard. "A loan for luxuries! How can you be so blind to your son's highest needs?" Maud stormed. Indeed, she declared, "It would be far more worth while to him, to have the lesson, that luxuries, pleasures, success of any sort in this life are to be his only through his own efforts. It is a lesson your three sons are all in need of. Manliness! Manliness! Manliness! Nature has dowered the three sons so handsomely with mind and talents, do you help them to the third good—character!"[44]

There were other issues as well. Everyone worried about Julia Romana and Flossy's mental health—both were naturally given to nervousness, plus Julia Romana had odd notions about diet and vegetarianism. Then there was the problem of infertility. Harry and his wife Fanny were never able to have children. Maud and her husband Jack Elliott also failed to conceive, and Maud was—at least in Laura's mind—jealous of Laura's six children (whom Laura characteristically dubbed the "Noble Six").[45] Problems also arose about where to live, and how properly to maintain family ties. Maud periodically argued with her husband Jack over her desire to live with her mother and run Julia's home. Maud usually won, but when Jack prevailed, he and Maud were off to Europe for years at a time, leaving Julia's household to the care of various granddaughters.[46] Laura lived in what all the others regarded as the middle of nowhere ("you think of this as a dreary little hole," she accurately observed to Maud), wrapped up in her husband, her children, and her writing.[47] There was no question in her marriage that patriarchy ruled; the family name for her husband was the "Skipper," and Laura freely confessed that she paralleled his rule with that of her father's.

Behind all these tensions lay the unresolved currents of their parents' marriage, continually replayed in the children's desire to convince their mother to conform to a more reasonable schedule. Guilt, power, love, resentment—all the old currents continued to flow. They would emerge with special fierceness at moments of stress, as the children strove both to deny and to resolve the strain of being part of an accomplished, but not perfectly harmonious, family.

A DEATH IN THE FAMILY

Nowhere did these currents show more clearly than in 1886, with the serious illness of Julia Romana. Her mother was lecturing when she received word on February 25 that her oldest daughter was sick. Julia returned to Boston on February 27 to find Julia Romana "seriously, but not dangerously, ill."[48] The next day, Julia Romana asked her mother if she remembered a dream she had had "when Flossy & I were little children, & you were in Europe? You dreamed that you saw us in a boat, such that the tide was carrying us away from you. Now the dream has come true, and the tide is bearing me away from you." Julia did remember; she had had the dream while on the European trip in 1850–51, when she and Chev had separated.[49] That Julia Romana should mention the dream now saddened her, and she resolved to herself that "death was not to be thought of."[50] The doctor diagnosed rheumatic fever that had advanced into typhoid fever.

By March 1, Julia was writing to tell Maud that Julia Romana was more at ease and that the doctor "says that my coming has saved her life. This of course is not true," she reflected, "but it shows how much comfort my presence has given her. This week will probably decide the turn of the disease."[51] March 3 found Julia at a conference in Poughkeepsie. She returned on the morning of March 4 to find her daughter comfortable. Julia then went to Providence to speak at the Rhode Island Woman Suffrage Association and returned in the evening to her daughter's sickbed.[52] She spent the entire day with Julia Romana on March 5 and wrote Maud, "I have only good news for you from Julia. She has turned the corner, and is looking toward recovery. The fever has left her, and there seems to be no mysterious danger lurking about her, anywhere . . . the rest of her advance to health is, humanly speaking, only a matter of time . . . Now darling understand that there is nothing dangerous in Julia's condition, and that I can be away for two or three days without any risk or inconvenience to her." Leaving Julia Romana in the care of two nurses, Julia departed on March 6 to attend the board meeting of the New England Woman's Club. Afterwards, she went to New York to meet Maud, reasoning that she would return to Boston later in Julia Romana's recovery, when the private nurses had been discharged and her help would be more valuable.[53]

On March 9, Julia sent a telegram asking about her daughter's health, only to receive word that Julia Romana had taken a turn for the worse. After a night of misery and anxiety, Julia caught a morning train and returned to Boston on March 10. She brought with her a bottle of champagne, hoping it might cheer Julia Romana. To Julia's relief, she found her daughter glad to see her. But Julia Romana was not well. Julia's diary recorded the details: with her husband Michael on one side of her and her mother on the other, each holding one of her hands, Julia Romana mused, "[I]f one has one's parents and one's husband, what more can one want?" When Michael stepped out of the room, Julia Romana asked her mother: "What does the Lord want to kill me for?" Julia remonstrated that she would get well, but Julia Romana knew she was dying. When Michael returned to the room, she urged the two of them to stand by one another. Her last words, her mother recorded, were: "If this is not the right one, call another priestess-truth, truth." Finally, her breathing stopped, film covered her eyes, and Julia Romana was gone. Her husband fell to the floor in agony.[54]

The family would revisit and revise the story of Julia Romana's death in the decades to come. Julia assumed that her daughter's last words referred to the Metaphysical Club Julia Romana had founded in the winter of 1883–84.[55] Years later in her *Reminiscences,* Julia improved upon the death scene by insisting that in her parting words Julia Romana had instructed her husband to "Be kind to the little blind children, for they are papa's children." Those words were later inscribed on the wall at the Jamaica Plain Kindergarten for the Blind.[56] In her autobiography, Flossy pronounced her sister's last words to be "Take care of the little blind children."[57] Laura agreed, noting in her biography of Laura Bridgman that Julia Romana's "last words on earth, 'Take care of the little blind children!' are graven on the walls of the kindergarten which is the enduring monument of her and her husband."[58] The family seems to have actively mythologized (and amended) Julia Romana's final moments.

In their biography of their mother, Julia's daughters addressed another issue that made them uneasy: Had their mother reacted with lightning speed to the news of her daughter's illness? The biography answered yes, explaining that Julia had been working out of New York that winter. Upon hearing of Julia Romana's illness, her daughters wrote, she "went at once to South Boston." Julia's diary, however, told a different story. Her entry for February 25 reported that upon hearing of her daughter's illness she resolved to leave for Boston the next day, not immediately. The diary further noted that she did not do so; on February 26, she went to a meeting at the home of Mrs. M. A. Stone and gave an address. Julia did not arrive in Boston until early on the morning of February 27.[59] Julia's April 12 letter to Louisa confirmed that she had not gone immediately to Julia Romana. She observed that Maud had probably already written Louisa how it all happened: "How I, very anxious about her, was detained in New York, whither we had gone, last winter, in order to be with Flossy and to take her out with us in N.Y. where she has always remained a stranger." When she did arrive in Boston, Julia reported, Julia Romana's "typhoid symptoms were not severe."[60]

In the end, the question of how quickly Julia went to Julia Romana was no more than a matter of appearances. But the Howes felt the need to improve on the actual chronology, perhaps in part because none of them had found Julia Romana the easiest person in the world to love. In their guilt and grief, they castigated themselves for not appreciating her more. Laura wrote to Aunt Annie: "You always understood dear Julia; that means so much now. Everybody has kindest words of praise and sympathy, but not many people really knew her, I think."[61] Brother Harry, disturbed that his mother had stayed on at the Institute after the funeral, became convinced that she was hysterical with sorrow and urged Laura to help him find a way to convince Michael to take a trip. "Mama's health as well as Michael's will suffer heavily if this mourning keeps on," he worried. "She feels that she must not leave Michael, and so we must induce Michael to go away himself."[62] Three days later, he repeated his concern: "Mama must leave the Institution. They must be bombarded till she is driven out. . . . She is too old a woman to stand the trying ordeal she has to go through every day." As Harry reflected on Julia Romana, he realized that he, like the others, had never appreciated her enough. "We never know our blessings till we lose them," he mused, adding, "I have reproached myself much and bitterly for my impatience to that sweet lovely soul, whose very blemishes, superficial as they were, arose from a rare and precious simplicity and unworldliness."[63]

And what of the grieving mother? She had mixed feelings. "Like you, darling, we too must feel that we often did sweet Julia injustice," she wrote Laura on March 14, adding that it had been infirmities of body that had clouded Julia Romana's temperament. Still, Julia professed relief at having appreciated Julia Romana when others had failed. "I thank God," Julia continued, "that I always greatly valued her, and that, however unfashionable she might at times appear, I always thought of her beauty and her talent, or rather genius, and felt that neglect she experienced from the world was its loss, not hers." Indeed, Julia confided, "Maud neglected her and now feels it deeply."[64] To her children, Julia was at peace. But to her sister Louisa, she castigated herself. "Why did I not know that I might lose my sweet Julia some day?" she asked. "Why did I leave her for months and years at a time, when there was to be only so much of her lovely life for me to enjoy!"[65]

Julia's diary also revealed profound misgivings. On March 24, 1886, she wrote, "My heart agonises [sic] again with the question 'could dear Julia have been saved?' oh! the dreadful pain of uncertainty about this. I can bear every thing else. God help me from thinking that all was not done that might have been done."[66] Six days later, on March 30, she confessed that she could still find no comfort in her daughter's death. "If God says any thing to me now," Julia sighed, "he says: 'thou fool!' The truth is that you have no notion of the value & beauty of God's gifts until they are taken from us." The next day, still uneasy, she wrote, "I seem to myself only dull, hard, and confused under this affliction. I pray God to give me comfort by raising me up, that I may be nearer to the higher life into which she and her dear father have passed."[67]

The specter of both Chev and Julia Romana accusing her from the spiritual realm was hard to shake. In early April, Julia spent a week with Maud in New York. After her return to Boston, she determined to sleep in Julia Romana's room. "This was hard for me & was at first formidable & full of a ghostly tremor," she acknowledged. "Then, I seemed to rise to a spiritual communion with my dear ones, Julia and her father, and so, I lay down & slept in quietness." On April 27, Julia announced that she had received an "uplifting of the soul." At last, she contended, she was "getting to stand where I can have some spiritual outlook—the confusion of 'is not' is giving place to the steadfastness of 'is.'" Finally, on May 9, Julia attended church, where the congregation sang "Nearer My God to Thee," a hymn that had also been used at Julia Romana's funeral. It was a good experience, Julia said: "the 'nearer' really appeared to me something definite, & not a mere vague desire. The singing of the hymn brought back the picture of dear Julia's funeral, the white form in the white coffin; the whiter soul departed. But the remembrance was tender, not terrible."[68]

Perhaps. In their biography of Julia, her daughters would write that her dreams "often brought back the gracious figure [of Julia Romana]; these visions are accurately described, each detail dwelt on with loving care."[69] Julia's diary, however, revealed more anguish than grace. In June 1886, Julia dreamed that Julia Romana was speaking to her through the clock in her back parlor. "Dearest Dudie, why can I not feel that you are near me?" Julia asked. Her daughter's answer was accusatory: "Because you do not care about it." Julia responded: "Oh yes, I do care about it very much." The next night, Julia recorded another encounter with her daughter: "Dreamed I had my sweet Julia in my arms, looking like herself, in a black silk dress. I said to her: 'dear Dudie, I do miss you so much.' That was all."[70] Julia Romana returned again in the night before the year was out. This time, she was bright and joyous. "I held her in my arms & found that she was really in the body," Julia explained. "I said: 'oh darling! Why don't you come oftener?'" Julia Romana then talked of some mixture that Julia did not recognize. She could remember no more of the dream. Still, she said, she had had "a good moment" in her morning prayers. "It really seemed like communion."[71]

Was it traveling while her daughter was on her deathbed that haunted Julia? Was it guilt over her lifelong ambivalence toward Julia Romana? Probably it was a combination of the two. Certainly, she was determined not to go down that particular road again. Flossy reported in her autobiography that she came down with rheumatic fever some months after Julia Romana's death. Her mother was frantic. "In the midst of her distress," Flossy explained, "my mother had a strange feeling that she could save my life by an effort of will. She did not content herself with praying only, but strongly opposed the administration of narcotics which the nurse in attendance was only too ready to give in order that she herself might sleep. My mother determined that I should no longer be dosed with these. She sat at my bedside one night till the small hours of the morning, when I dropped off into a natural sleep. To her vigilance I probably owe my life."[72]

Unfortunately, Flossy's return to health did not resolve Julia's anxieties about Julia Romana's death. In the midst of Flossy's illness, Julia had found herself arguing with God, "I gave up Julia, I can't give up Flossy—she has children."[73] Clearly Julia realized that her feelings toward Julia Romana had been mixed, and she feared—terribly—that she might have done too little in her daughter's final days. Julia also fretted that she had not esteemed Julia Romana highly enough during her life. Her daughter had been exceedingly bright; like her mother, she had written poetry and drama at a tender age. She had also followed her mother's love of philosophy and was active in the Concord School of Philosophy. She shared, as well, Julia's indifference to housework.[74] But in many ways Julia Romana was far closer to her father than to her mother. Like Chev, she was stubborn and quick-tempered. Julia noted in 1846, when Julia Romana was very young, "that violence and whipping do her no good, and that perfect sweetness and gentleness are the only thing with her. The very phrase: 'naughty girl,' if uttered harshly, will often throw her into spasms of rage."[75] Two decades later, things were much the same. Julia remarked in her diary in

1867 that Julia Romana had "disturbed me much, this year, by her uncontrollable & passionate self-will."[76]

No one in the family doubted Julia Romana's temper—she had been known to throw dinner out the window when it displeased her—and brother Harry, for one, was convinced that "her headstrongness and unwillingness to listen to others really killed her."[77] In addition to being stubborn, Julia Romana was also phenomenally timid in public settings. Though even Chev encouraged her to get out more, her bashfulness in social situations was unyielding.[78] Years later, when faced with the awkwardness of her daughter Alice, Laura recalled Julia Romana: "Do we not remember dear beautiful Julia, and the anguish that she and Mamma went through, trying to introduce her into a society that she was never meant for?"[79] Julia Romana's shyness was so pronounced that, at a memorial meeting held after her death by her Metaphysical Club, John S. Dwight remembered her as "slender, drooping her head like a modest violet, shrinking from much converse with others." One of his triumphs in life, Dwight concluded, was that Julia Romana "would talk freely with me, while, like a sensitive plant, she shrank from most others."[80]

Timorous though she was, Julia was the child whose work most closely coincided with her father's. If she shared her mother's dedication to philosophy and the life of the mind, she also managed a kind of selflessness toward Chev that Julia never adopted. As early as 1856, he was praising Julia Romana for having "all her mother's intensity" but none of her need to "shine & be pleased herself." Instead, he contended, Julia Romana strove "to make others happy."[81] In a similar vein, Chev explained to Julia's sister Louisa in 1866 that his wife was in the flower of her maturity and "more taken up in her literary reputation & its influence than she is aware of." Julia Romana, on the other hand, he described as a "great comfort," who had "been very useful to me."[82]

Everyone in the family knew that the two of them were closest. As Flossy said, "The bond of affection between her and my father was especially strong. 'Darlingest, Firstest, and Best Born' he calls her in one of his letters. It was a pleasure to see them start together for the daily trip to the Institution."[83] Maud agreed: "Our eldest, Julia Romana, was the child most intimately connected with my father's life. She shared his labors for the blind, gave her heart and hand to a Greek, and is remembered as a sort of patron saint of the Perkins Institution, where her husband, Michael Anagnos, succeeded my father as director."[84] Julia concurred, noting in her autobiography that Julia Romana was Chev's "constant companion and faithful ally." Chev had long ago forbidden his wife to teach at the Institute; to his daughter, he opened the door. Clearly, she was his legacy.[85]

She also faced difficulties about which no one wanted to speak—and which her sisters did their best to hush up. Julia Romana's "nervousness" expressed itself in periodic bouts of depression so deep that her family feared for her sanity. Harry was certain that Julia Romana was afflicted by insanity and that that condition, combined with her stubbornness and strange dietary preferences, led to her early death.[86] After Chev's death in January 1876, the family was petrified that Julia Romana would suffer a breakdown. Their fears were well founded. As late as June 1876, her mother recorded incidents in which Julia Romana became upset and "poured out poem after poem" for her to write. A few days later, her mother reported that Julia Romana was so "excitable" that Julia felt compelled to call in a doctor. The next morning at five o'clock, Julia Romana came to her mother's room and sat on the bed, her right hand jerking uncontrollably. This time the doctor diagnosed hysteria.[87] Julia Romana informed her Uncle Sam in July that she had recovered, but undoubtedly such episodes were unsettling, even terrifying, for the family.[88] When Flossy and Maud wrote their biography of Laura Bridgman, they described Julia Romana's sorrow at her father's death in vague yet heroic terms, recalling, the "great hopeless blank seemed too much at first for his daughter Julia, his first-born, the star child, the nearest to his great heart of all his children. She, like Laura [Bridgman], pined and for months stood at the gate of the valley of the shadow of death. Then she took courage, she put her hand to his work, which for ten years she was spared to carry on, at the side of her husband, who had been a son in love and loyalty to her adored father."[89]

The closest the public ever came to candid disclosures about Julia Romana's mental health was at the memorial meeting held after her death by her Metaphysical Club. At that time, speakers dropped hints about the afflictions Julia Romana had endured, although even then the speakers implied that her problems belonged to the distant past. Ednah D. Cheney delicately observed that Julia Romana's life "had not been without its pain and suffering," and confessed, "in her early years it did not seem to us that her heart was so formed for joy." Fortunately, Cheney contended, Julia Roman's life had taken a turn for the better, because "with the development of her life-work all her nature seemed to light up with radiant happiness." The Rev. Edward F. Hayward hinted at "the difficulty, under which she labored for a great many years, of not finding voice for her faculties," but asserted that she "had worked herself clear of all those chaotic feelings, and had emerged into a self-possession which was giving the true expression of her thought and life."[90]

In their public descriptions of Julia Romana, her family focused on portraying her as eager, open, innocent, and selfless. "The exaltation of her mother's spirit deeply influenced the mind and character of sister Julia," Flossy claimed. "She was so unworldly she did not know what worldliness was."[91] Laura averred that Julia Romana "had a look as if when she came away from heaven she had been allowed to remember it . . . she walked in a dream always, of beauty and poetry, thinking of strange things. Very shy she was, very sensitive."[92] Her mother wrote in the *Woman's Journal* that Julia Romana had been a "presence wonderfully radiant," with a childlike soul. "We will think of her," Julia intoned, "with the lyre still in her hand, with the song still in her heart, with starry glory of innocence in her eyes. . . . We may sum it up in these words: Worship of the beautiful, charity for all mankind, faithful love for one's own, but after and above all, truth! truth!" In her *Reminiscences,* Julia concluded simply, "beautiful in life, and most beautiful in death, her sainted memory has a glory beyond that of worldly fame."[93]

In real life, however, they had hardly known what to do with her. Of all the Howe children, Julia Romana had the most highly developed sense of irony, and she knew how to skewer people. Sometimes her dry humor brought her down from the clouds, making her more accessible to her family. Laura described her sister as "dreamy and absent, absorbed in severe study and composition, yet always ready with the brilliant flashes of her wit, which broke like sunbeams through the mist of dreams."[94] On other occasions, family members simply could not follow Julia Romana's banter. She complained in one letter to Flossy: "Your talent for misunderstanding has almost as delicate an edge as if it were satire. Don't you see, that that first letter of mine was meant as a gooch?"[95]

In her published poems and prose, Julia Romana found rich opportunities for employing her gift for satire. Her mother always described Julia Romana's participation in the summer school of philosophy at Concord as nothing short of blissful. "I cannot think of the sittings at the school without a vision of the rapt expression of her face as she sat and listened to the various speakers," Julia remarked in her *Reminiscences,* adding, "something of this pleasure" found expression in Julia Romana's *Philosophiae Quaestor.*[96] Even a casual examination of that work, however, indicates that no matter how fascinated Julia Romana may have been by the Concord School of Philosophy, she also found it hilarious. Transcendentalist culture was never better satirized than in her account of this "Mammoth Cave of thought" in which, during the "Emerson Season," the greats and the lesser lights gathered to consider the eternal verities. There, she wrote, the "most perfect courtesy, and a beautiful, sincere ignoring

of inequality, prevailed. . . . The Alpine summits kindly conversed with the little hills." No one who dismissed Thoreau's death as the result of bad weather at
Walden ("an attempt which, though most interesting and poetic in itself, was
yet and must ever prove, a suicidal one in our unfriendly climate") or who
described the author of a paper on Homer as a "sculptor-monk adoring in a
chapel-shrine the saintly statue of his own creation" could have taken the Concord School too seriously.[97]

Then there were her poems. All who knew Julia Romana agreed that
poetry was in her blood. The inimitable John Dwight put it most dramatically:
"Poetry seemed to her to be a natural element; she breathed it and lived in it;
she took it with the most childlike trust; it seemed as if she thought the whole
atmosphere was full of poetry and beauty. . . . She seemed to gather roses all the
time from invisible bushes, where we saw only brick walls, and weave them into
wreaths and throw them about broadcast for every one to pick up and enjoy."[98]
In 1883, Julia Romana published a book of verse entitled *Stray Chords*. Contemporaries invariably pointed to "Paean" as a description of her father. There,
Julia Romana implored her reader to

Weep not for him! He is gone to his glory
Weep for the many, who live to their shame!
Write his name high 'mid the World's sacred story:
"Here was a life that was spotless from blame!"[99]

What readers failed to note, however, was the similarity between another selec-
tion, "The Bard to the Rose-Tree," and a poem that her mother had written
long ago in *Passion-Flowers*: "Mind Versus Mill-Stream." The latter poem had
caused Samuel Gridley Howe exquisite pain with its story of a Miller who
made a fool of himself trying to tame a millstream. "Mind Versus Mill-Stream"
had ended (at least in its original version) with a section entitled "Moral" that
advised men who would marry happily to choose a placid wife, warning that
those who "woo the tempest" will find "their peace is lost!" Julia Romana's
"Bard to the Rose-Tree"[100] adopted a similar structure: it began with a narrative
of conflict followed by a concluding section entitled "Moral." The two characters in Julia Romana's poem were a male narrator and a female Rose-tree.

The poem began with the male narrator lauding the beauty of the Rose-
tree:

༄

Mine of sweetness, budding out,
Goddess hedged with pain about;
Beauty ruddy both and fair
Wedding York and Lancaster

༄

but warning, also, of the hidden barbs:

༄

Woe! for she has pricked my hand,—
Cruellest Rose-tree in the land!
By the pain I'm all unmanned,
Losing pleasures I had planned.
Knows the man whom Beauty scorns
That the Rose-tree's full of thorns?

༄

Unlike the Miller in "Mind Versus Mill-Stream," however, the male narrator in Julia Romana's "The Bard to the Rose-Tree" managed to subdue his female adversary. The Bard responded to the Rose-tree's thorns with a threat:

༄

But I know a sickle sharp
In the tones of Blondel's harp,
Rose-tree, thou may'st shake and carp,
Minstrel's strings did never warp.
Dreams the desert she adorns
That I'll cut the Rose-tree's thorns?

Sing that there will come a day
When the Rose-tree'll fade away,—
When her haughty yea or nay
Without victims she may say,
Let her choose while she adorns,—
Transient Rose-tree, full of thorns!

༄

At this rebuke, the Rose-tree wept and blushed red with "sudden shame" at her "well-earned blame," prompting the narrator to proclaim, "Mine's the Rose-tree full of thorns!" The concluding "Moral" then followed:

⤆⤇

> And for thee, thou damask dame,
> Scorning Minstrel's earnest flame,
> Catch the singer while he's tame:
> Bird two seasons never came.
> Scornful Beauty often mourns;
> Minstrel's love not ladies' thorns.

⤆⤇

Whatever else this poem may have been saying, it was surely Julia Romana's answer to the humiliation her father suffered with the publication of *Passion-Flowers*. The images were clear: the wedding of "York and Lancaster" suggested that most famous of civil wars, England's War of the Roses. As an image of her parents' marriage, the War of the Roses worked admirably. The Rose-tree with its beauty and its thorns represented Julia Romana's mother, who "unmanned" and wounded her father. "Rose" was also a play on her mother's red hair—Julia was, as she celebrated with James Binney Wallace in Rome—a "rossa." In "Mind Versus Mill-Stream," Julia had described the millstream as "coiffed with long wreaths of crimson weed" so that no one would miss the connection she was drawing between herself and the stream; in Julia Romana's poem, the link between the Rose-tree and her mother was equally manifest. In "The Bard to the Rose-Tree," however, the male narrator had the capacity to do what the Miller (or Julia Romana's father) never quite managed: tame (or trim) the Rose-tree to his will. "Mind Versus Mill-Stream" ended with the millstream sweeping away "to utterness of waste" both the Miller and his dam.[101] "The Bard to the Rose-Tree" ended with the Rose-tree repentant and seemed, in its moral, to offer a threat that Julia Romana's mother would have appreciated: the scornful woman of beauty mourning the loss of the Minstrel's love.

Lines like these could not have failed to demonstrate Julia's estrangement from her daughter. That she was attending one of her beloved meetings instead of sitting at Julia Romana's side when the fever turned fatal was agonizing. Would a more loving mother have worked harder to reconnect with her daughter? Would a more accomplished mother have helped her daughter overcome her shyness? Might a less self-absorbed mother have known better how to share her own brilliance with her children? Julia's surviving daughters would hardly have been human if they had not pondered such questions. Yet, as ever, they were hesitant to criticize; their mother was a great woman—a giant—and she was the rock of the happy Howe home. As Maud would counsel Flossy in 1893, when Flossy was out of sorts with her mother: "I want you to look at her in a new light. Don't worry as to whether she is a good mother to you, as you did last Spring . . . and the year before . . . that's her look out not yours—ours is to worry about being good daughters to her. If we can fill that bill, it's all thats' [sic] necessary."[102] In the end, Julia's surviving daughters could not follow their oldest sister; they would remember that their mother gave them the happy home, not the War of the Roses.

With an Edenic Green Peace in their past and a revered saint as their mother, Flossy, Laura, and Maud were hard put even to criticize Julia gently. In their biography, they simply argued that she was essential to their lives, as well as wise enough to relate to each of them in a particularly fitting way. Julia Romana, they claimed, was the most gifted of Julia's children, and in matters of philosophy, their mother's "special intimate"; in suffrage and club work, it was Flossy; in music, Julia turned to Harry; with Laura, she discussed books; and Maud "was the 'Prime Minister' in social and household matters." Thus, they contended, "till the very last, we gray-haired children leaned on her, clung to her, as in the days when we were children indeed."[103]

In private musings after her mother's death, however, Maud wondered. Had their mother's self-absorption prevented her from helping them over-come their own problems and shortcomings? In typical Howe fashion, Maud resolved the issue by crediting Julia with genius in leaving her children to the faults and errors that marred them. As she wrote after Julia's death in 1910, her mother

> didn't know how to cultivate graces in us—strange, but she couldn't—
> and yet what grace there was that was native, and had to be, delighted her
> beyond measure! We were her puppies—she didn't a bit know what to do
> with us—never could understand how Flossy could be prosaic, how I could
> be idle and frivolous, bad-tempered and passionate—or Julia awkward and
> shy—these things completely baffled her! A merely clever mother would
> have known how to combat the faults and develop the qualities but she just
> couldn't! She had to mind her own business, and her business was to grow
> as much into the image of God as is possible for a person to grow![104]

In short, self-absorption was the price of genius; the children had been obliged to do the best they could with their handicaps.

Another issue that emerged repeatedly in sibling discussions was the question of money. None of the children was well off, and—ironically—all three of the surviving daughters turned to writing or lecturing to help support their families. At times, their privations seemed unfair. As Maud said to Laura, "I used to feel rather grudgingly that we children of the most remarkably gifted pair of Americans of their time should know poverty, that one of us should know the real suffering of it, Flossy, when it seemed that with a little thought for the morrow on their parts it might not have been so."[105] There was no getting around the fact that Julia Ward had been financially secure when she married Chev and on the brink of financial ruin by the time she buried him. None of the Howes liked their relative poverty. Characteristically, however, Maud could find a bright side even to being poor. "Now I see," she explained, "that no inheritance that they could have left us is to be thought of in comparison to the poverty of which we have a right to be proud. They certainly both did neglect, according to the common view of the world, their children, but it was that they might serve the larger family of God's children. I wish Flossy could see that."[106]

Leave it to the Chevalier's children to turn his miserable financial skills into a character-building virtue. Julia's misgivings about her relationship to her children did not extend to financial problems; she was as generous with the little money she had as she possibly could be. Julia was haunted instead by the guilty fear that she may have loved her work too much and her children too little. Julia Romana would not disappear from her mother's dream life, but her visitations would become less frequent over the years. Julia knew she had unresolved feelings about her oldest daughter, as indeed she did about her husband. But the shock of Julia Romana's untimely death would not deter her mother from the remarkable career she was creating with such verve. By 1886, Julia was well on her way to becoming America's grand woman.

THE IDEAL WIFE AND MOTHER

Julia's professional activities after Chev's death were so varied and numerous that they are impossible to list—the number of meetings that she attended on behalf of suffrage alone would run for pages. Open meetings, board meetings, annual conventions—the list was voluminous. Highlights of Julia's work in clubs and associations included founding and serving for years (1876–97) as president of the Association of American Women, a group devoted to improving the educational and professional opportunities available to women. She was president of the New England Woman's Club until her death in 1910. She was, with Lucy Stone, the guiding force of the American Woman

Suffrage Association until its union with the National Woman Suffrage Association.[107] She was president of the Massachusetts Woman Suffrage Association from 1870 to 1878 and from 1891 to 1893. From 1868 to 1877, and then again from 1893 to 1910, she headed the New England Woman Suffrage Association. She helped found the General Federation of Women's Clubs in 1893 and served as its director from 1893 to 1898. She headed the Massachusetts Federation of Women's Clubs, begun in 1893, and founded the Century Club of San Francisco in 1888 as well as the Wisconsin Woman's Club in 1876. With T. W. Higginson, she also founded the Town and Country Club of Newport, Rhode Island.[108]

In addition to these labors, Julia helped to found the *Woman's Journal* in 1870 and served as an editor and a writer for the next twenty years. She continued to publish books as well. Her biography of Margaret Fuller was issued in 1883. Books of essays analyzing American society appeared in 1881 *(Modern Society)* and in 1895 *(Is Polite Society Polite?)*. She published her autobiography in 1899, and two additional volumes of poetry: *From Sunset Ridge: Poems Old and New* in 1898, and *At Sunset,* issued posthumously in 1910. While her volumes of poetry never sold particularly well after *Passion-Flowers,* Julia's reputation as a poet endured. She was frequently asked to write and deliver poems for ceremonial occasions, so her fears that the poem she delivered at the Bryan festival in 1866 would be the highlight of her career proved unfounded.

Julia was devoted to other causes in addition to woman suffrage. She became increasingly interested in Christian spirituality after Chev's death and preached in pulpits across the country. She founded a women ministers group in the early 1870s that met annually to provide support and encouragement to women in the ministry. She was chief of the Woman's Department of the World's Industrial and Cotton Exposition, held in New Orleans in 1885. In 1891, she helped found and then served as vice-president of the American Friends of Russian Freedom. In 1893, she spoke at the World Parliament of Religions as well as at the Chicago World's Fair. In 1894, Julia became the first president of the United Friends of Armenia.[109] She spoke frequently at the Massachusetts State House in support of woman suffrage, but also for pure milk for children. And she remained an active intellectual, reading papers before the Radical Club and the Concord School of Philosophy and participating regularly in the Boston-based Authors Club. The only woman elected to membership in the American Academy of Arts and Letters until 1930, Julia was probably also the only American woman to deliver an address on women and education to the Florence Philological Society in fluent French and Italian or to chair a Paris suffrage convention.[110] The woman was a dynamo.

Unquestionably, her voice was no longer frozen to silence. Freed to speak her mind, Julia was able to develop fully her views on marriage, women's rights, and domestic duties. Not surprisingly, her defense of women's rights in marriage became increasingly sharp. In her newfound role as domestic sage, on the other hand, she became far more sanguine about the demands of running a household than she had ever been during the years when she actually did so. It was easy to forget the miseries of her clashes with Chev once he was no longer present to challenge her.

Two things stood out about Julia's later considerations of marriage: her inclination to relate the traditional role of the wife to that of the slave, and her insistence that only marriages founded upon equality could prosper. Marriage as she had known it in her youth was a form of bondage for wives, Julia concluded. "The old institution, like Judas," she said, "betrayed freedom with a kiss."[111] Julia unfolded that idea in greater detail in a sermon entitled "The Liberty Wherewith Christ Has Made Us Free." There Julia proclaimed that she had indeed been in slavery "as a woman, when my avenue of advancement was carefully guarded, & the flaming sword of criticism waved over every thing wh[ich], as a woman, I could undertake." How bad was it? As bad as possible, she answered; this slavery was "very absolute and cruel." Yet, as she preached, Julia declared herself free from this bondage, free because of the "inner voice" that urged her "to do the greatest thing I could do, to rise to the greatest height I could attain."[112]

Julia wanted her listeners to be clear about this inner voice. It was the cry of conscience, a vital impulse that enabled women to experience what the New Testament called a second birth. "Conscience is the master," she explained, "who makes us free from all others." Christian freedom—the freedom promised by Jesus—was then nothing less (or more) than autonomy. "Will men ask us what we mean by freedom?" she queried. "We will ask them what they mean by self-government. The very word self-government implies that the governing principle resides primarily" in the individual. What women sought, Julia concluded, was simply the freedom to govern themselves in "all that concerns individual action," and the freedom "to be represented in all that concerns collective action." Christian salvation, in short, was nothing other than individual autonomy; and true spiritual progress was unattainable to couples mired in patriarchal relationships. "But I ask you," Julia challenged, "if Man and Wife are to be one, as Christ says they are, why should one half keep the other half of itself in darkness and ignorance? I tell you, my brethren, the gospel of Christ is coming today to save the womanhood which is lost to poor training and unequal discipline".[113]

Never did Julia indicate more clearly the immense importance she assigned to personal autonomy; it was the essence of spiritual salvation in this sermon. And never did she argue more forcefully for her notion—first expressed in the romance of Eva and Rafael—that men and women would either progress toward salvation together, or not at all. As Eva and Rafael were perfectly united and transfigured after death, so the wife and husband were to become one in marriage. Julia concluded in an 1893 lecture on the "Moral Equality of the Sexes," "the sense of equality is a most important condition in marriage, and the surest guarantee of its sacredness." Men who regarded their wives as subordinates, Julia warned, ultimately degraded and demoralized their spouses, because "such a feeling, latent in his mind, will always tend to lower the moral tone of a woman, who looks to him for guidance & approval." If marriage was to succeed, Julia claimed, it could do so only when both partners granted one another "mutual dignity and equality."[114]

Those presuppositions made it easy for Julia to contend that no inequitable marriage could thrive. In an 1888 speech on "Marriage and Divorce" to the American Association of Women, Julia had earlier explored in greater detail the dire consequences of subjecting the wife to the rule of her husband. Julia did not cite personal experience, but she certainly drew on it, reciting a litany of married woes. First there was the signing away of the woman's birthright of equality at the marriage altar. "The man endows her with the obligation to cede to him the possession of her worldly goods, which she is required to receive meekly, as a favor at his hands." Then there was the possibility of infidelity—which would result in "social death" for the woman, while the man "will be easily excused." Next were the disheartening consequences of a tyrannical marriage: "all injustice will bear, sooner or later, its inevitable fruit of insubordination and rebellion, and though these may never take the form of scandal or offence, they will yet be able to eat out the heart of married life, and will render it a grievous burthen to one or both partners." She spoke of the agonies endured when one partner was intolerant of the interests of the other. "Much heroism is often shown in married life by those who endure such tyranny," she remarked, "but it is difficult to endure it long without a loss of will power which in the end is seriously demoralizing."[115]

In cases of physical abuse, Julia continued, the law should forcibly annul the marriage, because in such situations "Divorce is as religious as Marriage." Where endurance and growth of character seemed possible, however, she urged partners to continue in marriage. Ideally, marriage should "represent freedom of choice, spontaneity of affection, and a stable and steadfast purpose." Julia had been around long enough to know that the ideal was rarely achieved. "My own views on this subject are colored by the sunset light of a life which has long passed the meridian," she explained. "Looking back on what it has taught me, I see a world of conflicting attraction and of uncertain relations in which principles of duty are the only guide." In many households, Julia admitted, she saw "an arid waste surrounding those in which the selfish principle has been enthroned and worshipped."[116]

Ultimately, as Julia asserted in an 1883 speech on suffrage, women had to learn their own worth. "When the daring to be womanly shall become general among women," she argued, "among them will pass away those miserable caricatures of womanhood which result from a life shaped to satisfy the excess and capriciousness of masculine views." She conceded, however, that "all that is brutish in man resists this ennobling process" and that many women lacked the courage necessary to claim autonomy. "These," she explained, "are women crippled by their own love of approbation, fearing to lose the favor of men by the exercise of their own judgment, of their own sensibility."[117] No one knew better than Julia the agony of a bad marriage or the terror of daring to break free.

Still, as she looked back over the nineteenth century, Julia could hardly help but rejoice. At the start of the century, she said, women had been universally regarded as men's inferiors. But at century's end, women were at last coming into their own, claiming their rights and finding ways to support themselves financially. No longer were they forced to marry in order to have a roof over their heads.[118] In time, Julia believed, women would receive full citizenship, and the equality of men and women would appear self-evident. "No one could be more opposed to woman suffrage than I was twenty years ago," she announced in an 1885 address, predicting that the day was close when respectable women would be self-governing, not meek and docile. "Let me say to fashionable women . . . that the time is coming when suffrage will be fashionable," she asserted.[119] No more would women have to choose—as Julia had—between autonomy and social respectability.

Julia's critique of marriage, however, did not entirely abandon the traditional recitation of its joys. While she railed at the abuses women suffered in patriarchal marriages, she was conventional enough also to celebrate the joys of properly ordered families. Safely removed from the stresses of mothering children and running her own household, she felt free to instruct others, becoming—ironically—a kind of sage of domesticity. That was no small accomplishment for a woman who had depended on servants her entire life and who by her own admission was not adept in the kitchen.

As she considered the advantages of motherhood, for example, Julia denied that maternity should be the "supreme end" of a woman's life, but she concluded that it offered wonderful opportunities for self-sacrifice.[120] In a letter to her sister Annie, Julia commented that her son Harry and his wife Fannie had no children. Julia felt Fannie was thereby diminished: "she is certainly devoted to him, but lacks the education which motherhood, or barring this, the habit of self denial gives."[121] Indeed, additional reflection suggested to Julia that the "house without children is always in the end a sad one," even when the marriage was happy. "Whatever may be the delights of solitary study," she claimed, "the human mind at length claims a generation of its own. . . . Scholars whose learning is sterile become old maids, and bachelors of souls."[122] The days when Julia had been obliged to struggle with all her might to salvage her P.T. for study had definitely receded.

In her thoughts about keeping house, Julia waxed even more eloquent, offering the following advice in her *Reminiscences:* "I would say to every young girl, rich or poor, gifted or dull: 'Learn to make a home, and learn this in the days in which learning is easy. Cultivate a habit of vigilance and forethought. With a reasonable amount of intelligence, a woman should be able to carry on the management of a household, and should yet have time for art and literature of some sort.'" Julia recommended the study of art, literature, and philosophy for those women who could spare three hours a day; those who had only an hour to themselves ought to read philosophy or learn foreign languages; and those with only fifteen to twenty minutes should read the Bible along with the best commentaries, as well as fine poetry. Everyone should maintain a good attitude. "Surely no love of intellectual pursuits should lead any of us to disparage and neglect the household gifts and graces," she counseled. "A house is a kingdom in little, and its queen, if she is faithful, gentle, and wise, is a sovereign indeed."[123]

In many ways, Julia challenged conventional notions of womanhood and marriage, but sometimes the traditional rhetoric in praise of domesticity was irresistible—even if it was largely irrelevant to her own life.

POET, SEER, AND WOMAN TOO

As the nineteenth century ended, *what* Julia said began to matter less than *that* she said it. A biographical sketch written shortly after her death pointed out, "as her contemporaries one by one dropped away, the veneration of the young for an older, heroic generation came to center upon her, the only surviving member. Her distinction as the 'grand old woman,' the 'first lady,' the 'American queen' was firmly entrenched. She became a kind of an institution, a repository of the spirit of a vanished age. . . . People came on pilgrimage to see her, as they might to a historic monument."[124] All of which is not to say that Julia ceased to speak articulately on behalf of the causes she championed or that her wit and energy had forsaken her. She never lost her sense of urgency about social reform. Her diary recorded frequent prayers that she might be of use in the service of good, as well as corresponding sections describing actions she undertook on behalf of the good—an article written, a speech given, or a donation sent.

Public rituals of veneration began to form around her. The annual events surrounding her May birthday grew so involved that Julia's daughters despaired of the energy they required. The New England Woman's Club always gave a luncheon to commemorate Julia's birthday, complete with speeches and verses cleverly designed to praise her. Flowers came from all over the country, and Julia would hold an open house at her home on Beacon Street. Memorial Day celebrations fell on the same week as Julia's birthday, and she would be called on to recite her "Battle Hymn" before adoring audiences. Articles would invariably appear in the Boston papers describing the events of her birthday week.

Some of her birthdays drew special attention. The *Woman's Journal* dedicated its May 27, 1899 issue to Julia in honor of her turning eighty. The articles were effusive in their praise, even including selections from daughter Laura's *When I Was Your Age*, a book for children that was rapturous in its depiction of her sainted parents. Already, even before Julia was dead, the public's view of her was being shaped by her children's mythologizing. A report on speeches delivered at the New England Woman's Club indicated that some of her admirers were interested in assessing Julia's impact on American culture as well as in celebrating her family relations. William L. Garrison wondered how Julia had managed to maintain her place in society while championing relatively unpopular causes. He concluded that she pulled it off by the power of her personality. "Society was too selfish to forego the grace and charm which her inclusion lent it," he asserted. Henry Blackwell pondered what Julia's place in history would be, and decided that she was a "realization of the coming woman, as daughter, sister, wife, mother, and citizen—a leader and exemplar in public and in private life."[125]

Other honors poured in. The Boston Authors Club celebrated Julia's eighty-sixth birthday in 1905 with a volume of commemorative poems. Most were humorous, but the epithets revealed genuine respect. Julia was feted as the

"Lady of the Vision and the Voice," a "Type of noblest womanhood," a "queen, in realm of spirit," a "Poet, Seer, and Woman too," a "Voice prophetic against the wrong," and the poet who had "set us all asinging."[126] By 1905, Julia was long accustomed to being called a queen—she looked a good deal like Queen Victoria of England, who was the same age. A Philadelphia paper, for example, reported on the Memorial Day services held in the Boston Theatre in May 1899. The singing of the "Battle Hymn" focused attention on Julia, the reporter commented, and once people saw her, "you should have heard the yell. When Vic celebrated her eightieth birthday a few days before, she got no ovation equal to that given this octogenarian." As Julia raised her voice to join in the last verse, "the whole vast audience was on its feet sobbing, and singing at the top of its lungs. If volunteers were really needed for the Philippines, McKinley could have had us all right there."[127]

Occasionally even comparisons to Victoria were not good enough. A 1910 article on the open house at Julia's ninetieth birthday turned to the Bible for parallels. Impressed with the elevator her children had installed in Julia's Boston home, the author imagined that the heavens themselves had opened to receive Julia. When "we saw her slowly mounting to the regions above in an electric 'lift' which she manages as skillfully [sic] as the Wrights manage their aeroplane, it reminded one of the celestial rapture of Elijah," he marveled.[128]

Of all the honors that came her way, however, Julia particularly cherished the honorary degrees she was awarded. Julia was convinced that one of the most significant accomplishments of the women's movement was the opening up of higher education for women. Prior to the Civil War, Oberlin was the only college in the nation that admitted women. In the 1870s, Julia had fought a bitter battle with Dr. Edward Clark of Harvard, who had argued that higher education had a masculinizing effect upon women. By the turn of the century, times had changed. Women's colleges had been established on a firm footing—even in Cambridge, near Harvard Yard—and in time, many colleges and universities would become coeducational. So no awards were sweeter to Julia than the three honorary degrees she received: from Tufts University in 1904, Brown University in 1908, and Smith College in 1910. The scene was the same in each case: the "Battle Hymn," the aged but vibrant woman on the platform, and the roar of the appreciative audience. Julia had lived long enough to be adored.

The Smith College award on October 5, 1910, was Julia's last grand outing. Her health had been precarious throughout the summer of 1910, because of a fall she had taken on June 13. She suffered a broken rib, and reluctantly consented to the hiring of a private nurse. By early August, Julia had "a passage of

arms with Maud," announcing that the nurse had to go.[129] The doctor disagreed, and Maud was distraught, but, as she put it, "that last fiery flash of the
cold gray eyes and the red hot temper, completely cowed and quelled the old
daughters!" As she thought it over, Maud came to realize that Julia was making
her "last stand for freedom" and that she was dominating her family "by the
sheer force of her will." And why not? "I think she was balked so much in her
youth, first by her own father . . . then by papa, that her first ideal of happiness
was to be let alone, and allowed to have one's own way," Maud concluded. No
one could appreciate better than Maud that the "discipline of living with papa,
who was very irritable and strong willed; and with certain of her children who
had the same characteristics" could drive a person into headstrong acts. Julia
had sought and treasured autonomy her entire life, and if her caretaker daughter did not always yield to her, at least Maud could recognize that Julia's strong
will was "the great basic element in her."[130]

The end came swiftly. On October 12, a week after her excursion to Smith
College, Julia developed a cough, which soon advanced into pneumonia.
Breathing became progressively difficult and, despite medical attention, she
died on October 17 in her own bed at her summer home in Rhode Island. "No
distortion, no agony, or ugliness," Maud reported—just a quiet passing.[131]
When Laura Bridgman died in 1889, Julia had imagined Chev's heavenly triumph, "standing before the face of the Highest and pointing to his work."
Three years later, Julia had had another dream about her dead husband. This
time, she and Chev were traveling. With no other means available to cross a
river, they jumped in, "he swimming, & supporting me, clinging to his neck.
This naturally suggested to me the silent river he has already crossed."[132] Julia
had now forded that river too. Whether she expected Chev to stand before God
in praise or condemnation of her, only she knew. One thing was certain: she
had made the journey on her own terms.

IN MEMORIAM

Nothing demonstrated Julia's success in creating the public image she desired
more than the memorial exercises held in her honor by the city of Boston.
Mayor Fitzgerald set the tone in his opening address when he declared that
Julia "typifies and stands for the nineteenth century, for womanhood itself, for
America, and for Boston."[133] Mary E. Woolley, in discussing Julia's club work,
noted that she had for years been president of the New England Woman's Club,
or "rather, its queen!"[134] Yet another speaker noted that Julia had not merely
been a reformer, but a "devoted wife and mother." Nor, the speaker concluded,

"did it injure her public service that she was to the end in every sphere emphatically a womanly woman."[135]

An ideal woman, a queen, a civic institution—and yet there was more. William H. Lewis gave Julia credit for Chev's work. "Fifty years she reigned over us, queen of all our hearts, the idol of those who knew her best," he intoned. Just as three decades earlier, Boston had mourned the passing of her "Prince Consort, Dr. Samuel Gridley Howe . . . so Boston now honors the memory of the ideal wife and mother who inspired the work of the great philanthropist and helped to make enduring the name of Howe." Chev had energetically resisted Julia's public career, and he had at times been jealous of her fame, but even he had not entertained the fear that he would be reduced to her prince consort. Or that she would be elevated to the status of deity. But Lewis spared no words. To him, Julia's "very presence seemed a benediction, sublime, Godlike."[136]

Julia could hardly have asked for a more glowing send-off. Against all odds, she had defied the gender conventions of her day without damaging her reputation. If anything, people admired her daring. In the end, she had achieved exactly what she had desired: independence and respectability. Her children, however, were not content to leave her legacy to the vagaries of public memory. By 1910, they had already published several books about their parents, and they were eager to write the definitive biography of their mother to ensure both that posterity knew all that was great and good about her and that nothing untoward was printed. Laura had already shown, in publishing her father's biography, what kind of a study she would like to do of her mother—her *Letters and Journals of Samuel Gridley Howe* designated him "the servant of humanity" and reprinted poetry depicting him as a knight-errant.[137] Any doubt that she would treat her mother's story as less legendary had earlier been dispelled in an essay that Laura had written in 1893 on "Woman in Literature." There she had declared her mother "the foremost literary woman of today" and added the highly tendentious claim that "it was not till some years after her marriage that she thought of publishing any of her work."[138]

In 1903, Maud and Flossy had also published a book on behalf of their father. They intended their study of Laura Bridgman to offset the fame that Helen Keller and her teacher Annie Sullivan had enjoyed in the late 1880s and 1890s. Helen Keller might seem an unlikely villain, but the enormous public attention focused on her was, to the Howes, a threat to the Chevalier's legacy. Annie Sullivan had trained at the Institute under Michael Anagnos and had known Laura Bridgman as well. The Howes found it supremely irritating that Helen, unlike Laura, had learned how to speak aloud, and they were determined to prove that the "miracle" by which Annie Sullivan had brought Helen

Keller into communication with the rest of humanity ought properly be credited to Samuel Gridley Howe. As far as the Howes were concerned, Annie Sullivan was no genius; she had simply (and rather poorly, in their opinion) adopted the methods invented by their father and passed along to their brother-in-law. And Helen Keller, to the Howes, was just another Laura Bridgman, only less demure and refined.

As they worked on their manuscript, trying to complete it as quickly as possible so that the public would give proper credit to the Chevalier, Maud told Flossy her strategy: they would document the case of Laura Bridgman carefully, since Chev kept detailed records of Laura's daily progress. Then they could briefly analyze the case of Helen Keller "from the superior point of view" and trust their readers to draw the proper conclusions.[139] The title of their book, *Laura Bridgman: Dr. Howe's Famous Pupil and What He Taught Her*, indicated clearly that they had written a study not so much of Laura Bridgman as of their father's triumphs. To further dispel doubt as to the book's central character, opposite the title page was a picture of Chev instructing Laura Bridgman. The book's consideration of Helen Keller covered less than two pages, in which Maud and Flossy managed to refrain from voicing the Howes' suspicions that Annie Sullivan, not Helen, had written many of Helen's celebrated public speeches.[140]

As the Howes turned to the task of writing the story of Julia's life, the family aspiration to manage history set off a series of fierce sibling conflicts that lasted for years. The biography wars were the biggest brouhaha yet in a family that had already experienced its fair share of discord. The initial dispute arose over the question of which of the Howes should author Julia's biography. Harry thought Laura should do it, and he thought she should do it unaided by her sisters.[141] But Maud and Flossy were determined to be a part of the biography. There was already tension among the family members over Julia's estate— both Maud and Flossy wanted the Rhode Island summer home, but neither could afford to buy out the others, and it was not clear that Flossy could afford the upkeep even if she were to take possession of the house. Maud was also upset over the question of designating an artist to paint the memorial portrait of Julia that would eventually hang in the Massachusetts State House. She thought her husband Jack should get the commission and was horribly wounded when Harry wrote a letter to the art commission saying he would accept another artist.[142]

During these squabbles, Harry continued to pressure Laura to take a stand against her sisters as the sole author of the projected biography. He promised to hire a secretary to help Laura work through the family papers. The secretary was hired, but reported for work at Julia's home in Boston, where Maud was sorting through Julia's effects. Harry wanted the secretary in Gardiner, Maine, where Laura lived. Maud did not see how she could work much faster. Both she and Jack contracted sore throats from packing up the contents of Julia's dusty home (the doctor blamed the elevator shaft for the accumulation of dust and germs), and Maud was moving as fast as she could, grumbling on occasion that Harry addressed his sisters "as the Czar to his subjects."[143] The cracks in the Howe armor—cracks that not only never appeared publicly, but which the Howe literary works were designed to conceal—were beginning to emerge.

Harry had real doubts about Maud, who took Julia's death harder than the other children did. Laura was able to say, in 1913, that Julia "never seems far way" and that death was a partial thing. "We shall never lose her altogether," she told Maud. "Why, I am talking to her—with her, all day long, you too; let us be thankful!"[144] Maud did not share Laura's optimism. She was having enormous difficulty concentrating on her work, and she missed Julia desperately. She reported having a miserable Christmas in 1911, and despaired that she was so paralyzed with grief at losing Julia that she had no energy to devote to her husband Jack. Maud observed in her diary on December 31, 1911: "Mama is still the dominant personality & takes up most of my thought when not taken up with actual practical things." On May 27, 1912, Maud remarked that she now understood why Jesus' followers had looked for a second coming. "When a great personality has enwrapped and dominated you it does not seem possible that it can be really permanently taken away from you. It must come back." On June 2, 1914, Maud wrote, "the savage pain of the time of Mama's death is always in the memory, at the back of one's mind." In October 1914, Maud was still suffering. "The sense of loneliness never lessens, and I find myself calling 'Mama, Mama!' in such a way that must seem strange to any who overhear me," Maud confessed.[145]

Harry was at a loss as to what to do with Maud. Even in the early months after Julia's death, Harry thought Maud needed to temper her grief. "Why, if she is that [desolate] she ought to be in a sanitarium," he said. "Really, Laura, I feel much troubled about her. She seems to me absurdly fat. . . . I don't know enough to say whether this sort of fatty degeneration to which she and dear Julia [Romana] seemed so subject is allied to dropsy or not. . . . the sort of intensity in which she lives is terrible. I always come home about sick after being with her."[146]

None of this was settling the question of who would write the biography. Harry appealed to Maud's sense of chivalry, asking her, as the Chevalier's daughter, to do the noble thing: let Laura, a proven biographer, work alone.

Maud replied that she was closer to Julia than Laura had been. Maud apparently had an additional card to play. After her mother's death, Maud had written a long account of Julia's last summer. That information would be of great use to the biography. According to Laura's daughter Betty, Maud used that document as leverage to force Laura to collaborate with her in writing the biography.[147] Flossy also worked hard to convince Harry and Laura that she ought to have a hand in drafting the biography. She pointed out that she as the oldest could provide information about events that occurred before the others had been born. Moreover, in their book on Laura Bridgman, she and Maud had proven that a jointly authored biography was a practical endeavor.[148]

In the end, a tenuous partnership was formed. Laura would act as head writer, but Maud would collaborate as well, and Flossy would assist, though not actually write copy. Harry would continue to pay for the secretary. "What would our poor parents say if they could see such senseless quarrels, with no real justification?" he wondered.[149] Unfortunately, the infighting was just picking up steam, as the collaboration produced endless agonies. Flossy and Laura made each other utterly miserable. Flossy was convinced that Laura was not giving sufficient attention to Julia's suffrage and club work—subjects, Flossy said, close to *her* heart, but not Laura's. To ensure that the public got a sufficient taste of Julia's suffrage activities, Flossy published *Julia Ward Howe and the Woman Suffrage Movement* in 1913. But she still wanted the biography to do a better job with the suffrage material. And she, too, had a card to play. Laura was convinced of the need to incorporate more of Julia's correspondence into the biography. Laura's early drafts quoted Julia's diary frequently, but the diary lacked the sparkle and good humor so characteristic of her letters. Laura coveted the correspondence from Julia that Flossy had saved, but so far, Flossy had not offered to share her cache. "Oh for more letters!" Laura wrote to Maud, lamenting, "Flossy must have plenty, if I could only get at them."[150]

Flossy, for her part, complained that Laura's draft chapters highlighted the role that her own children had played in Julia's life and deliberately slighted Flossy's offspring. At one point, Laura tried to pacify Flossy by assuring her that the number of references to Flossy's children was exactly the same as the number of references to Laura's children. Flossy was not impressed. "When you wrote me this," she chided Laura, "I made no answer, the unfairness of the test being obvious. Length and quality count as well as number."[151] Laura was so frustrated that she informed Harry in July 1914 that Flossy "has actually become unbalanced on some points." Like Harry, Laura hated to think of the spectacle they were making of themselves. But then, she asked Harry—in another break with Howe solidarity—what could be expected from someone as hostile as Flossy? "It is unseemly for sisters of our age—or any age—to wrangle and bicker; wrangling has been the habit of her whole life, and it does not affect her in any way afterwards, apparently; it makes me, and it makes Maud, in these days of her quieted and chastened spirit, sick! so no more of it for us!"[152]

But of course there was more. A September 1914 letter from Laura to Maud and Harry indicated that the bickering was continuing full force. This time Laura was on the offensive. When we started this biography, Laura exclaimed, Maud promised that Flossy would have no hand in the writing. "Then,—what happened? That which has always happened, ever since I have known that dear good woman. . . . First she wept and wailed to Maud; and Ma'am Greatheart was softened and promised to intercede, and did intercede, begging that after all F. might do such and such a part of the work. Then she wept and wailed to Harry; and Sir Greatheart smote his breast, and thought he had been harsh and promised to intercede." The result of this mess, Laura concluded, was that she was being held up as a tyrant, "and must bear the odium of resisting Flossy's petitions. Now, fellers, this ain[']t fair." More hidden dynamics of Howe family life then emerged. "Flossy has always got her own way in just this manner," Laura complained. "Papa, Mammy, every one of us, has always said, 'Oh, poor dear Flossy, she has had such a hard time, we must do all we can for her.'"[153]

As the process of revising rough drafts continued, Harry grew concerned that Laura was revealing too much about the family. In particular, he objected to a section in which Laura had written that a strain of insanity ran in the Howe family. "In what way will your readers and our fellows in general be the better for your informing them that there is a strain of insanity?" he asked. "What good will they receive to compensate for the pain which your descendants and Flossy's will receive from such a disclosure? Have you an ethical right to disclose matters which may injure her children, unless there is a clear benefit to mankind from the disclosure?"[154] Harry was determined that no reader would learn anything negative about the Howes.

For her part, Maud was wavering between lethargy and anxiety. Her depression over Julia's death had made it hard for her to do much writing, and she admitted to her diary in May 1914 that partly through her own fault and partly through Laura's design, her role in the biography "now is so small that it hardly counts." That produced anxiety, since Maud believed Laura's prose was overly exuberant. And—God help her—Maud agreed with Flossy that the suffrage chapter needed work.[155] An editorial conference at Gardiner in January 1915 caused as many problems as it solved. Maud reported being greatly discouraged "by the United Richards Front. Everything Laura does is impeccable in the eyes of the 8 great powers [her husband and children]." Working with Flossy was not any more cheering. Maud and Flossy spent an entire day on the suffrage chapter, only to have Maud conclude that Flossy "is so full of temper that it[']s very difficult to work with her." It was all difficult, in fact. Laura was indifferent to suffrage, Flossy was utterly absorbed in it, and Maud was stuck in the middle. "To oppose Laura is like striking a feather bed, to fight Flossy a nutmeg grinder," she sighed. "I don't know which is worst, but the feather bed wins in the end, I have seen."[156]

One point Maud did push with Laura—Laura's assertion in the biography's original draft that Julia "disliked" Dr. Howe after first meeting him. Maud was certain that was the last thing they wanted to say. "It is to us valuable," she contended, "but is part of just what we don[']t want to throw light on too much. They certainly attracted and repelled each other in a queer way!" The final edition of the biography followed Maud's suggestion, ignoring their parents' initial encounter with one another and highlighting the dramatic approach of the Chevalier on his black steed to meet—and impress— Julia Ward.[157] On other points, however, Laura would not yield. She wrote Harry to tell him just how miserable Flossy in particular was making her. "I feel that F's constant hammering is insensibly warping, or at least tampering with, your literary judgment," she complained to Harry when he sided with Flossy. "I agree that her suggestions are often valuable, and we are certainly using many of them," Laura explained. "But we must never forget that of literary judgment she has none. The notes she sends me—I could weep over them for pity and sorrow."[158]

When the book was finally published in 1916, even the title page proved problematic. Laura and Maud were listed as authors, and Flossy was said to have assisted them. Laura was certain, however, that they had decided not to have Flossy's name on the title page, and although Maud had written Laura in 1913 that both she and Laura agreed that Flossy's name should be there, by 1917 Maud could no longer remember what they had decided, and agreed with Laura that seeing Flossy's name on the title page was a "distinct shock."[159] None of that would have mattered much except that the book won a Pulitzer Prize, and there was prize money to divide, as well as royalties from sales of the biography. Laura was willing to divide the prize money, but not the royalties.[160] Flossy was apoplectic, protesting that all of them shared equally in Julia's estate. Since Julia's papers were part of her estate, and Laura had used those papers in writing the biography—and received considerable assistance from her two sisters—it was only fair that they share the royalties.[161] Flossy did not expect an equal share of the royalties, since Laura and Maud had done more work on the biography than she had, but she did expect to receive something. Flossy conceded that they had all been under considerable strain in writing the biography but pointed out that she and Maud had had no such difficulties when they had collaborated on a biography of Laura Bridgman in 1903. The problem this time had been Laura, Flossy said. She and Maud had stood up for themselves as best they could, "but it was hard . . . to oppose your entire family."[162]

Laura sent a blistering letter in reply, informing Flossy that her "name on the title-page was a matter of affection and courtesy, and of those alone." As far as Laura was concerned, Flossy had contributed very little to the book—"some good advice, some valuable letters, and a chapter which could not be used. That is the naked, brutal truth, my dear old girl." Laura closed by advising Flossy to take her share of the Pulitzer money ($333.33) to buy a Liberty Bond.[163] Brother Harry advised Laura to have patience and remember that Flossy "is our parents' daughter, born from them with an unfortunate disposition, born to be unhappy and to give unhappiness, born to a rather sad fate." It was Flossy who was to be pitied, Harry said. "We rub against her disposition only at times, but she must sleep and wake with it to the end." Envy, vanity, and a generous supply of cantankerousness—Flossy had it all. But what could they do? "One cannot afford to take note of the defects of those whom you must cherish out of love for their parents," Harry concluded. Or, "at least you cannot afford to act as if you took note."[164]

So much for the much cherished myth of the "happy family." The Howes were human, not superhuman, and nothing revealed their powers of persuasion more than their abilities to hide their family flaws in print.

STRIKE HOME!

In spite of the enormous frustration that went into the production of *Julia Ward Howe, 1819–1910*, Julia's children had written a book so inspiring that the Pulitzer Prize committee praised it as the "best American biography teaching patriotic and unselfish services to the people, illustrated by an eminent example." The biography was a success, and Julia's reputation was spotless. One final task remained: to keep it so. This job eventually involved the grandchildren as well.

That the family was touchy about Julia's reputation was eminently clear in a dispute that arose during World War I. A Navy chaplain named Henry Van Dyke had responded to a request from enlisted men to write a stanza to the tune of "John Brown's Body"—the same melody that Julia had used for her "Battle Hymn"—that the men might sing after completing the "Battle Hymn." Maud wrote Van Dyke and ordered him to stop, arguing, "the Integrity of a Literary Reputation forbids any addition or change to an author's work." The chaplain was stunned. "I have neither changed nor emended" the original hymn, he protested; there was no danger that his stanza would "ever be confused with your mother's completed work." Van Dyke was willing to follow any instructions Maud might give him, but he could not help but point out that the "great gain of freedom, won by the Civil War, is in peril by the ruthless German Power.... I cannot find in my heart any regret for having written the stanza and given it to the brave American boys who are going out to fight, and if need be to die, for the cause of our country and world-wide freedom."[165] The Howes fought tough when it came to protecting their own.

The family was alarmed once again in 1945, when Bobbs-Merrill published a children's biography of Julia written by Jean Brown Wagoner. Laura's daughter Rosalind Richards was especially furious at Wagoner's account of her grandmother's childhood. Rosalind had been a house companion for Julia for nine years, and then she moved back to Gardiner to care for her parents. She had devoted her life to the Howe legacy, and she would handle the prodigious archival materials passed on by Laura at her death. Rosalind was incensed that a scene from Wagoner's biography depicted the childish Julia impulsively throwing her arms around an Indian chief, and Rosalind charged that Wagoner had done the family a grave injustice by depicting Julia doing something so out of character. Wagoner replied that she had taken the vignette straight from Julia's autobiography. Upon consulting *Reminiscences,* Rosalind had to concede the point, but still she complained that Wagoner had failed to "present its heroine as she was." Rosalind also found it both puzzling and disturbing that Miss Wagoner had not allowed the family to read her manuscript before its publication. If Miss Wagoner had talked to the family, she would have learned that even though she was correct in depicting Julia hugging the chief, she had entirely misconstrued Julia's subsequent conversation. "It is probably impossible for the younger generation to realize the stateliness of speech of that day," Rosalind concluded. To her, it was not a minor point.[166]

An examination of books that Maud was writing about the family before this incident also indicates the lengths to which the Howes would go to tell their own versions of family history. Maud's 1938 biography of her Uncle Sam Ward had the potential to be a spicy read. Sam had run rather wildly through Europe in his student days, and had gone on to quite a checkered career. Lobbyist, Copperhead, gold miner, and financier—Sam Ward had made and lost several fortunes, but Maud's biography was entirely circumspect. Likewise, Maud's 1934 biography of her cousin Frank (F. Marion Crawford) had been so guarded that even Laura found it excellent. Like Daisy Terry Chanler, a cousin who had also done a study of Crawford, Maud had chosen not to tell her readers just how miserable Crawford's marriage had been. Laura thoroughly approved. "She, like Daisy Chanler, gives no hint of the bitter sufferings of his later life," Laura observed. "His wife was extravagant to frenzy, jealous, suspicious; many things a wife should not be. He was desperately unhappy. They [Maud and Daisy] are quite right in not unveiling this."[167]

In addition to policing public perceptions of the family and of Julia's legacy in particular, the children and grandchildren had to decide what to do with the family papers. Although Julia had burned letters relating to her 1850–51 separation from Chev and to Chev's extramarital affairs, many other sensitive documents remained. Should future generations have access to these documents? The Howes were concerned that the family name continue to be prominent, but not at the cost of respectability. They did not hesitate to destroy documents. Laura did not think twice about destroying her father's youthful letters and journals because they were so candid. "Somebody might read them, and see what S. G. H. thought of many, if not most, of the men for and with whom he was fighting," she explained.[168]

Also bound for the flames—*especially* bound for the flames—were Julia Romana's letters and notebooks. "Strike home!" Laura urged Maud in 1924, announcing that she had just burned "about half a ton" of family papers, including Julia Romana's letters to Aunt Annie. "I felt like a butcher, but could do no[t] otherwise," Laura said.[169] In 1928, Laura wrote Maud, urging her to follow her example. "Destroy dear Julia's notebooks! I know it isn't easy to do. I still have one, and so help me, I will make an end to it today . . . we do her no kindness by preserving her writings."[170] Very few of Julia Romana's papers survived these purges. A few letters remained in Laura's collection and Flossy kept a few. Some innocuous plays she wrote at age ten also survived, as did Julia Romana's two published works. The most intellectual Howe of all has virtually disappeared from history except as a vague character described as shy and otherworldly. Given Julia Romana's wicked sense of humor and her sympathy for her father's experience of his marriage, the loss is particularly keen. Yet the destruction of Julia Romana's papers did exactly what the Howes intended—it froze the story of Julia and Chev, making it impossible to discover the insights on the family dynamics that their oldest daughter might have shared. And the loss of Julia Romana's papers ensured that no curious eyes would ever explore the depths of her madness—if indeed she *was* insane.

More purges were ahead. Laura was burning her mother's papers in 1935 and asked Maud to send what she thought worth saving and destroy the rest. "Is it conceivable that that page should be turned again?" Laura queried. "I think not. Her place is secure; we must be content with that. I think—hope—mean, to destroy much of what I have; I have destroyed much already, A.A.W. addresses, etc etc. Oh dear! how she worked!"[171] Association for the Advancement of Women (AAW) addresses, of course, would have been covered by the press, so they were not lost; but many private papers were forever destroyed. The Richardses continued to employ a secretary to transcribe the family papers. After transcribing the correspondence between Julia and Chev, the secretary presented the materials for Rosalind "to read, or destroy, or both, at her leisure and discretion." A note on the surviving letters from June 1950, told the result: "Most of correspondence destroyed."[172]

In time, however, the Richardses made arrangements for scholars to examine, under carefully controlled conditions, the materials that remained. Louise Tharp was the first author permitted to read Julia's diaries, which were essential sources for *Three Saints and a Sinner,* Tharp's biography of Julia, Annie, Louisa, and Sam Ward. Tharp included few notes—meaning that no one who read the book would be able to follow her tracks—but even then, Rosalind was not pleased with what Tharp had written. Publication was delayed for a year until Rosalind and the author could come to an agreement.[173] *Three Saints and a Sinner* was finally released in 1956. By then, Rosalind and her brother John had begun a series of donations to the Houghton Library at Harvard University, limiting access to most entries to the discretion of Harvard or the family, and restricting access to Julia's diaries for thirty years, except by special waiver.[174] In 1975, two scholars (Deborah Pickman Clifford and Anne Stokes Alexander) were given permission to examine the Houghton's holdings.[175] Clifford then wrote the first modern biography of Julia, published in 1979, and Alexander completed a dissertation on Laura in the same year.[176] At her death, Maud made Rosalind the executor of her literary estate, and Rosalind donated Maud's papers to the John Hay Library at Brown University.[177]

Even when Rosalind donated materials, and even when she restricted access to them, she could not resist the urge to purge offensive passages. Current users of the Howe papers at Harvard and at Brown know her touch all too well. Rosalind did not hesitate to cut or ink out sections of letters and diary entries that were best left unseen, and she was not afraid to rip pages out of diaries. No one will ever be able to reconstruct the lost pages (or figure out how so many provocative texts were permitted to survive), but in the records that do remain, Julia Ward Howe emerges as a complex and fully human character. Her private agonies and triumphs stand alongside her relatively sanitized public persona. The American icon who seemed to glide through life effortlessly and the courageous woman determined to find her own voice in an age and in a marriage that regarded wives as extensions of their husbands intersect; and this cross need not be, like Eva's, the opposition of two desires. Julia's descendants presented a view of her that made light of her struggles and ignored the considerable tensions that continued to mark family dynamics long after she died. It is possible, however, to accept the demons of Julia's private life without rejecting her reputation as a dignified and accomplished woman of the Victorian age.

In a review of Julia's written works published a few months after her death, Jeanne Robert saluted her as the "Grand Old Woman of America" and celebrated Julia's daring and breadth of vision. "Most women realize their responsibility to the family, to the community, even to the state and to the country; Mrs. Howe, with a recognition of a far off ideal of womanhood, realized her responsibility to the world,—to the Cosmos," Robert intoned. Julia, for Robert, had had the courage to go her own way, to be independent in thought and action. And therein lay her genius. "It is right that she should be venerated; for she was in the truest sense a liberator and a reformer; she pleaded for the rights of womanhood with audacity and eloquence," Robert asserted. "In a century of marvelous achievement she was eminently usefully; she stands for the noblest womanhood and the highest standard of citizenship."[178] Surely Julia would have been pleased with Robert's assessment of her work—pleased not simply because Robert found her praiseworthy, but because Robert saw the audacity, as well as the eloquence, that had been required of her.

In the end, Julia had helped to create new roles and wider purposes for women; she had seen, as Robert phrased it, a far-off ideal of womanhood that could be attained only through the assertion of her own autonomy. Julia had taken a chance; she had dared to raise her voice in ways that her culture and her family found inappropriate for a genteel lady. As Julia understood it, the progress of civilization and increased autonomy for women went hand in hand. Working together, the new woman and the new man would not be ashamed to learn from one another or to aspire to realize capacities and virtues that had heretofore been thought to belong to one gender only. There is no way to appreciate Julia's accomplishments without also recognizing her boldness in defying the gender conventions of the Victorian age. It is, in short, impossible to tell her story of her life—the *whole* story, which includes her inner agonies as well as her magnificent public triumphs—and omit the gritty parts. If she had been merely respectable, she would not have been remarkable; instead, she would have faded quietly into the background of her husband's reputation.

Flossy once argued, the "sacred fires of noble tradition must not perish. To pass on to our descendants the lighted torch received from our predecessors, glowing ever brighter with the fervor inspired by the heroic deeds of the present hour, is for us an imperative duty and a splendid privilege."[179] With great vigor, the Howes attended to their duty, but they believed that the only way to honor their mother was to present a sanitized portrait that robbed Julia's character of its complexity and ignored the considerable agonies she endured in stepping outside the gender constraints prescribed for Victorian women. What I have tried to show in this book is that duty is no less fulfilled by telling the whole story—public and private—of Julia Ward Howe's extraordinary life.

Notes

INTRODUCTION

1. Laura E. Richards, *Two Noble Lives: Samuel Gridley Howe,* Julia Ward Howe (Boston: Dana Estes, 1911), pp. 49, 58.

2. Samuel Gridley Howe to Charles Sumner, 16 March 1844, Howe Family Papers, Houghton Library, bMS Am 2119 (908). The number in parentheses indicates the number used in the Houghton guide to designate the particular document being cited, and the call number identifies the collection's shelf number. Future references to materials from the Houghton will provide the collection's shelf number, the parenthetical document number (if available), and the abbreviation "HL" (Houghton Library). The publication of Houghton materials is by permission of the Houghton Library, Harvard University.

3. Julia Ward Howe to sister Louisa Ward Crawford, ca. 16 February 1846, bMS Am 2119 (450), HL.

4. Julia Ward Howe, "Address in a Prison," n.d., box 1, "Speeches and Writings," Julia Ward Howe Collection, Library of Congress.

5. Julia Ward Howe, 23 April 1865, Julia Ward Howe diaries, bMS Am 2119 (814).

6. Aileen Kraditor, *The Ideas of the Woman Suffrage Movement,* 1890–1920 (New York: Columbia University Press, 1965), p. 262.

7. The literature on separate spheres is enormous. Barbara Welter's 1966 essay in *The American Quarterly* on "The Cult of True Womanhood" (vol. 18, 151–74) was the first in a series of significant discussions on the topic. For an excellent survey of the literature up to 1988, see Linda K. Kerber's "Separate Spheres, Female Worlds, Woman's Place: The Rhetoric of Women's History," in *The Journal of American History,* 75, no. 1 (June 1988): 9–39.

8. For a more detailed discussion of the connection between evangelical piety and the reforming impulse, see my *Advocates of Peace in Antebellum America,* Religion in North America, ed. Catherine Albanese and Stephen Stein (Bloomington: Indiana University Press, 1992), pp. 10–15.

9. Mary Kelley, "At War with Herself: Harriet Beecher Stowe as Woman in Conflict within the Home," *American Studies* 19, no. 2 (fall 1978): 23–37.

10. Ziegler, *The Advocates of Peace,* pp. 59–60; Dorothy C. Bass, "'In Christian Firmness and Christian Meekness': Feminism and Pacifism in Antebellum America," in Clarissa W. Atkinson, Constance H. Buchanan, and Margaret R. Miles, eds., *Immaculate and Powerful: The Female in Sacred Image and Social Reality,* The Harvard Women's Studies in Religion Series (Boston: Beacon Press, 1985), pp. 20–25.

11. An example of such an argument can be found in the Rev. Celia Burleigh's "Spinsters and Step-Mothers" article from 1872. Burleigh asserted that for too long women had assumed that they could exert legitimate influence on the world's development only through their roles of wife and mother. "But God is not partial," Burleigh contended. "The best gifts, like the rain and the sunshine, are there for all. Womanhood is the great fact, not wifehood nor motherhood. . . . I can conceive of no higher mission, no holier trust, no more beneficent ministry than that of woman simply as woman, without reference to wifehood or maternity" (*Woman's Journal* 3, no. 33 [17 August 1872], p. 258).

12. Julia Ward Howe to Louisa Ward Crawford, 31 January 1847, bMS Am 2119 (465), HL.

13. Carolyn G. Chute, *Writing A Woman's Life* (New York: Ballantine, 1988), p. 18.

14. A long but no means exhaustive list numbers over twenty works. Volumes by Maud Howe Elliott include The *Eleventh Hour in the Life of Julia Ward Howe* (Boston: Little, Brown, 1911); *Three Generations* (Boston: Little, Brown, 1923); *Lord Byron's Helmet* (Boston: Houghton Mifflin; Cambridge: Riverside Press, 1927); *John Elliott: The Story of an Artist* (Boston: Houghton Mifflin; Cambridge: Riverside Press, 1930); *My Cousin F. Marion Crawford* (New York: Macmillan, 1934); *Uncle Sam Ward and His Circle* (New York: Macmillan, 1938); *This Was My Newport* (Cambridge, Mass.: Mythology Co./A. Marshall James, 1944); and *Memoirs of the Civil War, 1861–1864* (n.p., n.d.; proceeds of sale given to Newport Chapter of the Red Cross).

For Florence Howe Hall, the list includes *Flossy's Play Days* (Boston: Dana Estes, 1906); *Julia Ward Howe and the Woman Suffrage Movement* (Boston: Dana Estes, 1913; repr., Arno & New York Times, 1969); *The Story of the Battle Hymn of the Republic* (New York: Harper, 1916); and *Memories Grave and Gay* (New York: Harper, 1918).

For Laura E. Richards, see *When I Was Your Age* (Boston: Estes & Lauriat, 1894); *The Julia Ward Howe Birthday Book* (Boston: Lee & Shepard, 1889); *Letters and Journals of Samuel Gridley Howe,* 2 vols. (Boston: Dana Estes, 1906 and 1909); *Two Noble Lives: Samuel Gridley Howe, Julia Ward Howe* (Boston: Dana Estes, 1911); Julia Ward Howe, *The Walk with God,* ed. Laura E. Richards (New York: Dutton, 1919); Laura E. Richards, *Laura Bridgman: The Story of an Opened Door* (New York: Appleton, 1928); *Stepping Westward* (New York: Appleton, 1931); and *Samuel Gridley Howe* (New York: Appleton-Century, 1935).

Maud and Flossy collaborated in writing *Laura Bridgman: Dr. Howe's Famous Pupil and What He Taught Her* (Boston: Little, Brown, 1903). Laura and Maud authored, with assistance from Flossy, the Pulitzer Prize-winning *Julia Ward Howe 1819–1910,* 2 vols. (Houghton Mifflin, 1915). In 1925, Laura produced a revised one-volume version also entitled *Julia Ward Howe, 1819–1910* (Boston: Houghton Mifflin; Cambridge: Riverside Press, 1925). Future references in this work will be to the original two-volume biography, which will be abbreviated as Richards and Elliott, *Julia Ward Howe.*

Other documents were never published. At her death, Laura left behind a manuscript intended for family use that she called "Side Shows." In it, she whimsically noted that she had been writing about her parents for at least forty years and could not shake the habit. She intended "Side Shows" to offer reflections on other family members important to her parents (Yellow House Papers, Gardiner Public Library, collated and typed by Danny D. Smith, October 1989). For more information on the Yellow House Papers, see n. 15.

At her death, Maud left behind several unpublished memoirs. Two of them (*Afternoon Tea* and *Memories of Eighty Years*) offer more reflections on her parents (John Hay Library, Brown University, Ms. 89.13).

15. Danny D. Smith, conversation with author, 1 April 1999. When she wrote her autobiography, *Stepping Westward,* Laura chose to omit a historic meeting with President Theodore Roosevelt in the White House. Roosevelt was a fan of the books for children that Laura had written, particularly of her nonsense verse. He invited her to lunch (along with her brother Harry and his wife Fanny), and while the attorney general looked on in wonder, the president treated his guests to fervent recitations of his favorite passages. Laura reported feeling both embarrassed and pleased. She wrote an account of this memorable occasion for the family log she routinely kept (see "Mammy's Great Frisk," *Family Log,* vol. 3, 1906, Yellow House Papers, Gardiner Public Library, Gardiner, Maine). Danny Smith's point is that Laura felt including such a triumphant story in her autobiography would be boastful and thus inappropriate.

Danny Smith's knowledge of Laura E. Richards and the Howe materials contained in the Yellow House Papers at Colby College and Gardiner Public Library is unsurpassed. In addition to personally knowing several generations of Howes, Smith is also responsible for arranging and cataloging the Yellow House Papers. His *Yellow House Papers: The Laura E. Richards Collection: An Inventory and Historical Guide* (Gardiner, Maine, compiled for the Gardiner Library Association and Colby College, 1991) is the last—and indeed, the only—word on the subject. These archives are of central importance to Howe research; it was from them that Rosalind Richards (Laura's daughter and Julia's granddaughter) culled materials to donate to the Houghton Library at Harvard and to the John Hay Library at Brown University. Access to the Houghton materials was restricted for decades, but is so no longer. The Houghton collections have been and will continue to be crucial to studies of the Howe family. The materials in the Yellow House Papers have received almost no scholarly attention and deserve to come to light. As I was conducting this research, access to the Yellow House Papers at Colby College was severely limited by the availability of library staff. Materials at the Gardiner Public Library in Gardiner, Maine, were freely available to researchers during the library's regular hours of operation. Future references to these collections will be abbreviated as YHPCC for the Colby College papers and YHPGPL for the Gardiner Public Library collection.

There is considerable overlap between the two Yellow House collections. The Howe family employed a secretary to organize their family papers after Julia's death in 1910, and in the process much of the family correspondence was typed and duplicated. The Gardiner Public Library contains many typed copies of original correspondence housed in the Yellow House Papers at Colby College. Whenever it was possible to gain access to the materials in the Colby collection, I have quoted from original Yellow House sources; in every instance that I have cited copies of the originals, I have indicated that fact in the notes. A further note on citations to Yellow House materials: to aid other scholars, I have provided informal names for each file folder from which I have cited information. These folder names are not official titles, but they summarize the contents of each folder and enable persons searching through the various record groups to easily locate the materials cited in these notes. Those wishing a more systematic description of the contents of the Yellow House record groups, as well as of the individual file folders in each group, should consult Smith's *Yellow House Papers.* Finally, as this book was going to press, I learned that the Yellow House Papers at Colby College were being transferred to the Maine Historical Society in Portland. Once the collection has been placed there, scholars will have unrestricted access to it, which should prove a boon for Howe studies.

16. Hall, *Memories Grave and Gay,* p. 342.

17. Richards, *Stepping Westward,* p. 329.

18. Laura E. Richards to Annie Howe Mailliard, 6 August 1886, bMS Am 2119 (1605), HL.

19. President Nicholas Butler of Columbia University to Maud Howe Elliott, 4 June 1917, box 1, folder 25, Maud Howe Elliott Papers, John Hay Library, Brown University.

20. Linda S. Schearing, Gonzaga University, Spokane, Wash., conversation with author, 20 November 2001.

21. Surprisingly little scholarly work on Julia Ward Howe exists. The most important book-length studies began with Louise Tharp's *Three Saints and A Sinner* (Boston: Little, Brown, 1956). The first outsider to gain access to the Howe family papers, Tharp provided biographical portraits of Julia, her sisters Louisa and Annie, and their brother Sam. Tharp's book continues to serve as a valuable resource, although its usefulness is limited by two factors. First, Tharp did not use footnotes, and second, her freedom to cite Howe family materials was limited by Rosalind Richards (one of Julia's great-granddaughters), who served as executor of the Howe literary estate in the 1950s.

The most comprehensive biography to date is Deborah Pickman Clifford's *Mine Eyes Have Seen the Glory: A Biography of Julia Ward Howe* (Boston: Little, Brown, 1979). Clifford's book is out of print, as is a more recent study that considers Julia's life up to 1869, Mary H. Grant's *Private Woman, Public Person: An Account of the Life of Julia Ward Howe from 1819 to 1868* (Brooklyn: Carlson Publications, 1994). Grant's book was a revision of her dissertation, which also spawned a fine article in Mary Kelley's *Woman's Being, Woman's Place: Female Identity and Vocation in American History* (Boston: G.K. Hall, 1979) entitled "Domestic Experience and Feminist Theory: The Case of Julia Ward Howe," pp. 220–32. The most recent study is Gary Williams's *Hungry Heart: The Literary Emergence of Julia Ward Howe* (Amherst: University of Massachusetts Press, 1999).

All of the volumes listed above are helpful in entering the world of Julia Ward Howe. With Williams and Grant, I share a desire to analyze the public/private split that appears in so much of her work. All three of us have discovered much autobiographical material (whether acknowledged or masked) in Julia's public papers.

Clifford is the only author who used footnotes (crucial to a study that depends on archival materials) to consider Julia's entire life. Grant is the only author to provide a lengthy consideration of Julia's philosophical lectures from the 1860s. Williams is the only author to analyze Julia's works from the vantage point of a literary critic. While Williams's study covers only the years from 1835 to 1857, his attention to detail is exceptional, and his consideration of Julia's early works of poetry constitutes the current standard in the field. His book is essential reading.

CHAPTER ONE

1. Richards, *Two Noble Lives: Samuel Gridley Howe, Julia Ward Howe*, p. 45.

2. Julia Ward Howe, *Reminiscences*, pp. 13, 45–48, 60; Richards and Elliott, *Julia Ward Howe*, vol. 1, pp. 32, 41–45.

3. Julia Ward Howe, *Reminiscences*, pp. 4–10; Richards and Elliott, *Julia Ward Howe*, vol. 1, p. 17.

4. Julia Ward Howe, *Reminiscences*, pp. 8–10.

5. Julia Ward Howe, typescript draft of "Religious Education for the Young," Boston, April 1902, bMS Am 2119 (812).

6. Richards and Elliott, *Julia Ward Howe*, vol. 1, p. 21.

7. Julia Ward Howe, *Reminiscences,* pp. 12–13, 18; Richards and Elliott, *Julia Ward Howe,* vol. 1, pp. 21–22.

8. Richards and Elliott, *Julia Ward Howe,* vol. 1, p. 29; Julia Ward Howe, *Reminiscences,* pp. 14–18.

9. Richards, *Two Noble Lives,* p. 45. The younger sister, Annie, agreed to write poetry, but Louisa refused to relinquish her toys.

10. Richards and Elliott, *Julia Ward Howe,* vol. 1, p. 31.

11. Ibid., p. 31.

12. Ibid., p. 33.

13. Julia Ward Howe, *Reminiscences,* pp. 43–44. Julia's brother Sam had also considered himself a scholar of note. Convinced that he possessed extraordinary mathematical gifts, Sam persuaded his father to purchase an expensive mathematical library for him, assuring a friend, "Before all else I desire that a history of mathematics shall crown my career, and perpetuate the name of my father. There lies my life's work." Sam also regarded himself a poet and for a time functioned as Henry Wadsworth Longfellow's literary agent. Unlucky in love—his first wife died within two years of their marriage, and his second marriage resulted in separation—Sam suffered periodic business reversals and eventually, after false starts that included gold mining in the West, become a Washington lobbyist renowned for serving exquisite meals. He never wrote his history of mathematics (Maud Howe Elliott, *Uncle Sam Ward and His Circle,* pp. 51, 133, 150, 155, 170–71). See also Tharp, *Three Saints and a Sinner,* and various newspaper obituaries, including the *New York Times,* 20 May 1884; *New York Tribune,* 20 May 1884; and *New York World,* 20 May 1884.

14. Richards and Elliott, *Julia Ward Howe,* vol. 1, p. 46. Julia was willing to endure physical discomfort to enjoy her "precious time." Daughter Laura remembered that in their summer home in Lawton Valley, near Newport, Rhode Island, Julia "worked all morning . . . in the strange little place of her choice . . . she thought a north light essential for study; the only north light to be had in conjunction with anything approaching quiet was at the top of the attic stairs. . . . in a place some six feet square she set her little pine table, shut the door at the foot of the stairs, and with a skylight above her, and wasps buzzing around her, wrote her five-act drama, 'Hippolytus,' for Edwin Booth and Charlotte Cushman. . . . The heat in the attic must have been excessive, the wasps I know were myriad; I can see them now crawling, and hear them buzzing, all about her paper, but she never faltered till the morning stint was done" (Richards, *Stepping Westward,* pp. 31–32). Daughter Maud observed that all the children knew that if the house were to catch fire, it was their first duty to save the black walnut chest in which Julia kept her manuscripts (Elliott, *This Was My Newport,* pp. 60–61).

15. Julia Ward Howe, *Reminiscences,* pp. 43–46, 57–60; Richards and Elliott, *Julia Ward Howe,* vol. 1, pp. 136–37.

16. Richards and Elliott, *Julia Ward Howe,* vol. 1, p. 47.

17. Elliott, *Uncle Sam Ward and His Circle,* pp. 183–84.

18. Julia Ward Howe, *Reminiscences,* p. 46; Richards and Elliott, *Julia Ward Howe,* vol. 1, p. 48.

19. Elliott, *Uncle Sam Ward and His Circle,* pp. 51, 150.

20. Julia Ward Howe, *Reminiscences,* pp. 47–49; Richards and Elliott, *Julia Ward Howe,* vol. 1, pp. 57, 49.

21. Elliott, *Uncle Sam Ward and His Circle,* pp. 175–77.

22. Ibid., p. 183.

23. Ibid., p. 177.

24. Richards and Elliott, *Julia Ward Howe*, vol. 1, p. 22.

25. Julia Ward Howe, *Reminiscences,* pp. 65–66; Richards and Elliott, *Julia Ward Howe,* vol. 1, p. 50.

26. Richards and Elliott, *Julia Ward Howe*, vol. 1, pp. 47–48.

27. Ibid., pp. 50–52.

28. Ibid.

29. Ibid., p. 65. See Williams (*Hungry Heart,* pp. 16–18) for an excellent discussion of the significance of Julia's early published works, which consisted of a review of Lamartine's *Jocelyn* in the *Literary and Theological Review* 3 (December 1836): 559–72, and a review of John Sullivan Dwight's *Select Minor Poems of Goethe and Schiller* in *New York Review* 4 (1839): 393–400. Julia was also interested in publishing her poetry, a scheme that her brother Sam took seriously. See Williams, pp. 18–23, and a letter from Julia to her brother Sam, dated Wednesday, 4th, n.d., in *Women's Studies Manuscript Collections from the Schlesinger Library, Radcliffe College,* Series I: Woman's Suffrage, Part A: National Leaders, Julia Ward Howe Family, series 1, reel 8, no. 14, M-133, MC 272. Future references to this microfilm collection will be identified as Women's Studies Manuscript Collection, Julia Ward Howe Family, Schlesinger Library. Appropriate reel numbers will also be noted. Publication of these materials is by permission of the Schlesinger Library, Radcliffe Institute, Harvard University.

Julia's father was as unimpressed with the usefulness of her musical talents as with that of her literary accomplishments. When her brother Sam urged Samuel Ward, Sr., to purchase a new piano in the summer of 1839, Samuel answered: "I confess I lay very little stress on Julia's proficiency in music. It is but an accomplishment, it neither heals the sick, nor feeds the hungry, nor consoles the afflicted. It will not make her a better wife or companion" (Elliott, *Uncle Sam Ward and His Circle,* p. 186).

30. Julia Ward Howe, *Reminiscences,* pp. 48, 62–63; Richards and Elliott, *Julia Ward Howe,* vol. 1, pp. 66–67.

31. Ibid.

32. Julia Ward Howe, *Reminiscences,* p. 62; Richards and Elliott, *Julia Ward Howe,* vol. 1, pp. 68–69.

33. Richards and Elliott, *Julia Ward Howe*, vol. 1, pp. 57–58.

34. Ibid., p. 59.

35. Julia protested to Sam in one letter: "What has possessed you with the idea that at twenty-two I am not able to take care of myself and behave myself with propriety? I really want to laugh at you [and Uncle John] for a couple of old grannies . . . cannot I be trusted away from the shadow of your wing?" But Julia also gave signs of wanting to shepherd her younger sisters, writing Sam from Washington, D.C., in March 1841: "This is an evil place, I would not have my sisters even breathe its air. . . . Never did I so truly feel the blessing of our sacred, private home, as now" (Elliott, *Uncle Sam Ward and His Circle,* pp. 227–28).

36. Richards and Elliott, *Julia Ward Howe*, vol. 1, pp. 70–71. The letter quoted by the authors was undated; they assigned it a date of 1842. Probably they should have chosen 1841, as subsequent notes will explain.

37. Julia Ward Howe to her sisters, Saturday, n.d., bMS Am 2119 (382), HL. This would appear to be Julia's first encounter with her future husband. She says that at this dance "I met the Chevalier there, for the first time, but did not talk to him, as he does not dance, and went away early." Williams dates this letter to February 1841 (*Hungry Heart,* p. 24). See the next note for a fuller discussion.

38. Julia Ward Howe, *Reminiscences,* p. 81. Her daughters' biography gives the date for this visit as 1842 (*Julia Ward Howe,* vol. 1, p. 74), but the *Reminiscences* state 1841. Tharp (*Three Saints and A Sinner,* p. 80), Clifford (*Mine Eyes Have Seen the Glory,* p. 52), Grant (*Private Woman, Public Person,* p. 57), and Williams (*Hungry Heart,* p. 25) also set the year as 1841. The confusion in the biography probably related to Julia's correspondence style—in the headings of her letters she rarely recorded the year in which they were written, thus compelling later readers to reconstruct the dates as best they can.

39. Richards, *Samuel Gridley Howe,* pp. 4, 71.

40. Ibid., pp. 74–75.

41. Julia's daughters' biography describes the visit to the institution as the initial meeting and omits reference to Julia and Chev's encounter the previous winter. Julia's autobiography does not indicate when she first met Chev. But the first scene with him that it describes is the visit to Perkins Institution, when he made such an impression on Julia as he galloped on his black horse. Clifford (p. 51) and Grant (p. 57) consider this to be their initial meeting; Williams (p. 24) opts for the earlier encounter discussed above—in February 1841, when Julia met Chev at a ball, only to learn that he did not dance. Williams's opinion seems to me to be the correct one, although it is easy to see how the dramatic encounter at the Institute better served the literary purposes at work in the biography and the autobiography. In her book *Memories Grave and Gay,* daughter Florence Howe Hall described her parents' initial encounter under the following heading: "The Romance of Philanthropy Causes the First Meeting of Dr. Samuel Gridley Howe and Julia Ward."

42. Howe invariably chose black horses. He was, as his daughter Laura remembered, "the ideal of the perfect rider. . . . Our horses usually black; always swift; their names were 'Breeze,' 'Blast,' and the like, and they were required to live up to them." The stories Howe's children told about him abounded in feats of exquisite skill with horses, as they depicted Howe leaping about (much like John Wayne in *Stagecoach)* to save innocent bystanders from runaway teams (Richards, *Samuel Gridley Howe,* pp. 185–86).

43. Richards and Elliott, *Julia Ward Howe,* vol. 1, p. 75.

44. Julia Ward to Sam Ward, 8 February 1843, Julia Ward Howe Letters (bMS Am 2214 [168]), Houghton Library. Hereafter designated as bMS Am 2214, HL.

45. Sam Ward to Julia Ward Howe, 22 February 1843, bMS Am 2119 (1777), HL. Maud Elliott Howe quoted this letter on p. 376 of *Uncle Sam Ward and His Circle.*

46. Julia Ward Howe, *Reminiscences,* pp. 82–83.

47. Sam Ward to Samuel Gridley Howe, 4 March 1843, bMS Am 2119 (778), HL.

48. Julia Ward Howe to [Uncle] John Ward, Tuesday, n.p., n.d., bMS Am 2215 (410), HL.

49. Cornelius Felton, one of Howe's closest friends, wrote Sam Ward in August 1842 that the Chevalier thinks "as I do that your incomparable sister writes extraordinarily natural poems with high intellectual culture, and that all this is lighted up with a play of fancy and wit which makes her conversation the most brilliant and delightful entertainment a man of sense can ever hope to enjoy" (Elliott, *Uncle Sam Ward and His Circle,* p. 356).

50. Julia Ward Howe, *Reminiscences,* pp. 83, 151. Laura Richards commented on her father's work at the Institute: "First, last and always, he must direct every detail, watch over every child, teach, admonish, cheer, and comfort." A blind man named Francis Campbell was Chev's chief assistant for eleven years at the Institute, and Chev controlled him as well. Laura remembered Campbell as "an indomitable man, something of whose character appears in his climbing the Matterhorn, stone-blind as he was, for a holiday exercise. Yet he could be dominated." Her father was the man for that job (Richards, *Samuel Gridley Howe,* pp. 77, 110–111).

51. Sam Ward to Samuel Gridley Howe, 4 April 1843, bMS Am 2119 (1782), HL.

52. Elliott and Richards, *Julia Ward Howe,* vol. 1, pp. 75–76.

53. Samuel Gridley Howe to Charles Sumner, n.d., n.p., record group 20, folder "Correspondence between SGH and JWH," YHPCC. See Williams (*Hungry Heart,* pp. 40–65) for a discussion of Chev's entreaties to Sumner to fall in love with a woman.

54. Samuel Gridley Howe to Julia Ward, n.d., Boston, record group 20, folder "Correspondence between SGH and JWH," YHPCC.

55. Samuel Gridley Howe to Julia Ward, Sunday, n.d., n.p., record group 20, folder "Correspondence between SGH and JWH," YHPCC.

56. Samuel Gridley Howe to Julia Ward, Saturday morning, n.d., n.p., record group 20, folder "Correspondence between SGH and JWH," YHPCC.

57. Samuel Gridley Howe to Julia Ward, Friday, 2 p.m., n.d., n.p., record group 20, folder "Correspondence between SGH and JWH," YHPCC.

58. Julia Ward to Sam Ward, Tuesday morning, n.d., bMS Am 2214 (168), HL. Quoted in Richards and Elliott, *Julia Ward Howe,* vol. 1, pp. 77–78.

59. Richards and Elliott, *Julia Ward Howe,* vol. 1, p. 99.

Chapter Two

1. Julia Ward Howe to Eliza Ward Francis, 1843, bMS Am 2119 (395), HL. Chev was working to separate Julia in one important way, at least, from the Wards, as his letter written prior the wedding indicated: "As touching the ceremony, have you decided? This only would I whisper in thy private ear, that be it morning or evening I think we had better leave your house soon after . . . we can . . . run away to Philadelphia a few days, or up to West Point. But still, I incline to think that my idea of leaving Bond St. for quarters at some Hotel from which we can start . . . the next morning on our expedition will please you better than remaining there: I think you would like the privacy of a crowd, in steam Boat, Car, or Hotel, to being the observed of all observed at home" (Wednesday, n.d., n.p., record group 20, folder "Correspondence between SGH and JWH," YHPCC).

2. Julia Ward Howe, *Reminiscences,* pp. 84–85, 88–89.

3. Julia Ward Howe to Louisa Ward, 12 May 1843, bMS Am 2215 (381), HL.

4. Julia Ward Howe, "La Veille des Noees" and "Mary's Tears," from a bound set of poems dated 1843 and titled "Life is strange, and full of change." Found in a folder labeled "Poems" in box 3 of a collection called "Julia Ward Howe: Three Boxes of Poetry," bMS Am 2214 (321), HL.

5. Julia Ward Howe, "Sailing" and "The Past Lives," "Life is strange, and full of change," bMS Am 2214 (321), HL.

6. Julia Ward Howe, "The present is dead," from "Life is strange, and full of change," bMS Am 2214 (321), HL. The poem's ending indicated that Julia was not overly optimistic: "Tis true, our blended life on earth is sweet, / But can our souls within one heaven rest? / I am content to live, content to die, / For life and death to me are little worth; I cannot know, through all eternity / A grief more deep than those I knew on earth."

7. Richards and Elliott, *Julia Ward Howe,* vol. 1, pp. 82–88; Julia Ward Howe, *Reminiscences,* pp. 91–104.

8. Julia Ward Howe, *Reminiscences,* p. 110; Richards and Elliott, *Julia Ward Howe,* vol. 1, pp. 85–86; Richards, *Samuel Gridley Howe,* p. 138.

9. In a letter to Louisa written on August 4, 1843, Julia spoke of domestic strife, complaining that Chev had hired a Greek servant against her will: "I wished very much to have had no servant, but Howe rather liked this fellow, and engaged him without my consent." Julia also hinted at bigger news: "Can you keep a secret? but no, I am afraid to trust you—I will tell you in my next." The news was, of course, of Julia's pregnancy (bMS Am 2215 (382), HL).

10. Richards and Elliott, *Julia Ward Howe,* vol. 1, pp. 95–96; Julia Ward Howe, *Reminiscences,* pp. 122, 128, 133.

11. Richards and Elliott, *Julia Ward Howe,* vol. 1, p. 96.

12. Julia Ward Howe, no title (though Dublin is designated as the place of origin). Found in "Life is strange, and full of change," bMS Am 2214 (321), HL.

13. "The dawning of light," a poem begun in Rome and finished in England. In a folder labeled "Poems" in box 3 of bMS Am 2214 (321), HL.

Julia's poems of emotional turmoil penned in the early months of her marriage were in sharp contrast to a series of letters that Chev wrote to her during occasional separations during the honeymoon. He repeatedly pointed to his joy at their union and even ventured to apologize for being occasionally irascible. In a letter written six months after their wedding, Chev said, "Julia, it gives me inexpressible happiness to find that my heart yearns so strongly towards thee. . . . But how your letter made me ashamed! You speak of what I have done to erase certain slight spots which diminished the beauty of your nature! alas, dear love, how many times since we parted have I reproached myself in that very particular; how have I regretted that I ever expressed the slightest impatience. . . . " Still, even in these tender times, he could not help but try to remake her. "I do not promise any thing, much less promise not to try to make the crystal of your soul still clearer, but I will try to do all that my imperfect nature allows to prevent the slightest cloud concealing for a moment the ardour of my affection. . . . I have faith firm as in nature's laws that we shall be ever happy together" (Paris, Friday 28, record group 20, folder "Correspondence between SGH and JWH," YHPCC; additional letters in this folder—typically signed "Husband"—continue in this vein).

There are signs that Chev's absences also made Julia's feelings toward him warmer. In a poem written in Milan entitled "Widowhood and exile," she mourned, "My dearest love my side has left," and asked God to "Soon give me back to my dearest home, / And my husband back to me." In "Life is strange, and full of change," bMS Am 2214 (321), HL.

14. Samuel Gridley Howe to Charles Sumner, 8 November 1843, bMS Am 2119 (897), HL.

15. Julia Ward Howe, *Reminiscences,* pp. 81–143, reference to Julia Romana, p. 128; letter to John Ward, 12 March 1844, bMS Am 2119 (870), HL. Though receiving just a paragraph's attention in Julia's autobiography, Julia Romana's birth was relatively well documented. Julia passed over the births of Florence, Laura, and Maud entirely and failed to mention her sons Harry and Sammy at all.

16. Samuel Gridley Howe to Charles Sumner, 16 and 20 March 1844, bMS Am 2119 (908). Sumner was Chev's dearest friend, and Julia at times despaired that the two of them made a better couple than she and Chev did. "As Julia often says," Chev mentioned to Sumner, "Sumner ought to have been a woman and you to have married her" (11 September 1844, bMS Am 2119 [920]). Gary Williams has aptly observed the triangulated nature of this relationship. Sumner and Chev had been accustomed to spending long hours in each other's company; Chev's marriage to Julia upset that arrangement. Chev often urged Sumner to marry and find happiness as he had with Julia. And Julia undoubtedly was vexed at the special place that Sumner held in Chev's affections (Williams, *Hungry Heart,* pp. 40–65). Ultimately, of course, the emotional dis-

tance that characterized Chev's relationship to Julia had more complex roots than Chev's affection for Sumner. Had there been no Sumner, Julia's estrangement from Chev would have nonetheless been a central feature of their marriage.

17. I have found only three instances in which Julia adopted such language. After returning from her honeymoon, Julia went to New York to visit her family and to join in the debate about her sister Louisa's tangled love life. (Louisa fell in love often, and the argument among family members at this point was whether or not she should marry the artist Thomas Crawford. She did.) In a letter to Chev, Julia indicated that she had left baby Julia Romana behind and begged him to send the baby to her in New York. "I am half wild without my baby—oh Chev, if you love me send her on—the journey is one of little or no exposure," Julia pleaded. She added, "I am suffering with my breast, & think that the sudden weaning will do me no good. I have to extract the milk artificially. I cannot bear to dry it up. I must nurse her again, little angel! it kills me to think of her as no longer dependant [sic] on me. . . . I am not alive, till I have her in my arms once more." Julia sent another letter soon, thanking Chev for sending Julia Romana to her. "Baby is wonderfully well," Julia reported, "laughs all day, and is much admired. I have her in my arms constantly, and love her better every moment." Neither letter is dated, though the first one gives "Tuesday" as the day of its composition. See record group 20, folder "Correspondence between SGH and JWH," YHPCC.

Finally, in a poem Julia wrote for Julia Romana in 1845, she claimed to weep "tears of rapture" at the mere sight of her baby, and observed, "How paltry are the ties I break / To give myself to thee alone. / How poor the pleasures I forsake, / To make my heart and life thine own" (box 3 of "Julia Ward Howe: Three Boxes of Poetry," bMS Am 2214 [321], HL).

18. Julia Ward Howe, *Reminiscences,* pp. 137–38. Laura Richards reported her father as giving a longer answer: "My dear Miss Florence, it would be unusual, and in England whatever is unusual is apt to be thought unsuitable; but I say to you, go forward, if you have a vocation for that way of life; act up to your inspiration, and you will find that there is never anything unbecoming or unladylike in doing your duty for the good of others. Choose your path, go on with it, wherever it may lead you, and God be with you!" (Richards and Elliott, *Julia Ward Howe,* vol. 1, p. 97; Richards, *Samuel Gridley Howe,* pp. 144–46).

19. Richards and Elliott, *Julia Ward Howe,* vol. 1, pp. 103; Julia Ward Howe, *Reminiscences,* p. 151.

20. Richards and Elliott, *Julia Ward Howe,* vol. 1, p. 102.

21. Julia Ward Howe to Annie Mailliard, Saturday 13, n.d., bMS Am 2119 (334). Daughter Laura later wrote that, in the first year of her parents' marriage, Chev was gone so late to a meeting that Julia assumed he was dead. She sent Chev's assistant on the two-mile walk to town to look for him (or his body). When Chev was discovered, he was amazed that Julia was worried about him (Richards, *Stepping Westward,* p. 15).

22. Julia Ward Howe, *Reminiscences,* p. 150.

23. Ibid., pp. 214–15; Richards and Elliott, *Julia Ward Howe,* vol. 1, p. 110.

24. Julia Ward Howe to Louisa Ward Crawford, 15 May 1847, bMS Am 2119 (467).

25. Julia Ward Howe scrapbook, pp. 31–32, bMS Am 2119 (815).

26. Julia Ward Howe to Louisa Ward Crawford, 31 January 1846, bMS Am 2119 (449).

27. Although the family did not sell Green Peace until after Chev's death, they did not live there exclusively. Laura remarked, "My father had a passion for change, and we were whisked about from place to place, often from motives that we never knew." Between moves, she claimed, they often lived at the Institute for long periods. Living at the Institute spared Chev the two-mile

ride from Green Peace to his office. Julia found the frequent moves disruptive, and when the girls were older, the moves occasionally had comic results when bewildered suitors knocked on the door only to find to their astonishment that the family had vanished overnight (Richards, *Stepping Westward,* pp. 12, 55).

28. She followed her dramatic declaration of "my voice is still frozen to silence" with the claim that "I am quite happy, nowadays my children are a great delight to me." The juxtaposition of two such variant statements is striking, though it was not unusual in Julia's letters.

29. Julia Ward Howe to Louisa Ward Crawford, 5 November 1844, and 23 July 1845, bMS Am 2119 (411, 418).

30. Julia Ward Howe to Louisa Ward Crawford, bMS Am 2119 (414). Reprinted in part in Richards and Elliott, *Julia Ward Howe,* vol. 1, p. 116, and dated November 1845.

31. Julia Ward Howe to Annie Ward Mailliard, ca. 1846; Julia Ward Howe to Louisa Ward Crawford, ca. August 1846, bMS Am 2119 (440, 545). The letter to Annie is partially reproduced in Richards and Elliott, vol. 1, *Julia Ward Howe,* pp. 117–18.

32. Julia Ward Howe to Louisa Ward Crawford, ca. 16 February 1846, bMS Am 2119 (450).

33. Julia Ward Howe to Louisa Ward Crawford, 13 June 1848, bMS Am 2119 (486).

34. According to family lore, Chev had hoped for a son when his second daughter was born. Disappointed to greet another little girl, he announced to Julia, "I will forgive you, if you will name her for Florence Nightingale!" (Richards and Elliott, *Julia Ward Howe,* vol. 1, p. 112).

35. Richards and Elliott, *Julia Ward Howe,* vol. 1, p. 109.

36. Julia Ward Howe to Annie Ward Mailliard, ca. 1846, bMS Am 2119 (439).

37. Julia Ward Howe to Louisa Ward Crawford, 31 January 1847, bMS Am 2119 (465).

38. Julia Ward Howe to Louisa Ward Crawford, 20 September 1847, bMS Am 2215 (383), HL.

39. Julia Ward Howe to Louisa Ward Crawford, 23 January 1848, bMS Am 2215 (383), HL.

40. Samuel Gridley Howe to Louisa Ward Crawford, 5 April 1848, bMS Am 2119 (998).

41. Julia Ward Howe to Louisa Ward Crawford, 18 April 1848, bMS Am 2119 (485); partially reprinted in Richards and Elliott, *Julia Ward Howe,* vol. 1, p. 131.

42. Julia Ward Howe to Annie Ward Mailliard, 1850; Julia Ward Howe to Louisa Ward Crawford, ca. 25 January 1850, bMS Am 2119 (525, 583).

43. Samuel Gridley Howe to Louisa Ward Crawford, 1 March 1850, bMS Am 2119 (1024). An editor's note identifies this letter as Chev's only announcement of Laura's birth.

44. Julia Ward Howe to Annie Ward Mailliard, March 1850; Julia Ward Howe to Louisa Ward Crawford, May 1850, bMS Am 2119 (528, 529), HL.

45. Julia Ward Howe to Louisa Ward Crawford, 11 November 1845, bMS Am 2119 (414), HL; partially reprinted in Richards and Elliott, *Julia Ward Howe,* vol. 1, pp. 115–17. This was the letter, quoted earlier, in which Julia mocked Chev and Sumner for pitying unmarried women. At the end, Chev added his own note. "I would not have you judge her feeling by what she says just now because she is a little homesick for N.Y.," he told Louisa. "We are getting on pretty well, but looking forward to the time when we shall be better."

46. Julia Ward Howe to Louisa Ward Crawford, 17 May 1847, bMS Am 2119 (467), HL; quoted in Richards and Elliott, *Julia Ward Howe,* vol. 1, pp. 125–27.

47. Julia Ward Howe to Samuel Gridley Howe, 22 April, n.d., bMS Am 2119 (347), HL.

48. Julia Ward Howe to Louisa Ward Crawford, 13 June 1848, bMS Am 2119 (486), HL.

49. Julia Ward Howe to Annie Ward Mailliard, ca. 8 November 1854, bMS Am 2119 (559), HL. Julia asked Annie to take care of her children if she did not survive childbirth and instructed Annie to see that her manuscripts were given to Ripley.

50. Julia Ward Howe to Louisa Ward Crawford, ca. 31 November 1847, bMS Am 2119 (476), HL.

51. Julia Ward Howe to Annie Ward Maillaird, ca. 27 December 1854, bMS Am 2119 (560), HL.

52. Chev told Longfellow in 1845 that he could feel his life slipping remorselessly away; in 1850, he assured Longfellow that there was little time left to him (Williams, *Hungry Heart*, pp. 78, 244).

53. Julia Ward Howe to Louisa Ward Crawford, 4 March 1845; Julia Ward Howe to Annie Ward Mailliard, ca. 1846, bMS Am 2119 (422, 441), HL.

54. Richards, *Samuel Gridley Howe*, pp. 184–85.

55. Julia Ward Howe to Samuel Gridley Howe, October 1846; Julia Ward Howe to Annie Ward Mailliard, ca. 1846, bMS Am 2119 (457, 441), HL.

56. Richards and Elliott, *Julia Ward Howe*, vol. 1, p. 121.

57. Julia Ward Howe to Annie Ward Maillaird, ca. 12 January 1856, bMS Am 2119 (572), HL.

58. Julia Ward Howe to Samuel Gridley Howe, ca. 1846, bMS Am 2119 (376), HL.

59. Julia Ward Howe to Samuel Gridley Howe, ca. 1846 or 1847, bMS Am 2119 (463), HL.

60. Julia Ward Howe to Annie Ward Mailliard, 30 December 1860, bMS Am 2119 (590), HL.

61. For full bibliographical information on these books, see the Introduction, n. 14.

Ironically, some historians have inadvertently entered into the Howes' bickering over which of them was to be dominant by noting that Julia's brilliance overwhelmed Chev's. In a popular biography of Chev, John Jennings ended his book with Chev proposing marriage to Julia. Jennings was no fan of Julia's. When he wrote scenes depicting Julia's reading her poetry to Chev, Jennings commented, "the true marvel was that he could bear it." With Chev's marriage, however, Jennings argued, the rest of his life "might best be left in shadow." Jennings concluded by observing, "there is much beyond that is not told . . . [but] all this seems to me to be far more her story than his. All the rest is somehow overshadowed by Julia" (*Banner Against the Wind* [Boston, Toronto: Little, Brown, 1954], pp. 286–88, 297).

Lucia Gilbert Calhoun, who wrote a biographical sketch of Julia in 1869, asserted that Julia's resentment of Chev began on their honeymoon. "In England, the petted child, the young heiress, the idol of her own circle, the haughty belle found that her only claim to social distinction was her husband's fame," Calhoun argued. "To a woman of her strong, self-centred nature, of her conscious power, and stately pride, this acceptance of her as the appendage of another, this carelessness of what sovereignty might be in herself was an abasement as bitter as salutary. She had dreamed of literary fame; but this sudden humiliation, the new cares, the alien interests that crowded upon her, postponed her career for years" ("Mrs. Julia Ward Howe," in James Parton, Horace Greeley, et al., *Eminent Women of the Age; Being Narratives of the Lives and Deeds of the Most Prominent Women of the Present Generation* [Hartford, Conn.: S.M. Betts, 1869], pp. 623–24).

62. Richards, *Samuel Gridley Howe*, pp. 135, 178–83.

63. Ibid., p. 135; Richards and Elliott, *Julia Ward Howe*, vol. 1, pp. 104–5.

64. Richards, *Samuel Gridley Howe*, p. 183.

65. Ibid., pp. 182–83, 185.

66. Richards and Elliott, *Julia Ward Howe*, vol. 1, pp. 146–48.

67. Ibid., pp. 148, 150.

68. Ibid., pp. 148–50.

69. Richards, *Two Noble Lives*, p. 58.

70. Richards, *Stepping Westward,* pp. 30–31.

71. Richards, *When I Was Your Age,* p. 102.

72. Richards, *Samuel Gridley Howe,* p. 188.

73. Richards and Elliott, *Julia Ward Howe,* vol. 1, pp. 154–55, 166.

74. Laura E. Richards to Annie Ward Mailliard, 6 August 1886, bMS Am 2119 (1605), HL.

75. Richards, *When I Was Your Age,* p. 210.

CHAPTER THREE

1. Almost no one had read this novel—perhaps only three people—at the time I drafted this chapter. The manuscript resides (with pages and even some sections out of order) in one of the Houghton collections of Howe material that is largely uncatalogued (bMS Am 2214 [320]), and can be found in a folder in box 4. A librarian or editor with the initials A. W. C., or possibly A. M. C., at an unknown point in the past wrote a note on the manuscript's first page suggesting an 1847 date of composition, based on the letter from Julia to Louisa that I have cited above.

Deborah Clifford worked in the bMS Am 2214 collection in researching her 1979 biography of Julia Ward Howe. She initialed the folders she examined and appears not to have read this particular folder, since it is not initialed. She can hardly be blamed—she was working in collections that contain an incredible variety of materials, from clumps of hair found on the floor of the Houghton and preserved because they might have belonged to Julia Ward Howe, to folders full of scrap paper that Julia had saved for no apparent reason. Because the pages of the opening section, as filed, were out of order, the manuscript would have been utterly mystifying to any reader for at least the first hour.

Mary Grant's 1982 doctoral dissertation was the first work to discuss the manuscript. Faced with a complicated—and at times bizarre—text, Grant noted that the novel came "as something of a shock. Not all biographers get their subject's fantasy life handed to them in such direct form. The possible interpretations seem both limitless and limited" (*Private Woman, Public Person,* 1994, p. 227). Grant clearly recognized the endless layers of meaning that such a work of literature suggested.

Gary Williams's treatment of the Laurence story in his 1999 *Hungry Heart* sought to tease out those layers. He saw the novel as a crucial stage in what he called Julia's "literary emergence," and provided valuable information on the probable literary and artistic antecedents of the manuscript. He raised a series of perceptive interpretive issues in a lengthy discussion (pp. 80–105, 235–41) that stands as the most detailed and sophisticated analysis the Laurence story has ever received. Readers interested in the story of Laurence should begin by consulting *Hungry Heart* and a forthcoming edition of the novel (by the University of Nebraska Press) edited by Williams, which contains his excellent preface, "Introduction to Julia Ward Howe's Laurence Manuscript."

2. Williams, *Hungry Heart,* pp. 16, 96–98; draft version, "Introduction to Julia Ward Howe's Laurence Manuscript," pp. 5–14; Julia Ward Howe, *Reminiscences,* p. 58; Julia Ward Howe, "George Sand," *Atlantic Monthly* 8 (November 1861): 514; Maud Howe Elliott, *Uncle Sam Ward and His Circle,* pp. 342–43. Williams pointed to Balzac's *Seraphita* (1834–35) and Theophile Gautier's *Mademoiselle de Maupin* as particular influences on Julia's novel. See draft version, "Introduction to Julia Ward Howe's Laurence Manuscript," pp. 7–9.

3. Williams, *Hungry Heart,* pp. 96–98; draft version, "Introduction to Julia Ward Howe's Laurence Manuscript," pp. 11–14. Williams concluded in the latter that "Lamartine, Sand, Balzac,

possibly even . . . the louche Theophile Gautier . . . provided certain specifics—a character's name, a narrative circumstance, a theme—for a story that, in 1836, she certainly could not have foreseen the need to write."

4. Julia Ward Howe to Louisa Ward Crawford, 15 May 1847, bMS Am 2119 (476), HL.

5. Julia's 1843 diary—which she apparently used after 1843 as a scrapbook—has a number of passages from the novel (including the poem about Eva to Rafael that Julia sent to Louisa) pasted into it. Also pasted into the diary is a passage apparently taken from a letter Julia wrote. The intended recipient remains unknown, but in this fragment Julia claimed that her "pen had been unusually busy during the last year." She conceded, "the golden tide is now at it's [sic] ebb," but explained that she had been "deeply engaged for three months past" in a "stranded wreck of a novel, or rather story." She noted that she had written not "a moral and fashionable work" but rather "the strange history of a strange being." She did not know, Julia concluded, if she would ever publish or even finish the work, but she would like to discuss it with her unnamed correspondent (Julia Ward Howe scrapbook, 1843, bMS Am 2119 [815], HL). I am indebted to Williams for this discussion of Julia's use of the 1843 diary pages in composing the Laurence story. See *Hungry Heart,* pp. 81, 236–38.

6. Laurence manuscript, D 1–10, bMS Am 2214 (320), HL. Gary Williams divided the manuscript into the following strands: (A) the story of Laurence from childhood through his encounters with Ronald: pp. 2–163—though missing pp. 118–32; (B) Lawrence with his father, his brother Philip, and his friend Berto in Roman society: pp. 50–171 of the other long, numbered section of the manuscript; (C) the reading of the uncle's manuscript; (D) the romance of Eva and Rafael; (E1) and (E2) the effect of the story of Eva and Rafael on Nina; (F) the aftermath of the story; and (G) additional material about Ronald (*Hungry Heart,* pp. 82, 87, 90).

I am not concerned here with delineating such a detailed account of the various manuscript strands. For my purposes, it is enough to examine the relationship between the story of Laurence and the romance of Eva and Rafael. Nevertheless, I have chosen to use Williams's nomenclature in giving page references, in the hopes that readers will find the consistency between our referencing useful. Where the original manuscript is numbered, I will provide page references; in sections that are not numbered, I will not provide page references.

Like Williams, I have attempted to put the plot into a chronological sequence for the reader. It is impossible to know how Julia would have arranged the manuscript had she finished the novel. The romance of Eva and Rafael (D) is numbered from pages 1 to 27, and at least since the manuscript has been at the Houghton Library, this story has been the manuscript's first section. The card describing the microfilm contents for this reel (film 93) designates the novel as "Composition beginning 'Eva stood by the tomb of Rafael . . .'" And it is on the first page of the Eva and Rafael story that the librarian/editor wrote a note suggesting 1847 as a possible date of composition.

7. Laurence manuscript, D 11–27, bMS Am 2214 (320), HL.

8. Ibid., A 2–27, bMS Am 2214 (320), HL.

9. Ibid., A 28–35, bMS Am 2214 (320), HL.

10. Ibid., A 50–116, bMS Am 2214 (320), HL.

11. Ibid., A 136–40, bMS Am 2214 (320), HL.

12. Ibid., A 158–62, bMS Am 2214 (320), HL. Williams (*Hungry Heart,* p. 86) transcribes "man-like" for the word I have quoted as "swan-like" (A 158). Julia's writing is notoriously difficult to read (certainly it has driven me to bifocals), and her "sw" looks like her "m." But Laurence

floating "man-like" makes no sense in the context of this quotation, where Ronald is begging Laurence to be for him a woman. If readers check the last word of the twenty-third line of A 157, they will see the word "sweet." A comparison of the "sw" in "sweet" with what I have quoted as "swan-like" (the last word of the fifth line of A 158) justifies my reading "swan" rather than "man."

13. Laurence manuscript, B 147, 152, bMS Am 2214 (320), HL.

14. Ibid., fragments C and D, bMS Am 2214 (320), HL.

15. See n. 3 for a discussion of the various manuscript sections.

16. Laurence manuscript, fragment G, bMS Am 2214 (320), HL.

17. Ibid., fragment F, bMS Am 2214 (320), HL.

18. Maggie Kilgour, *The Rise of the Gothic Novel* (London: Routledge, 1995), p. 8. Numerous critics have argued that Gothic literature functioned as a defense of patriarchal Euro-American institutions, since the restoration of order is an enormous relief to the reader after the disruptive terror that preceded it. Of course, as Kilgour also notes, the pleasure of reading the transgressive sections is what attracted readers to the genre, and in that sense Gothic fiction also functioned as a critique of social norms.

19. Laurence manuscript, A 2, bMS Am 2214 (320), HL.

20. Ibid., B 117, 126; fragment F, bMS Am 2214 (320), HL.

21. Ibid., fragment F, bMS Am 2214 (320), HL.

22. Ibid., fragment F, bMS Am 2214 (320), HL.

23. Williams interprets the Laurence manuscript as a form of "encoded autobiography" as well. Although he feels that the figure of Laurence might represent Julia's "guilty sense of herself," he also suggests that another way—perhaps the most important way—to read the story is as a commentary on Chev's inability to be as emotionally available to Julia as he was to Charles Sumner. Williams noted that Julia was the same age as the character Emma, and that the seduction scene between Emma and Laurence could represent Julia's disgust at Chev's inability to love her wholeheartedly and open his life to her completely. The divided loyalty here involved Chev's emotional intimacy with Sumner, who, as Julia had often noted, ought to have been a woman, so that Chev could have married her.

In an age that sharply distinguished the natures of men from those of women, Julia's remark about Sumner (and the fact that Chev shared it with his friend, who could hardly have seen it as a compliment to his masculinity) was striking. Equally noteworthy were Chev's frequent appeals to Sumner to find himself a wife and enter the same kind of bliss that Chev enjoyed with Julia. Chev was clear; he felt guilty leaving Sumner behind. Sumner was equally direct; he feared that Chev's marriage would ruin their friendship. Sumner wrote Julia's brother Sam before the wedding, "I feel sometimes that I am about to lose a dear friend; for the intimate confidence of friendship may fly away, when love usurps the breast, absorbing the whole nature of a man." Still, Sumner hoped, all might yet be well: "Howe's nature is too generous, I believe, for such a fate. His heart is large enough for her to whom he has given it, and for his friends besides" (21 February 1843, bMS Am 2119 [1659], HL). On a later occasion, Sumner told Chev that participating in Longfellow's wedding would only rekindle the grief he had felt at Chev's wedding. "In all these ceremonies," Sumner confessed, "I have seemed to hear a knell; for a friend becomes dead to me. I ask pardon, dear Howe, for your most affectionate letters tell me I am wrong" (31 August 1843, bMS Am 1.61, no. 1, HL).

Julia's characterization of Sumner as the woman Chev ought to have married is unforgettable, and in my first reading of the Laurence manuscript, I thought of it often. Both in her comment about Summer and in the Laurence manuscript, Julia was probing the complexities of what it means to be a woman or a man. I have no doubt that Julia's musings about Sumner, Chev, and gender were part of the impetus behind her writing the novel.

I am not ready, however, to say with Williams that the Laurence manuscript "chiefly . . . became a means for trying to conceptualize her husband's nature, for understanding his indifference to her (and responsiveness to Sumner) as somehow corporeal, a principle of his very constitution rather than the result of shortcomings on her part" (Williams, *Hungry Heart*, p. 99). The parallel of Laurence/Chev being unwilling to respond to the sensuous Emma/Julia because of a divided heart is intriguing, but the metaphor is difficult to sustain.

The problem between Julia and Chev was the reverse of that of Laurence and Emma. Laurence freely offered Emma emotional intimacy, but she wanted physical intimacy too. Julia's dilemma with Chev was his inability to enter into her emotional world, not his hesitancy about physical intercourse. Chev jokingly hinted at just such a dimension in their relationship in the courtship letter where he depicted Julia as spiritual, but himself as appreciative of earthly pleasures and determined to clip her wings and bring her down to his level (Chev to Julia, Sunday, n.p., n.d., record group 20, folder "Correspondence between SGH and JWH," YHPCC).

In any case, the aspect of the Laurence manuscript most interesting to me is the way in which Julia used the characters of Laurence and the transfigured lovers Eva and Rafael to work out her own identity as an exceptional woman in a man's world.

24. Julia may have earlier toyed with a more conventional version of this image. A poem captioned "On My Leaving for Greece, dear Julia wrote as follows," attributed to Julia Romana in the Schlesinger archives, seems more likely to have been written by her mother to her father, when Chev left Rome for Greece after the birth of Julia Romana. The poem begins by acknowledging the recipient as the "centre and orbit of my soul" and rejoices that "thou" and God "have me a mother made." The author then notes that, as a mother, she is "doubly thine," but "no longer *all* thine." The poet acknowledges that she was once haunted by "wildest visions, strivings, hopes and fears," but was convinced that "joy and duty now walk hand in hand."

Foreseeing a life in which the recipient will daily leave the home to labor, while the poet "will sing among my household cares," the author describes marriage and parenthood as a union of souls:

ဢ

For, in the being of our little one
Our spirits are made one forever more;
Without a separate wish, or thought, or pride,
One soul, which death itself cannot divide.

ဢ

After returning to Boston, and confronting the dreary life of a homebound mother at the Institute, Julia discarded the notion that motherhood could serve as the catalyst of spiritual union between herself and Chev. (I am quoting here from a typed microfilm copy of the poem, marked "Thine own, Dudie," at the end. Underneath, an editor or librarian has written "Julia Romana Howe." Since Julia Romana was never a mother, I doubt that she wrote the poem. See Women's Studies Manuscript Collection, Julia Ward Howe Family, series III, no. 70, reel 10, Schlesinger Library.)

25. Williams, *Hungry Heart*, p. 111. One of the selections for Griswold's *Female Poets of America* was Julia's "To a Beautiful Statue." The poem contained elements reminiscent of the Laurence

manuscript; the poet urged the statue to "wake to life and love," seeking a spell that could "release thee from this seeming death." The poem ended with the assurance that the statue "shall not sleep forever," for thy "frozen heart its pulses shall resume" (bMS Am 2214 [322], box 1, HL). The latter phrase also brings to mind Julia's 1846 comment to Louisa, "my voice is still frozen to silence" (to Louisa Crawford, 31 January 1846, bMS Am 2119 [449], HL).

26. Julia Ward Howe to Louisa Ward Crawford, 12 December 1848, bMS Am 2119 (490), HL.

27. Clifford, *Mine Eyes Have Seen the Glory,* pp. 101–4; Richards and Elliott, *Julia Ward Howe,* vol. 1, pp. 133–35; Julia Ward Howe, *Reminiscences,* pp. 188–204; Florence Howe Hall, *Memories Grave and Gay,* pp. 21–22.

28. See Tharp, *Three Saints and A Sinner,* p. 173, chap. 4 of this book, and Julia's diary for 15 January 1876 (bMS Am 2119 [814], HL). Tharp notes that Chev asked Julia to burn his letters to Sumner from this period as well.

29. Julia Ward Howe to Samuel Gridley Howe, ca. 1850, bMS Am 2119 (524), HL.

30. Samuel Gridley Howe to Julia Ward Howe, Sunday, 27 October [1850], record group 20, folder "Correspondence between SGH and JHW," YHPCC. This citation comes from a type-script copy of the original letter.

31. Julia Ward Howe to Julia Romana and Flossy, Rome, 5 November [1850], bMS Am 2214 (435), HL.

32. Clifford, *Mine Eyes Have Seen the Glory,* p. 150; Florence Howe Hall, *Memories Both Grave and Gay,* pp. 4–5; Anne Stokes Alexander, *Laura E. Richards, 1850–1943: A Critical Biography* (Ph.D. diss., Columbia University, 1979), p. 95.

33. Julia Ward Howe to Louisa Ward Crawford, 28 October 1851, bMS Am 2119 (533), HL.

34. Julia Ward Howe to Louisa Ward Crawford, April 1852, bMS Am 2215 (384), HL; Louisa Ward Crawford to Julia Ward Howe, 18 August 1852, 54M-83, box 1, HL.

35. Julia Ward Howe to Maud Howe Elliott, 6 March 1899, folder 21: "Letters from JWH and Ward Family: Three," YHPGPL. This letter is a typed copy of the original housed in the Colby College collection.

36. Julia Ward Howe, *Reminiscences,* pp. 198–200.

37. Julia Ward Howe to Annie Ward Mailliard, 18 February 1852, bMS Am 2119 (543), HL.

38. Julia Ward Howe to Horace Binney Wallace, 7 January 1853, bMS Am 2215 (401), HL. Julia wrote that she missed Wallace and was anxious "to have my best friend on the same side of the water again."

39. Tharp, *Three Saints and A Sinner,* p. 173.

40. Grant, *Private Woman, Public Person,* pp. 97–99.

41. Annie Ward Mailliard to Samuel Gridley Howe, Rome, 29 April 1851, bMS Am 2215 (565), HL.

42. Williams, *Hungry Heart,* pp. 115–22.

43. Julia Ward Howe, "What Life Means to Me," *The Cosmopolitan* (Rochester, N.Y.: Schlicht & Field, 1925), p. 287.

44. Julia Ward Howe, *From the Oak to the Olive. A Plain Record of a Pleasant Journey* (Boston: Lee & Shepard, 1868), p. 45; *Reminiscences,* pp. 203–4.

45. Julia Ward Howe to Louisa Ward Crawford, 28 October 1851, bMS Am 2119 (533), HL.

46. Julia Ward Howe to Annie Mailliard, ca. 1851, bMS Am 2119 (493), HL.

47. Julia Ward Howe to Annie Mailliard, "Wednesday 17th," ca. 1851, bMS Am 2119 (513), HL.

48. Julia Ward Howe to Annie Mailliard, ca. 1851, bMS Am 2119 (493), HL.

49. Julia Ward Howe to Annie Ward Mailliard, 8 November [1852], bMS Am 2119 (534), HL.

50. Julia Ward Howe to Annie Ward Mailliard, 27 December [1854], bMS Am 2119 (560), HL. Julia speaks in this letter of her last meeting with Wallace in a Bordentown garden. See Williams, p. 131.

51. Julia Ward Howe to Horace Binney Wallace, 7 January 1853, bMS Am 2215 (401), HL.

52. Julia Ward Howe to Louisa Ward Crawford, 18 February 1853, bMS Am 2119 (543), HL. Julia also wrote the philosopher August Comte a letter in French about Wallace at this time. See Williams, *Hungry Heart,* pp. 121–22 for a discussion.

53. Julia Ward Howe to Annie Ward Mailliard, 8 December [1853], bMS Am 2119 (540), HL.

54. Williams, *Hungry Heart,* pp. 134–35, 251.

55. Julia Ward Howe to Annie Ward Mailliard, n.d., bMS Am 2119 (555), HL. In this letter, apparently written in the summer of 1853, Julia told Annie that she was readying a book of poems for publication but could not decide whether to issue them anonymously or under her own name. Using her own name might appear inappropriately forward for a woman, but Julia conjectured that the poems might sell better if people realized she was the author. She had considered asking Chev's advice, but admitted that Chev would "probably make a fight about the name. I have a great mind," she added, "to keep the whole matter entirely secret from him, and not let him know anything until the morning the volume comes out. Then he can do nothing to prevent it's [sic] sale in it's [sic] proper form."

56. Julia Ward Howe to Annie Ward Mailliard, December [1853], bMS Am 2119 (548), HL.

57. Julia Ward Howe to Annie Ward Mailliard, Thursday, 29 December [1853], bMS Am 2119 (550), HL. As Williams notes, critics were not unanimous in their praise for *Passion-Flowers*. At least one reader found Julia's authorial voice officious and absurdly egotistical. Francis J. Child wrote to Arthur Hugh Clough that the "vanity of the woman is most amusing throughout her poems; she sets up to be a good dancer, to be a famous musician, a dab at theology, cooking, languages, and all the accomplishments. She hints at a time when she was a leading belle and gives you to understand that her beauty as well as her cleverness entitled her to that distinction.... She does *not* pretend to be a model wife, and there are several obscure pieces addressed to different men unknown which might reasonably give offense to her husband, who by the way never saw the book until it was printed" (*Correspondence of Clough* 2:475, quoted in Williams, *Hungry Heart,* p. 252).

58. By far the most thorough and insightful critique of *Passions-Flowers* is Williams' *Hungry Heart,* pp. 134–70. Williams described Julia's authorial voice as a "poetics of defiance." He also observed that Julia's "decision to publish unmistakably autobiographical poems had few precedents, and none among women as prominently situated as she" (pp. 138–39).

59. With regard to a poem entitled "The Royal Guest," for example, Julia wrote to Edward and Ellen Twisleton that readers delighted in trying to break the poems' codes. "Would you believe it," she asked, "I am constantly being asked: 'who is the Master? who is the Royal Guest?' Now that of course I will not tell" (17 April [1854], bMS Am 2214 [164], HL).

60. Julia Ward Howe, *Passion-Flowers,* 1st ed. (Boston: Ticknor, Reed, & Fields, 1854), pp. 1–4, 8–11. Softening her delight in a grace more than maternal, Julia ended "Rome" back home with the children, watching the shadows of twilight deepen.

61. Julia Ward Howe, *Passion-Flowers,* pp. 91–92. In "The Heart's Astronomy," Julia called herself a comet "dire and strange," explaining to her children, "Among the shining I have shone, / Among the blessing have been blest; / Then wearying years have held me bound / Where darkness deadness gives, not rest." She urged her children to remember that "Comets, too, have holy laws," and asked them to "Pray that the laws of heavenly force / Would help and guide the Mother

star" (pp. 101–3). It is hard not to read the poem as a depiction of her struggle to find happiness as a wife and mother, in spite of the higher call to poetry.

62. Julia Ward Howe, *Passion-Flowers*, p. 95.

63. Ibid., p. 106.

64. Ibid., pp. 111–12.

65. Ibid., pp. 157–58. A poem called "The Dead Christ" (pp. 151–53) may also refer to Wallace. This work began with a curious call to "Take the dead Christ to my chamber, / The Christ I brought from Rome," and continued, "The name I bear is other / Than that I bore by birth; / And I've given life to children / Who'll grow and dwell on earth." Married with children or not, Julia proclaimed, the time was swiftly coming when "the dead Christ will be more to me / Than all I hold today." She knew, she said, this Christ was dead, and she expected no miracles; yet still, "I love and prize thee dead."

66. Julia Ward Howe, *Passion-Flowers*, pp. 117–19.

67. Ibid., pp. 170–71.

68. Ibid., pp. 80–85.

69. Ibid., pp. 128–31.

70. Julia Ward Howe to Annie Ward Mailliard, "Tuesday the seventh" [1854], bMS Am 2119 (554), HL.

71. Julia Ward Howe to Annie Ward Mailliard, Thursday [1854], and 27 May 1854, bMS Am 2119 (552, 557), HL.

72. Williams, *Hungry Heart*, p. 251.

73. I do not believe that anyone else has noticed the revisions in the second and third editions of *Passion-Flowers* before. No other poems were altered, not even "Philosoph-Master and Poet-Aster." I have not discovered any materials in which Julia discussed her decision to soften her book's later editions, although ample evidence documents Chev's fury at "Mind Versus Mill-Stream" in its original version. Omitting the "Moral" made the poem (and thus the book) a page shorter, so that the pagination of the second and third editions of *Passion-Flowers* differs from the original version after p. 84. All three editions had an 1854 date of publication and an 1853 copyright. Ticknor, Reed, & Fields of Boston was designated as the publisher of each edition. The first edition named Thorston, Torry, & Emerson as the printers; the second and third editions did not list printers.

74. Samuel Gridley Howe to Julia Ward Howe, Willard's Hotel, Washington, "Friday 24," n.d., record group 20, folder "Correspondence between SGH and JWH," YHPCC. No year is specified in the letter's heading, nor does Chev give the title of the book that he is critiquing. But he begins the letter by saying that he had stopped into Ticknor's publishing house and was told that the press was ready to issue a new edition of Julia's book—Chev thought it might be the fourth edition. Only one book that Julia published with Ticknor's went into a third edition: *Passion-Flowers*.

75. Julia Ward Howe to Annie Ward Mailliard, 19 June [1854], bMS Am 2119 (316), HL. Julia's suspicions were correct, as Chev confessed at his death. He had been unfaithful to her.

76. Julia Ward Howe to Louisa Ward Crawford, 23 July 1854, bMS Am 2215 (385), HL. This letter was not finished (or mailed) until months later. It continues with a November 4 date.

77. Julia Ward Howe to Louisa Ward Crawford, begun 23 July 1854, finished 4 November, bMS Am 2215 (385), HL.

78. Ibid.

79. Julia Ward Howe to Annie Ward Mailliard, 27 December [1854], bMS Am 2119 (560), HL.

80. Clifford, *Mine Eyes Have Seen the Glory,* p. 122.

81. Williams observes that *Words for the Hour* had an 1857 copyright date but was issued late in December 1856 (*Hungry Heart,* p. 263).

82. Williams observes that one review described *Words for the Hour* as "purely private and personal," while another commented upon the "wail of private sorrow which forms the keynote." The *North American* found many of the references so obscure as to prompt the reviewer to wonder if they were meant to be intelligible only to "the author's own coterie" (*Hungry Heart,* p. 179). Williams's analysis of *Words for the Hour* (pp. 178–99) is the most comprehensive yet written and is the best reference for readers interested in a fuller analysis.

83. Julia Ward Howe, *Words for the Hour* (Boston: Ticknor & Fields, 1857), pp. 40–43.

84. Ibid., pp. 64, 96–98.

85. Ibid., pp. 129–31.

86. Williams perceptively describes the differences between the full version of "Via Felice" and the abbreviated form Julia printed in her *Reminiscences* (pp. 200–201). Each contains lines depicting Julia watching from a window as Wallace purchased flowers for her. But in the edited version, the reader assumes that Julia is watching from the window in her apartment, whereas the unabridged poem indicates she is watching from Wallace's window (*Hungry Heart,* pp. 245–47).

87. Julia Ward Howe, *Words for the Hour,* pp. 43–44, 52–56, 75–78, 80–81.

88. Laura began chap. 8 of her 1935 biography of her father with this poem. See *Samuel Gridley Howe,* p. 8.

89. Julia Ward Howe, *Words for the Hour,* pp. 71–72.

90. Ibid., p. 54.

91. Julia Ward Howe, *Leonora, Or The World's Own,* in Arthur Hobson Quinn, ed., *Representative American Plays* (New York: Century, 1917), p. 393.

92. Julia Ward Howe, *Leonora, Or The World's Own,* pp. 422, 425–27.

93. Quinn, *Representative American Plays,* p. 388.

94. In the final scene Edward was direct that Leonora's sin was that of revenge, not lust:

∽

Not for the weakness of a second love
Or sordid need, or lust of leprous splendour,
But for the ruin of one wretched soul,
She gave, what God till then held innocent,
The glories of her youth.

∽

See *Leonora, Or the World's Own,* p. 426. Fanny Longfellow is quoted in Clifford, *Mine Eyes Have Seen the Glory,* pp. 126–27.

95. Quoted in Tharp, *Three Saints and A Sinner,* p. 231; and in Paul S. Boyer, "Howe, Julia Ward," in Edward T. James, Janet Wilson James, and Paul S. Boyer, eds., *Notable American Women, 1607–1950: A Biographical Dictionary,* vol. 2 (Cambridge: Belknap Press of Harvard University Press, 1971), p. 227.

96. Maud Howe Elliott, *Uncle Sam Ward and His Circle,* pp. 447–49.

97. Julia Ward Howe to Annie Ward Mailliard, 1 October [1857], bMS Am 2119 (576), HL.

98. Samuel Gridley Howe to Julia Ward Howe, 24 November 1859, record group 20, folder "Correspondence between SGH and JWH," YHPCC. By his own admission here, Chev remained a hypochondriac. In May 1858, Chev told Sumner he was all but done for, explaining, "I am not

well: the pent up suffering I have bourne so long, & in such sad loneliness is telling upon my brain, & I have had several unmistakeable [sic] symptoms, of tendency to paralysis. . . . I am prepared now at any moment for a shock, & if it is to incapacitate me from my only solace,— work,—then, may it end me." Chev's remarks indicate that he, too, felt keenly his alienation from Julia (bMS Am 2119 [1203], HL).

99. Julia told Chev in a November letter that she was in severe pain and "should give up altogether but for my red hair, wh[ich] won't let me give up to you, much less to your baby" (21 November 1859, record group 20, folder "Correspondence between SGH and JWH," YHPCC). By December 22, Julia was utterly miserable. "My nights have been weary with pain," she confided to her sister Annie. "I am so glad that the end, hard as it is, draws near. I have almost got to feel as if the miracle of recovery never could take place, and as if I were never again able to move without pain." Still, Julia said, she did not mean to complain, because the "physical miseries" were balanced "by the real compensation of Chev's on the whole kind treatment. This is more than an equivalent for the good health of former times. He has really been very good & has seemed quite fond of me" (22 December 1859, bMS Am 2119 [587], HL).

100. Julia Ward Howe, "Maidenhood" and "Matronhood" [ca. 1860], in vol. 3 of 6 vols. of "Miscellaneous and Fragmentary Poems," bMS Am 2119 (797), HL.

101. Richards and Elliott, *Julia Ward Howe,* vol. 1, pp. 136–54.

102. Samuel Gridley Howe to Charles Sumner, 25 August 1852, bMS Am 2119 (1097), HL. For a fuller quotation, see Williams, *Hungry Heart,* p. 131.

103. Julia Ward Howe to Samuel Gridley Howe, 2 December [1859], record group 20, folder "Correspondence between SGH and JWH," YHPCC. December 2 was the day of John Brown's execution, which might have offered Julia Romana relief if she feared that her father would be hanged with Brown. Grant claims that Julia Romana suffered a nervous breakdown in 1859 (*Private Woman, Public Person,* pp. 140, 230). As will be further discussed in chap. 5, it is virtually impossible to establish the condition of Julia Romana's emotional health at any period of her life, since her sisters destroyed most of her private papers after her death.

104. Hall, *Memories Grave and Gay,* p. 4.

105. Elliott, *Three Generations,* pp. 14–15; and *This Was My Newport,* p. 64.

106. Richards, *Stepping Westward,* p. 389; and *When I Was Your Age,* dedication.

107. Henry Marion Howe to Laura E. Richards, Bedford Hills, New York [ca. 1919 or 1920], record group 32, folder "HMH to LER, 1914–1919," YHPCC.

108. Richards, *When I Was Your Age,* pp. 14–15, 146.

109. Hall, *Memories Grave and Gay,* pp. 31–32. Julia Romana at age ten described Maud's birth in *The Listener* as follows: "A very curious little animal lies on the editor's table this week. It does not understand the use of cup, plate or spoon, yet it feeds itself. It does not know any language, yet it makes itself understood. It never bought itself a dress, yet it has a whole wardrobe full of clothes. It does not know anybody, yet it has plenty of friends. Can you guess what it is? It is our little baby sister."

110. Hall, *Memories Grave and Gay,* p. 36; Elliott, *This Was My Newport,* pp. 95–96; Elliott, *Three Generations,* pp. 33–34. Younger than the other children, Maud found herself unable to keep pace in Sdrawkcab. Little of Patagonian survived the Howes' childhood; Flossy was able to reconstruct only a few phrases in *Memories Grave and Gay:* "Bis von snout?" (Are you well?) and "Brunk tu touchy snout (I am very well). Laura remembered a few other phrases: 'Milldam' (yes); "Illdam" (no); "Mouche" (Mother); and "Ching Chu Stick Stumps?" (Will you have some doughnuts?). See Richards, *When I Was Your Age,* pp. 27–28.

111. Hall, *Flossy's Play Days,* pp. 29–37; Elliott, *This Was My Newport,* p. 96; Richards, *When I Was Your Age,* pp. 22–26. Laura, Maud, and Harry devoutly believed that Patty's balls were true, until Flossy made the error of telling Harry that he would be permitted to bring home a pair of diamond trousers from that night's revelries. The game was up when he awoke and saw no signs of his diamond pants. He wept bitterly, and a pall settled over the Patty tales.

112. Richards, *When I Was Your Age,* pp. 35–36.

113. Richards, *Stepping Westward,* pp. 19–20, 123; Richards, *When I Was Your Age,* pp. 36–39. Laura said that her father used to tell them stories of the many pranks he had pulled as a boy, including the most spectacular one from his college days, when he led the president's horse upstairs in one of the college buildings and left him there. Chev would invariably warn the children not to follow his example, but there was no stopping Harry (Richards, *When I Was Your Age,* pp. 90–91).

114. Richards, *When I Was Your Age,* pp. 70–76.

115. When Maud and Laura were working on the years 1852–1858 of their mother's biography, Maud noted in her diary that Julia's letters to her sisters in those years were bewildering and "beyond belief" interesting. "She seems to be like an opal flashing fire always, but sometimes violet wrath, red despairs, rosy hope, & blue hope and tender everlasting green of constancy to her own flesh & blood. They explain her more than anything. They explain myself nearly as much. Laura says that the blackest time of all, was before my birth. These tremendous depressions, these supreme elations, are all here, stamped in my poor little being, deep, deep! The temperament of genius is not a comfortable thing to possess without the genius that is its only excuse for being!" Maud Howe Elliott diary, 1 May 1912, John Hay Library, Brown University.

116. Richards, *When I Was Your Age,* pp. 134, 148.

117. Ibid., pp. 138–39.

Chapter Four

1. Hall, *The Story of the Battle Hymn of the Republic,* p. 7.

2. Ibid., p. 8.

3. Julia Ward Howe, *Trip to Cuba* (Boston: Ticknor & Fields, 1860), pp. 12–13, 234. Julia wrote another travel book in 1868 to recount her journey with Chev, Laura, and Julia Romana to Western Europe and Greece. *From the Oak to the Olive* was published by Lee & Shepherd. For a discussion of the strategies Julia employed in her travel books to present herself both as a "literary character" and as a "woman's woman," see Mary Suzanne Schriber, "Julia Ward Howe and the Travel Book," *The New England Quarterly* 62, no. 2 (June 1989): 264–79. Selected portions of *From the Oak to the Olive* are reprinted in a chapter entitled "Julia Ward Howe" in Schriber's *Telling Travels: Selected Writings by Nineteenth-Century American Women Abroad* (DeKalb, Ill.: Northern Illinois University Press, 1995), pp. 153–70.

William Lloyd Garrison would sharply rebuke Julia for her disparagement of Cuban blacks (see Clifford, *Mine Eyes Have Seen the Glory,* p. 136). The ways in which the Howes felt free to use disparaging terms for the Irish and for African Americans would make for a fascinating word study. Even in a family as identified with the Union cause as was the Howe family, there was— both before the war and well into the twentieth century—no reluctance to use the word "nigger." Youngest daughter Maud noted after a memorial service for Julia in 1911 that her mother would have been pleased to know that the best speaker was an African American Maud called "the nig" (diary, 8 January 1911, Maud Howe Elliott Papers, John Hay Library).

4. Scholars disagree as to when Julia became an abolitionist. Clifford believes Julia was in the antislavery camp by the mid-1850s and that her brother Sam's refusal to speak out against slavery caused Julia considerable pain. See Clifford, *Mine Eyes Have Seen the Glory,* pp. 129, 139. Grant, however, argues that in later memoirs, Julia was deliberately vague about the date of her entry into abolitionism, hoping to give the impression that she had been a contributor to the cause of freedom earlier than was in fact the case. Grant believes Julia was not wholeheartedly abolitionist until the arrest and execution of John Brown, in the last quarter of 1859 (*Private Woman, Public Person,* p. 133).

5. It was Sumner whom Preston Brooks caned into insensibility on the floor of the Senate because of a fiery antislavery speech. The case drew international attention. Sumner was absent from the Senate for months, recovering from the beating.

6. Clifford, *Mine Eyes Have Seen the Glory,* pp. 142–45. Julia was to use this method of inspiration frequently in later years on occasions when she had trouble preparing public speeches. In her diaries, she recalled several instances in which, upon rising in the morning, a speech had come together in her mind and needed only to be written down.

7. Quoted in Hall, *The Story of the Battle Hymn of the Republic,* pp. 49–50; also printed in Julia's *Reminiscences,* pp. 273–75.

8. Hall, *The Story of the Battle Hymn of the Republic,* p. 57. Both Julia's autobiography and her daughters' biography reprint the original handwritten manuscript as an insert. Anyone wishing to get an idea of how difficult Julia's handwriting is to read may profitably consult these inserts.

9. Julia Ward Howe, *Reminiscences,* p. 275.

10. Ernest Lee Tuveson has written an incisive analysis of the "Battle Hymn" in *Redeemer Nation: The Idea of America's Millennial Role* (Chicago: University of Chicago Press; Midway repr., 1980), pp. 197–202. As I have summarized Tuveson's argument elsewhere, "'the coming of the Lord' was an allegory for the millennial triumph of Christian principles, and its 'glory' was 'the wonder and terror of the transition to the millennium.' The 'grapes of wrath' recalled Revelation 14:19, where the angel of God ordered the figure 'like the Son of man' to gather with his sickle the grapes of the demonic Babylon and crush them in the 'great winepress of the wrath of God.' As Babylon fell and the reign of the Antichrist ended, the faithful shouted, 'Alleluja; Salvation, and glory, and honour, and power, unto the Lord our God'—or, as Julia Ward Howe wrote it, 'Glory, Glory, Hallelujah.' The 'terrible swift sword' recalled the horseman of Revelation 19. His name was the Word of God, and he wore clothes dipped in blood, while 'out of his mouth goeth a sharp sword, that with it he should smite the nations.' And so God was 'sifting out the hearts of men' as the judgment preparatory to the dawn of the millennium. Thus, true believers would exhort, 'Be swift my sword, to answer him! Be jubilant my feet!"(Ziegler, *The Advocates of Peace in Antebellum America* [Bloomington, Ind: Indiana University Press, 1992], p. 217).

Originally, there were six verses to the "Battle Hymn." Julia decided to omit the final verse, where the millennial overtones were most evident:

∽

He is coming like the glory of the morning on the wave
He is wisdom to the mighty, he is honor to the brave
And the world shall be his footstool, and the soul of wrong his slave
Our God is marching on.

∽

11. Florence Howe Hall, *The Story of the Battle Hymn of the Republic,* p. 55.

12. Julia Ward Howe, "What Life Means to Me," *The Cosmopolitan* (Rochester, N.Y.: Schlict & Field, 1925), p. 287.

13. She would go on to publish three more books of poetry: *Later Lyrics* (1866), From *Sunset Ridge* (1898), and *At Sunset,* published posthumously in 1910.

14. Richards, *When I Was Your Age,* p. 13.

15. Julia Ward Howe diary, 17–20 May 1863, bMS Am 2119 (814), HL.

16. Julia Ward Howe diary, 5, 7, 8, 26 June 1863, and 3 August 1863, bMS Am 2119 (814), HL.

17. Samuel Gridley Howe to Julia Ward Howe, 29 November [1863], record group 20, folder "Correspondence between SGH and JWH," YHPCC. Deborah Clifford published "'The Last Letter to Sammy' by Julia Ward Howe" in the *Harvard Library Bulletin* 25, no. 1 (January 1977): 50–62.

18. Julia Ward Howe diary, 7 October 1863; 16, 23, 30 November 1863; 7, 21, 28 December 1863; 11, 20, 27 May 1864, bMS Am 2119 (814), HL. Sumner did more than simply discourage Julia from reading her lectures in Washington; according to Julia's diary of 6 March 1864, he disrupted preparations she had made to read three papers in a private home in Washington. Julia was forced to make new arrangements.

19. Julia Ward Howe diary, 29 May 1864, bMS Am 2119 (814), HL. In their biography, Julia's daughters acknowledged Sumner's opposition to Julia's readings but said nothing of Chev's, only recalling, "there were various difficulties in the way, and she was uncertain of the outcome of the enterprise" (Richards and Elliott, *Julia Ward Howe,* vol. 1, pp. 205–6).

20. Julia Ward Howe diary, 11 November 1864, bMS Am 2119 (814), HL.

21. Julia Ward Howe, *Reminiscences,* pp. 277–80; Richards and Elliott, *Julia Ward Howe,* vol. 1, pp. 209–10.

22. Julia Ward Howe diary, 12 April 1866; 7 December 1866; 21 November 1867, bMS Am 2119 (814), HL.

23. The old pattern of Julia Romana and Flossy siding with their father against their mother continued. Deborah Clifford suggests that Laura was the child who was the most encouraging to Julia, which accounted for her nickname as "the Comforter" (*Mine Eyes Have Seen the Glory,* pp. 150–51). Julia remarked in a diary entry in 1865, "Laura is the most sympathetic and companionable of my children" (Julia Ward Howe diary, 9 June 1865, bMS Am 2119 [814], HL).

24. Julia Ward Howe diary, 7 February 1865, bMS Am 2119 (814), HL. Only Julia would have written a poem "On Leaving / for a Time / the study of Kant" (August 1866, bMS Am 2214 (322), notebooks, box 1 of 2, HL):

Dull seems the day that brings no hour with thee,
Oh master, lapse'd to eternity.

I am as loathe to leave thy guiding hand
As babes to quit the mother's house, and stand.
My memory shows the rude, chaotic ways
Wherein I walked, ere thou reformedst my days.

Truth was the air palace that I sought
Thro' many a wild adventure dreamed & wrought.

Lo! at the touch its crystal turrets rise,
Set in the gold gloom of evening skies;

Experience widening Wisdom's sacred scope,
The fixed ideals, the everlasting hope.

⟳

25. Julia Ward Howe diary, 11 February 1865, bMS Am 2119 (814), HL.

26. Julia Ward Howe diary, 12 March 1865, bMS Am 2119 (814), HL. Not coincidentally, Chev often expressed satisfaction with Julia Romana, who wished for nothing more than to assist him in his work. In 1856, he wrote to Sumner that Julia Romana "loves me tenderly. . . . She has all her mother's intensity & earnestness [?] of nature, but [?] little of it intellectually [?] [—] she pours it forth in an effort to make others happy—not to shine & be pleased herself" (S. G. Howe to Charles Sumner, 4 February [1856], bMS Am 2119 [1152], HL).

27. Julia Ward Howe diary, 17 March, 1865, bMS Am 2119 (814), HL.

28. Ibid., 18 March 1865.

29. Ibid., 19 March 1865.

30. Ibid., 18 April 1864.

31. Ibid., 24 and 26 March 1865.

32. Tharp notes that a Boston judge had invited Julia to speak to the women prisoners at the jail in Charlestown, Massachusetts. See *Three Saints and A Sinner,* p. 295.

33. Julia Ward Howe Diary, 23 April 1865, bMS Am 2119 (814), HL.

34. Ibid., 24 April 1865.

35. Ibid., 4 May 1865.

36. Ibid., 24 May 1865.

37. Ibid., 29 May 1865.

38. Ibid., 29 May 1865.

39. Ibid., 22 August 1865.

40. Ibid., 3 and 4 November 1865.

41. Ibid., 18 and 19 December 1865. The furnace wars continued for years. Julia noted in her diary entry for 28 January 1868 that she was "very angry with Chev for changing the heating apparatus of the house without consulting or even informing me. A most unnecessary and inconvenient measure, a feature of his mania for such changes. I certainly did not take it amiably, but cannot help considering the provocation extreme."

42. Julia Ward Howe diary, 26 January 1867. Grant argues that Julia wrote her essay on "Opposition" in January 1867. See *Private Woman, Public Person,* pp. 177, 236.

43. Grant makes the same point on p. 177 of *Private Woman, Public Person.* Grant's discussion of Julia's philosophical essays (pp. 159–92) is the most detailed study to date and provides the best resource for readers who wish to pursue this aspect of Julia's work.

44. Julia Ward Howe, "Opposition," pp. 1–2, bMS Am 2214 (320), box 5, HL.

45. The understanding of gender that Julia developed through her suffrage and peace advocacy changed her reliance on the "exceptional woman" theory. As she said, "I was made to feel that womanhood is not only static, but also much more dynamic, a power to move, as well as a power to stay. True womanliness must grow and not diminish, in its larger and freer exercise. . . . The new teaching seemed to me to throw the door open for all woman to come up higher" ("Mrs. Howe

on Equal Rights," *Women's Rights Collection Papers, 1633–1958,* Women's Rights Collection, box 6, folder 80, Schlesinger Library).

46. Julia Ward Howe, "The Woman's Rights Question," bMS Am 2214 (320), box 9, HL. There is no way to date this speech with precision, nor is it possible to know when (or if) Julia delivered it. Scholars generally assume Julia wrote it in the 1840s or 1850s; it is stored at the Houghton Library in a folder labeled "Speeches." Clifford suggests the late 1840s or early 1850s as the probable date of composition (*Mine Eyes Have Seen the Glory,* p. 171); Grant argues for a mid-1850s date (*Private Woman, Public Person,* p. 168).

The tone of this essay is so strikingly opposed to much of Julia's work that the only other document I can suggest that seems similar is the 27 March 1848 letter to Louisa previously cited in chap. 2. There, in addition to denouncing a woman (Clampit) who had rebelled against her husband, Julia had defined marriage as "not an affair simply of happiness," but as a relation in which wives owed grave obligations to others. Julia insisted that Chev had rights and privileges, even a kind of supremacy and dignity, which were proper to a husband (bMS Am 2119 (484), HL).

47. For a discussion of "masochistic discourses of womanhood" in the nineteenth century, see Marianne Noble, *The Masochistic Pleasures of Sentimental Literature* (Princeton: Princeton University Press, 2000), pp. 26–60. Noble argues, among other points, that the inability to submit happily to male authority prompted women like Julia to suffer feelings of guilt and inadequacy and encouraged them to embrace a "masochistic desire for domination." Noble sees Louisa May Alcott's *Little Women* as a text incorporating that dynamic (pp. 38–39). Perhaps a similar dynamic was at work in Julia's essay on "The Woman's Rights Question."

48. Julia Ward Howe, "The Woman's Rights Question," pp. 1, 18–20, bMS Am 2214 (320), box 9, HL.

49. Ibid., pp. 20–27, 40–47, 12. In this essay, Julia mentioned only one legal custom in need of reform. So long as husbands could trust their wives to exercise self-control, she argued, the laws restricting women's holding of property could be loosened. Since Chev had harassed her (and her uncle and brother) repeatedly until he gained control of all the money and real estate that Julia derived from the Wards, she knew that problem firsthand. But the question that she raised in this essay was not what to do with the man who squandered his wife's inheritance (which in her marriage was a genuine point of concern). Rather, she worried about the husband whose wife overspent her prenuptial income and left the husband to pay the household expenses entirely from his own resources.

Julia worried about that wife of independent means throughout this speech. In a passage that can only be described as incredible (given its eerie resemblance to her own sojourn in Rome in 1850–51), she lamented the behavior of the financially self-sufficient wife. "Having always money at her command, she leaves him when she likes, without permission or advice. The public prints inform him that his wife has taken the last steamer for Europe, carrying his child with her. Here, you see, the whole function of and idea of marriage is destroyed, and the proximate cause is the legal clause by which the married woman retains the independence of the unmarried one." Public opinion, Julia insisted, should condemn such derelictions of "womanly duty and virtue."

Therefore, Julia concluded, it was fine to consider changing the laws about women's holding of property. But all things in moderation: "I do not object to any wise and necessary modification in existing laws upon this point. I object only to the unphilosophical spirit which regards these laws as wrongs and outrages from the beginning, and ourselves, in all ages, as their victims" (pp. 38–42).

It is hard to imagine—given Julia's own history—that she wrote this speech after returning from Europe with "his" children. It seems equally unlikely that she wrote it after the publication of *Passion-Flowers* (when Chev, like the husband she pitied in this speech, discovered the latest news about his wife not from her, but in the newspapers). But anything is possible. It is hard to believe she wrote this essay at all. Marked by page after page of vituperation against women—whom she blamed for most of society's faults, including the ones committed by men—the level of animosity expressed for women who sought independence was overwhelming. Perhaps the guilty sense of self suggested in the Laurence manuscript ("monster!") received full expression here.

50. Julia Ward Howe diary, 21 December 1863, bMS Am 2119 (814), HL.

51. Julia Ward Howe, "Proteus," pp. 49–51, Julia Ward Howe Collection, box 5, Library of Congress.

52. Ibid.; this manuscript page was not numbered.

53. Julia Ward Howe, "Limitation," pp. 61–62, 67, 85–87, bMS Am 2214 (320), box 3, HL.

54. Grant, *Private Woman, Public Person,* pp. 174–75.

55. Julia Ward Howe, "Polarity II," Julia Ward Howe Collection, box 4, Library of Congress, pp. 74–75. Grant dates this essay to 1865. See *Private Woman, Public Person,* p. 249.

56. Julia Ward Howe, "Opposition," pp. 1–3, bMS Am 2214 (320), box 5, HL.

57. Julia Ward Howe, "Representation and How to Get It," pp. 19–21, 29. bMS Am 2214 (320), box 3, HL. Grant puts the date for this lecture as 1867. See *Private Woman, Public Person,* p. 249.

58. Julia Ward Howe, "Position of Women," bMS Am 2214 (320), box 5, HL. Grant estimates the date for this work as 1867. See *Private Woman, Public Person,* p. 249.

59. Julia Ward Howe, "Behold I Create . . . ," 1869, Julia Ward Howe Collection, box 1, Library of Congress.

60. Julia Ward Howe, *Reminiscences,* p. 376.

61. Henry Richards, *Ninety Years On: 1848–1940* (Augusta, Maine: Kennebec Journal Press, 1940), pp. 301–2. Laura's husband was called "Harry" or, later, "Skipper" in the family.

62. Hall, *Memories Grave and Gay,* pp. 12–13.

63. Samuel Gridley Howe to Laura E. Richards, Oak Glen, 5 September, n.d., record group 20, folder "Letters: Julia Anagnos," YHPCC.

64. Samuel Gridley Howe to Laura E. Richards, 21 December 1871, and 3 August 1874, record group 20, folder "Letters: SGH to LER, MHE, et al.," YHPCC.

65. Samuel Gridley Howe to George Finlay, 13 August 1874, bMS Am 2119 (1389), HL.

66. Julia Ward Howe, *Reminiscences,* pp. 372–73.

67. Ironically, Julia credited Theodore Parker with awakening her to the possibility that God was mother as well as father, recalling that in public prayer Parker had addressed God as "Father and Mother of us all," and that his prayers were so powerful that he "took us with him into the divine presence" (*Reminiscences,* pp. 166–67).

68. Julia Ward Howe diary, 27 August 1872, bMS Am 2119 (814), HL: Julia Ward Howe, "The Woman's Peace Festival—Mrs. Howe's Address," *Woman's Journal* 6, no. 23 (June 5, 1875): 180.

Numerous historians have noted the popularity of the "essentialist" argument in women's reform movements of the nineteenth century. Contemporary feminists are far less likely to argue for women's rights and public involvement in social reforms based on the presumed innately uplifting character of woman's nature. In the late nineteenth century, however, the essentialist argument was crucial to the women's suffrage movement, as well as to the woman's club movement. Karen J. Blair has contended that women like Julia were "feminists under the skin," as well as proper ladies who "utilized the domestic and moral traits attributed to the ideal lady to increase autonomy, assert sorority, win education, and seize influence beyond the home in the forbidden public sphere." Blair concludes that, despite public criticism, "thousands of nineteenth-century women effectively employed the lady's traits to justify their departure from the home to exert special influence on the male sphere" (Karen J. Blair, *The Clubwoman as Feminist: True Womanhood Redefined, 1868–1914* [New York: Holmes & Meier Inc., 1980], pp. 1, 4, 32).

As I have indicated in the text, I believe that Julia's appeals to woman's "nature" were essentialist in that she assumed that women, as mothers, shared a common moral character. But she did not argue that woman's (or man's) character was static or unchangeable. The point of civilized progress was that men and woman would come to share in the strengths associated with the "opposite" gender.

69. Julia Ward Howe, "Woman's Contribution to Christianity," *The Christian Register,* October 20, 1891.

70. Julia Ward Howe, "The Woman's Peace Festival—Mrs. Howe's Address," *Woman's Journal* 6, no. 23 (June 5, 1875): 181.

71. Julia Ward Howe, "The Halfness of Nature," 22 October 1875, Julia Ward Howe Collection, box 3, Library of Congress. For a published version that is largely verbatim, see "The Halfness of Nature" in Julia Ward Howe, *Is Polite Society Polite? And Other Essays* (Boston and New York: Lamson, Wolffe, 1895), pp. 172–73.

72. Hall, *Julia Ward Howe and the Woman Suffrage Movement,* p. 42; Edwin D. Mead, *Woman and War: Julia Ward Howe's Peace Crusade* (Boston: World Peace Foundation, 1914), pp. 6–9; *Minutes of the Pennsylvania Peace Society,* 1893–1928, 21 November 1907, Swarthmore College Peace Collection.

73. Julia Ward Howe to Annie Ward Mailliard, 8 April 1874, bMS Am 2119 (604), HL.

74. Julia Ward Howe diary, 16 December 1872, bMS Am 2119 (814), HL.

75. *Sex and Education: A Reply to Dr. E. H. Clarke's "Sex in Education,"* ed. Julia Ward Howe (Boston: Roberts Brothers, 1874).

76. K. N. D., "The Leaders of the Congress," *Woman's Journal* 5, no. 48 (November 28, 1874): 380.

77. Henry Richards, *Ninety Years On,* p. 299.

78. Several of Julia's diary entries in the 1860s referred to Chev's philandering. On January 18, 1864, she wrote, "[S]ome illusions left me today, giving place to unwelcome facts." These facts—related to Chev's unfaithfulness—left her utterly miserable. On January 25, 1864, she observed that some of the anxiety had lifted, and that she and Chev were getting along better. Still, if conditions did not continue to improve, she said, "I should have to leave home for a time, to avoid utter breaking down of body and of mind." Clearly, Julia was distraught.

On December 12, 1866, Julia offered to go the Institute with Chev for the evening, but he refused. She was already in trouble at home for having spoken at the Lexington Lyceum against his will on December 7, and the household was in furor. Julia observed on the morning of December 8 that she "went to bed last night full of mournful discouragement about my family, & especially Julia & Maud," who were squabbling (Julia Ward Howe diary, 8 December 1866, bMS Am 2119 [814], HL).

When Chev refused to allow her to accompany him to the Institute on December 12, she suspected the worst: "This caused me bitter pain & suspicion as the horrible reason for such an exclusion." To increase her misery, Chev "brought me very smartly to my own house, where of course my reception was such as I dreaded and expected" (Julia Ward Howe diary, 12 December 1866, bMS Am 2119 [814], HL).

79. Samuel Gridley Howe to "my dear Conway," 20 April [18]69, bMS Am 2119 (1365), HL.

80. Julia Ward Howe diary, 17 October 1872, bMS Am 2119 (814), HL.

81. Ibid., 19 March 1874.

82. Ibid., 1 April 1874.

83. Ibid., 26 November 1874.

84. Ibid., 31 December1874.

85. Ibid., 23 December 1874.

86. Ibid., 16 January, 1875.

87. Ibid., 26 July 1875.

88. Ibid., 13 August 1875.

89. Ibid., 23 November 1875.

90. Ibid., 8 December 1875.

91. Ibid., 9 December, 1875.

92. Ibid., 8 and 9 January 1876.

93. Ibid., 10 January 1876.

94. Julia Ward Howe, *Memoir of Dr. Samuel Gridley Howe* (Boston: Howe Memorial Committee/Albert J. Wright, 1876), pp. 61–62.

95. H. B. B., "Death of Dr. Howe," *Woman's Journal* 7, no. 3 (January 15, 1867): 20.

96. Julia Ward Howe diary, 13 and 15 January 1876, bMS Am 2119 (814), HL. Julia's journal entry for March 2 referred to "letters from the locked drawer," and she discussed on March 31 two letters that she found and burned at the Institute. She also destroyed a letter from April 1849, according to a diary note dated July 10. See also Clifford's discussion of the burning of the papers, pp. 205–7 of *Mine Eyes Have Seen the Glory*.

97. Julia Ward Howe diary, 23 January 1876, bMS Am 2119 (814), HL.

98. See her diary entry for April 30, 1876, bMS Am 2119 (814), HL.

99. Julia Ward Howe, "The Halfness of Nature," October 22, 1875, Julia Ward Howe Collection, box 3, Library of Congress. Reprinted in her *Is Polite Society Polite?* p. 170.

100. T. W. Higginson, "Julia Ward Howe," *The Outlook* (January 16, 1907), p. 167.

101. Julia Ward Howe diary, 25 May 1899, bMS Am 2119 (814), HL. Also quoted in Richards and Elliott, *Julia Ward Howe,* vol. 2, p. 263.

CHAPTER FIVE

1. Florence Howe, *Memories Grave and Gay,* pp. 201–2. Flossy also kept the family accounts and was inclined to be strict. Letters from her father indicated one "small storm" occasioned when Flossy forbade Maud to purchase ice cream for a party, because Flossy thought the ice cream was too expensive. Chev came to the rescue by buying a freezer so that they could produce ice cream at home. On another occasion, he sent Laura a check for ten dollars, apologizing, "I should have made it more, but Flossy the calculator, says ten is enough, & that you will spend all we send, be it ever so much. So dear if it is not enough[,] charge it to Flossy & send me word" (Samuel Gridley Howe to Laura E. Richards, 25 February 1869, and March 6, 1860,

record group 20, folder "Letters: SGH to LER, MHE, et al.," YHPCC; these letters are typed copies of the originals).

Even after she had married and started her own family, Flossy's culinary adventures continued. The first time she made gingerbread, she mistakenly used mustard in the recipe. The final product was not encouraging. "My family thought it hilarious," she remarked, "and I got $5 for an article about it in *Demorest's Magazine*." With practice, Flossy contended, she eventually produced admirable gingerbread (see *Memories Grave and Gay*, p. 217).

2. Harry Marion Howe to Laura Richards, 10 November 1910, record group 32, folder "Letters: HMH to LER 1910–1913," YHPCC. Chev described Maud to Laura in this way in 1874: "Maud is fluttering & floating over the field of fashion; the decided belle of the season. Poor child! she is becoming—undomesticated; has lost her balance;—what of higher aspirations she had; and (I fear) demoralized for the season. Silly Mama, has not the heart to restrain her; but lets her get intoxicated, daily, & nightly, by the admiration & compliments of silly men, by the fumes of fashion. Heaven grant she may not become permanently, & fatally injured, in moral character, in this flowery ordeal" (25 August 1874, record group 20, folder "Letters: Samuel Gridley Howe to LER, MHE, et al.," YHPCC; this letter is a typed copy of the original).

Julia tried in 1881 to defend Maud's ways to her brother Sam: "She is not worldly, though some of her inclinations might make you think so. She knows the value of recognised [sic] position, desirable neighborhood, etc etc, much better than I did, in my dream youth. Dear Father hated the fashionable world so sincerely, and Auntie . . . knew so little of the world at all that I grew up with an utter ignorance of the value of appearances which left me much to learn when I came to live in a strange place, as the wife of a man very conspicuous in position, and recognized as a 'come-outer' in politics and religion. These circumstances might naturally have led Maud to make some efforts in a contrary fashion" (22 May 1884, bMS Am 2119 [1682], HL).

3. Elliott, *Three Generations*, pp. 134–35.

4. Julia Ward Howe, "The New Year," *Woman's Journal* 6, no. 1 (January 2, 1875): 4.

5. Numerous Boston papers carried accounts of a dream (or vision, as she described it) that Julia had of the dawning millennium on April 2, 1908. See Clifford, *Mine Eyes Have Seen the Glory*, p. 270. For Julia's description of the dream, see "An account of my vision of the world regenerated by the combined labor and love of men and women," bMS Am 2214 (320), box 5, HL.

6. Julia Romana Anagnos to Laura E. Richards, 23 October, n.d., record group 20, folder "Letters: Julia Anagnos," YHPCC.

7. Julia Romana Anagnos to Laura E. Richards, Tuesday, n.d., record group 20, folder "Letters: Julia Anagnos," YHPCC. There are few preserved letters of Julia Romana Anagnos, as Laura burned most of them in the 1920s. The few letters that remain indicate that Julia Romana had a wickedly dry style, as evidenced in this letter written to Laura while Maud, Chev, and Julia were visiting Santo Domingo: "First of all, let me state, that [my husband] Michael is not dumb at all. We are a sedate & appreciative couple, especially appreciative of the extreme nastiness of those who abuse us. Second, that we are mostly bereft of family ties by the insane absence of our Dominican relatives. (Maud is to marry a Spanish nigger.)" Julia Romana Anagnos to Laura E. Richards, month unreadable, 1872, record group 20, folder "Letters: Julia Anagnos," YHPCC.

8. Julia Ward Howe to Laura E. Richards, 7 July 1871, record group 18, folder 1 of "Typed copies of letters from JWH to her relatives and friends," YHPCC.

9. Julia noted in a diary entry on October 5, 1872: "All life is full of trial, & when I hear literary performances praised, & remember my own love for it, & for praise, I think a little how much of all this I have sacrificed in these later years for a service which has made me enemies as well as

friends. I felt called upon to do this, and I still think that if I made a mistake, it was one of those honest mistakes wh[ich] it is best to make" (bMS Am 2119 [814], HL).

10. Elliott, *Three Generations,* pp. 88, 134–35.

11. Laura E. Richards, *Stepping Westward,* pp. 169, 388. Laura and her husband Harry moved to Maine in the summer of 1876. Both Laura and Julia were distressed about the move, but Laura's husband was called to work in his family's paper mill there. In time, Laura became a beloved figure in Gardiner, and the Richards home (the Yellow House) became a local icon of sorts.

12. Laura E. Richards to "Aunt" [Annie Mailliard], 24 October 1885, bMS Am 1595 (1462).

13. Laura E. Richards to "Dearest Own Auntie" [Annie Mailliard], 8 December 1890, bMS Am 1595 (1468).

14. Laura E. Richards to Mrs. [Annie] Mailliard, 8 November 1893, bMS Am 1595 (1473), HL.

15. Julia Ward Howe to Laura E. Richards, 21 June 1891, bMS Am 2119 (707i), HL.

16. Laura E. Richards to Louisa Crawford Terry, bMS Am 2119 (1601–1611), HL. This letter is one of the series between numbers 1601 and 1611, but its exact number is not indicated in the accession lists.

17. Laura E. Richards to Maud Howe Elliott, 1 June 1906, folder 41, "LER to MHE, 1900–1907," YHPGPL. These letters at Gardiner Public Library are copies of the originals housed at Colby College.

18. Maud Howe Elliott to Florence Howe Hall, 11 October 1898 [or 1899], Women's Studies Manuscript Collection, Julia Ward Howe Family, series 3, no. 76, reel 10, Schlesinger Library.

19. Julia Ward Howe to Florence Howe Hall, 20 April 1894, Women's Studies Manuscript Collection, Julia Ward Howe Family, series 3, no. 76, reel 10, Schlesinger Library.

20. Maud Howe Elliott to Florence Howe Hall [1893], Women's Studies Manuscript Collection, Julia Ward Howe Family, series 3, no. 75, reel 10, Schlesinger Library. Maud confessed with great regret after Julia's death, "alas! I so often did not have cream—for economy—she liked it better than anything!" See her "Notes on the Last Summer of J. W. H.'s Life," p. 15, record group 18, YHPCC.

21. Maud Howe Elliott, "Notes on the Last Summer of J. W. H.'s Life," record group 18, YHPCC.

22. Quoted in Smith, *The Yellow House Papers,* pp. 67–68.

23. Julia Ward Howe diary, 28 April 1908, bMS Am 2119 (814), HL.

24. Laura E. Richards to Maud Howe Elliott, 7 May 1900, folder 41, "LER to MHE, 1900–1907," YHPGPL. The letters in this folder are typed copies of the originals housed at Colby College.

25. Henry Marion Howe to Florence Howe Hall, n.d., Women's Studies Manuscript Collection, Julia Ward Howe Family, series 3, no. 80, reel 10, Schlesinger Library. Harry often was delegated as a go-between. Laura hoped he could convince Julia to accept a personal secretary at Harry's expense, but that plan never took hold (Laura E. Richards to the "Dear Three," 20 July 1903, folder 41, "LER-MHE, 1900–1907," YHPGPL; this citation comes from a typed copy of the original letter housed in the Colby College collection).

26. Laura E. Richards to Maud Howe Elliott, 23 April 1908, folder 42, "LER-MHE, 1908–1914," YHPGPL. This citation comes from a typed copy of the original letter housed in the Colby College collection.

27. Laura E. Richards to Maud Howe Elliott, 15 November 1900, folder 41, "LER-MHE, 1901–1907," YHPGPL. This citation comes from a typed copy of the original letter housed in the Colby College collection.

28. Laura E. Richards to Maud Howe Elliott, 10 March 1896, folder 40, "LER-MHE, 1881–1899," YHPGPL. This citation comes from a typed copy of the original letter housed in the Colby College collection.

29. Elliott, *Three Generations,* p. 209.

30. Laura E. Richards to Maud Howe Elliott, 17 June 1907, folder 41, "LER-MHE, 1901–1907," YHPGPL. This letter is a typed copy of the original housed in the Colby College collection.

31. Laura E. Richards to Maud Howe Elliott, 2 April 1906, folder 41, "LER-MHE, 1901–1907," YHPGPL. This letter is a typed copy of the original housed in the Colby College collection.

32. Laura E. Richards to Maud Howe Elliott, 26 May 1907, folder 41, "LER-MHE, 1901–1907," YHPGPL. This letter is a typed copy of the original housed in the Colby College collection.

33. Henry Marion Howe to Laura E. Richards, 2 January 1911, red notebook: "Correspondence, HMH to LER, 1876–1922," YHPGPL. These letters are typed copies of originals found in the Colby College collection. As Harry also observed, when Laura was reluctant to hurt her sisters by excluding them from the writing of their mother's biography: "We are Dr. Howe's children too, and not to be diverted from a line of duty by such considerations" (Henry Marion Howe to Laura E. Richards, 10 November 1910, record group 32, folder "Letters: HMH to LER, 1910–1913, YHPCC). A few days later, he wrote again: "The essence of chivalry, is it not to endure for the sake of others? You will yield to none in your chivalry, being pre-eminently your father's daughter. You will feel the sting, but after a while you will rejoice to endure the pain" (22 November 1910). When in their adult years the Howe children wrangled (a not infrequent occurrence), invoking the memory of the Chevalier could provide justification for pursuing their goals to another's detriment. Harry's point above to Laura was that, even though Maud and Flossy wanted to co-write their mother's biography, Laura was the best author for the job. Thus, he concluded, Laura should be brave like her father and insist on her own way, even if she thereby hurt her sisters.

Maud made a similar case about another family dispute to Laura in January 1910. Both Flossy's son Harry Hall and Laura's son Hal Richards wanted to be hired as headmaster of the Perkins School for the Blind. Both Maud and Laura agreed that Hal was the man for the job, and Maud urged Laura to tell Flossy so. As far as Maud was concerned, Flossy's feelings on this topic were irrelevant; what mattered was honoring the Chevalier and the school he had made famous. "If you believe as I do that your boy is the only one who could wear the Giant's robe properly," she told Laura, "just because the little sister will be hurt is a trivial reason for letting it go wrong. We owe papa more than we owe her, and if it came to making even a serious breach with her, and not honoring with all our might and main papa's memory, she must be hurt!" (n.p., n.d., record group 15, box 1, folder "Letters from MHE to LER, 1905–1910," YHPCC). Ultimately, neither Harry nor Hal was offered the job, and the directorship of the Perkins Institute passed from Howe family control.

34. Margaret Field, "Julia Ward Howe and Her Daughters," *Munsey's Magazine* (February 1895), p. 529.

35. Elliott, *This Was My Newport,* p. 177.

36. Maud's unpublished manuscript entitled *The Golden Special* is an account of her campaign work on behalf of Charles Evans Hughes, the Progressive presidential candidate of 1916. Maud Howe Elliott Papers, John Hay Library.

37. Danny D. Smith, *The Yellow House Papers,* pp. 129–30.

38. Laura E. Richards to Maud Howe Elliott, 11 February 1915, record group 12, folder 43, YHPGPL. This citation comes from a typed copy of the original letter, which is housed in the Colby College collection.

39. Hall, *Memories Grave and Gay,* pp. 258–62.

40. Maud observed in *Three Generations* (p. 62) that Julia Romana had been "the intimate of my childhood, but I remember a curious withdrawal the moment my feet touched the threshold of girlhood." Then the "beneficent and adored elder sister" became more distant, a development that Maud said eventually made sense to her. "I understand it all now, I could not then." Her mother never did comprehend it. In one diary entry, Julia complained that she was "almost crazed by the irritability & quarrelling of Maud & Julia," adding that she "felt broken hearted at this mutual unkindness, & unkindness to me" (Julia Ward Howe diary, 30 December 1867, bMS Am 2119 [814], HL).

41. Maud hinted at the family literary rivalry when she wrote, "In my family we all wrote books inevitably, and while we tried to be patient with each other, we were rather tried by each other's work. I rarely knew what my sisters, my mother, or [my cousin] Crawford were writing, and more rarely read their books when they were published" (*Three Generations,* p. 201). Undoubtedly many critiques of one another's works have been lost, but Laura clearly scoffed at Flossy's ability to write fiction. After Flossy published *Flossy's Play Days,* Laura told Maud that the memoir of Flossy's childhood played to her strengths. Flossy was unable to "write—make up—a story, but she relates the actual with a directness that will (or should) delight children," Laura concluded. (13 November 1906, folder 41, "LER to MHE, 1901–1907," YHPGPL. This citation is from a copy of the original letter housed in the Colby College collection.)

42. Maud Howe Elliott diary, 26 September 1911, Maud Howe Elliott Papers, John Hay Library.

43. Julia Ward Howe to Maud Howe Elliott, 21 August 1898, MS 88.12, "Letters from Julia Ward Howe to Maud Howe Elliott," John Hay Library.

44. Maud Howe Elliott to Florence Howe Hall, 3 May [1899], Women's Studies Manuscript Collection, Julia Ward Howe Family, series 3, no. 76, reel 10, Schlesinger Library. Perhaps in reply to Maud, Flossy noted in her autobiography that although her sons enjoyed Harvard, it "was fully borne in upon them . . . that study must be the principal aim of their college course. We could not afford to send them to Harvard simply for amusement." Flossy also noted (with justifiable pride) that all of Julia's grandsons (Laura had three and Flossy two) went to Harvard, but only her Jack had managed to win a varsity letter. Jack was the youngest of her sons, and he was obliged to help finance his Harvard education with scholarships and part-time employment (Hall, *Memories Grave and Gay,* pp. 254–57).

45. Laura actually had seven children, but a daughter died in infancy.

46. Laura wrote to her aunt Annie Mailliard on November 8, 1893, that Jack had been in Rome since the previous autumn, preparing a design for artwork to be submitted for inclusion in the new Boston Public Library. Maud and Jack, Laura reported, had "felt the separation keenly, but Maud has always given Mamma the first place, Jack gladly consenting thereto." When Jack found his design had won a commission from the library, however, he insisted that Maud join him in Rome.

That demand was traumatic for Maud. "I found poor Maud almost distracted, the two loves, the two desires, for the first time pulling opposite directions," Laura confided to her aunt. "On the one side, the sacred, blessed Mother, needing her more and more always, (far more than she is aware of) on the other side the husband whom she loves, and who, after all, only demands his right." In the end, both Julia and Laura advised Maud to go. Still, Laura was not pleased. "I don't in the least believe that a picture cannot be painted in Boston as well as in Rome," she concluded (bMS Am 1595 [1473], HL).

47. Laura E. Richards to Maud Howe Elliott, 18 December 1899, folder 40, "LER-MHE, 1881–1899," YHPGPL. Laura defended Gardiner to Maud, explaining that her husband's family and her own children cherished the sporting opportunities available even in the coldest months. "You think of this as a dreary little hole, in winter, I mean; but you see, it doesn't seem so to them; they love the cold and the snow, and the snuffy people, and every bit of it, yes, they do."

In 1906, Laura expounded further upon her years in Maine. "Humdrum they seem to you?" she asked Maud. "Yes; but I could not have lived at your pace, my darling, I am not big enough; and I couldn't have brought up the children either; and I should not—oh, why should I foolishly talk? you know how greatly and wonderfully happy I have been; and if you made the best match, as you say you did, then you made a Darned Good One" (17 June 1906, folder 41, "LER to MHE, 1901–1907," YHPGPL; both this citation and the one preceding it are taken from typed copies of the original letters housed in the Colby College).

Maud agreed that Laura's life was mundane, and, to her taste, over-regimented. She reported, after a visit to Gardiner in 1933, a stultifying daily routine that began with breakfast in bed at 7:30. Laura then set to work writing until 10:30, when she, Skipper, and daughter Rosalind met on the piazza for a fifteen-minute break. Laura invariably drank a cup of malted milk, while Skipper had buttermilk and a doughnut. Literary work then continued until noon, when Laura took a nap. Dinner was at 1:00. Afterwards, Skipper and Rosalind napped, while Laura returned to her work, occasionally mixing in reading with her writing. At 4:30, everyone adjourned to the parlor for tea, where they usually welcomed a steady stream of guests. After tea, Laura and Rosalind retired to their rooms, to emerge at 6:30 in evening clothes and jewels. ("I highly approve of this habit," Maud noted.) Supper was then served; afterwards, a silent period commenced during which people read from a variety of newspaper and journals—as Maud observed, the Richards subscribed to all the best of them. At 8:00, Laura read aloud for the family, and at 8:45, everyone joined in a game of cards. At 9:30, all retreated to bed.

Maud admitted she had not even heard of most of the books with which Laura, Skipper, and Rosalind busied themselves, and was rather stunned to live in a place where works like the *Manchester Guardian Spectator* were "not only taken but read." She observed that Rosalind's life was "dedicated, I might even say sanctified, to parental devotion," and concluded—not without irony—that she found the household routine "very instructive and almost super human." It is hard to disagree. Maud Howe Elliott diary, 3 and 7 October 1933, Maud Howe Elliott Papers, John Hay Library.

48. Julia Ward Howe diary, 25 and 27 February 1886, bMS Am 2119 (814), HL.

49. Julia Ward Howe diary, 7 May 1886, bMS Am 2119 (814), HL. Julia had written Julia Romana and Flossy from Rome: "Mother is often sad to think she cannot see your dear faces. Sometimes she dreams of you at night, and then when she wakes up, she is grieved to find out how far away you are, and that she cannot hope to see you for many long days" (bMS Am 2215 [435], HL).

50. Julia Ward Howe diary, 27 February 1886, bMS Am 2119 (814), HL.

51. Julia Ward Howe to Maud Howe Elliott, 1 March 1886, record group 16, folder "Letters from JWH to MHE, 1883–1895," YHPCC.

52. Julia Ward Howe to Maud Howe Elliott, 5 March 1886, record group 16, folder "Letters from JWH to MHE, 1883–1895," YHPCC. Julia told Maud that she had sent Maud a postcard from Providence and that she returned to find Julia Romana no worse.

53. Julia Ward Howe to Maud Howe Elliott, 5 March 1886, record group 16, folder "Letters from JWH to MHE, 1883–1895," YHPCC. See also Julia Ward Howe diary, 6 March 1886, bMS Am 2119 (814), HL.

54. Julia Ward Howe diary, 9–10 March 1886, bMS Am 2119 (814), HL; and Julia Ward Howe to Louisa Crawford Terry, 12 April 1886, bMS Am 2215 (389), HL.

55. Julia Ward Howe to Annie Mailliard, 9 May 1884, bMS Am 2119 (681), HL.

56. Julia Ward Howe, *Reminiscences,* pp. 441–42. I have used the following sources in reconstructing the death scene of Julia Romana: her mother's diary entries and her mother's April 12, 1886, letter to Louisa Crawford Terry (bMS Am 2215 [389], HL). Neither of these sources mentions Julia Romana instructing her husband to care for the blind children because they were Chev's. The diary gives a long account of Julia Romana's last day, and the letter to Louisa recaps that account. If Julia Romana actually told Michael to care for the blind children, her mother did not include that conversation in her earliest reconstructions of the scene.

57. Hall, *Memories Grave and Gay,* p. 310. Julia's April 12, 1886, letter to her sister Louisa disagreed. "You probably know her last words: 'if this is not the right one, call another priestess—truth, truth!" (bMS Am 2215 [389], HL).

58. Laura E. Richards, *Laura Bridgman: The Story of an Opened Door* (New York: Appleton, 1928), p. 76.

59. Julia Ward Howe Diary, 26 and 27 February 1886, bMS Am 2119 (814), HL.

60. Julia Ward Howe to Louisa Crawford Terry, 12 April 1886, bMS Am 2215 (389), HL.

61. Laura E. Richards to Annie Howe Mailliard, 6 August 1886, bMS Am 2119 (1605), HL.

62. Henry Marion Howe to Laura E. Richards, 26 March 1886, record group 32, folder "Letters: Copies of HMH to LER, 1876–1922," YHPCC.

63. Henry Marion Howe to Laura E. Richards, 29 March 1886, record group 32, folder "Letters: Copies of HMH to LER, 1876–1922," YHPCC.

64. Julia Ward Howe to Laura E. Richards, 14 March 1884, bMS Am 2119 (684h), HL. Maud continued to struggle with her relationship to Julia Romana long after her sister's death. Years later, Maud wrote Flossy that she did not especially like Julia Romana's husband Michael. She had invited him to Christmas dinner, but he had had another engagement, and Maud commented that Michael had not visited for quite some time. "I don't care for him," she admitted, "only I feel achey about dear Julia & somehow ashamed as I have failed towards him in affection" (26 December, n.d., Women's Studies Manuscript Collection, Julia Ward Howe Family, series 3, nos. 77–78, reel 10, Schlesinger Library).

65. Julia Ward Howe Diary, 9 and 10 March 1886, bMS Am 2119 (814), HL; and Julia Ward Howe to Louisa Crawford Terry, 12 April 1866, bMS Am 2215 (389), HL.

66. Julia Ward Howe diary, 24 March 1886, bMS Am 2119 (814), HL. Julia had reported the same kind of anguish over Sammy's death. She told her sister Annie in May 1863 that she was "still fighting over the dark battle of his death, still questioning whether there is any forgiveness for such a death. Something must have been wrong, somewhere—to find it out, I have tortured myself almost out of sanity" (May 22, [1863], bMS Am 2119 [594], HL).

67. Julia Ward Howe diary, 30–31 March 1886, bMS Am 2119 (814), HL.

68. Ibid., 21 April, 27 April, and 9 May 1886.

69. Richards and Elliott, *Julia Ward Howe,* vol. 2, p. 118.

70. Julia Ward Howe diary, 24 and 25 June 1886, bMS Am 2119 (814), HL.

71. Julia Ward Howe diary, 26 November 1886, bMS Am 2119 (814), HL.

72. Hall, *Memories Grave and Gay,* pp. 228–29. Maud referred to this incident in a letter to Aunt Louisa Crawford Terry, telling of her coming marriage to Jack Elliott. Flossy would not be well enough to attend the wedding, she explained, though Julia had nursed her through her "terrible rheumatic fever" (bMS Am 1595 [1104], HL).

73. Julia noted in her diary entry for December 27, 1886: "The day was a very distressing one to me. I sat much of the time beside F[lossy] with a strange feeling that I could keep her alive by some effort of my will. I seemed to contend with God, saying, 'I gave up Julia, I can't give up Flossy—she has children'" (Julia Ward Howe diary, bMS Am 2119 [814], HL).

74. Hall, *Memories Grave and Gay,* p. 201.

75. Julia Ward Howe to Louisa Crawford, 29 September 1846, bMS Am 2119 (456), HL.

76. Julia Ward Howe diary, 31 December 1867, bMS Am 2119 (814), HL.

77. Ibid., 5 September 1867; and Henry Marion Howe to Florence Howe Hall, 24 December 1916, record group 32, folder "Letters: HMH to LER, 1914–1919," YHPCC.

78. Chev wrote Laura in March 1869 that Julia Romana "went with Harry and Flossy to a party last evening. She also went out on Sunday eve; so you see she is getting into the world" (record group 20, folder "SGH Letters to LER, MHE, et al.," YHPCC; this letter is a typed copy of the original). Julia noted in an 1870 letter to Laura, "I took Julia to the Chas. Russell's, yesterday, a Croquet reception. She did pretty well" (13 August 1870, file 19, "Letters from Julia Ward Howe and Ward Family: One," YHPGPL; this letter is a typed copy of the original).

Occasionally even her father suffered Julia Romana's wrath. Chev reported from Greece in 1867 that Julia Romana did not have a natural appetite and had at times ignored him on the trip. She was not sociable, he concluded, and even when she had treated him well, she was "oh! so frigid & repellent to every body" (Samuel Gridley Howe to Laura E. Richards, 5 May 1867 and 8 June 1867, record group 20, folder "Letters: SGH to LER, MHE, et al.," YHPCC; this letter is a typed copy of the original).

79. Laura E. Richards to Maud Howe Elliott, 4 December 1895, folder 40, "LER-MHE, 1881–1899," YHPGPL. This letter is a typed copy of the original housed in the Colby College collection.

80. *Proceedings of the Metaphysical Club, at a Meeting Held March 24, 1886, in Memory of its late President, Julia Romana Anagnos* (Boston: Henry H. Clark, 1886), p. 6.

81. Samuel Gridley Howe to Charles Sumner, 4 February [1856], bMS Am 2119 (1152), HL.

82. Samuel Gridley Howe to Louisa Crawford Terry, 14 October 1866, bMS Am 2119 (1339), HL.

83. Hall, *Memories Grave and Gay,* p. 178.

84. Elliott, *This Was My Newport,* pp. 93–95. Numerous family members pronounced satisfaction at Julia Romana's marriage; generally, they claimed that Michael was a sensitive and caring husband. A letter from Julia to Chev prior to the marriage indicates the strain that the match introduced in their relationship: "Julia [Romana] writes to you today of something near to her heart, and surely to your's [sic]. She will not show me her letter, but I suppose that you and she will come to an understanding in the matter . . . the suddenness . . . took me much by surprise, and her peculiarities give me great anxiety for her future. But if this marriage can be arranged on a suitable footing, I suppose that we shall both of us consider her dreams of health and happiness as greatly increased." Clearly, Julia Romana's preference for her father

over her mother was a source of tension; equally evident was her mother's concern for what she considered her daughter's eccentricities (16 October 1870, record group 20, folder "Correspondence between SGH and JWH," YHPCC). In an 1871 letter to Laura, Chev reported, "Julia R—is about recovered from a long & tedious slow fever. Anagnos is in full feather; & is the most affectionate husband, of a year's standing, that I have ever known" (27 November 1871, record group 20, folder "SGH to LER, MHE, et al.," YHPCC; this letter is a typed copy of the original).

85. Julia Ward Howe, *Reminiscences.* p. 440. Like Chev, Julia Romana liked to be cared for when sick, and during a short illness in 1870 wrote Laura a letter marked "private." Chev, she explained, had been "very kind & tender, waiting on me, & winding up the music-box etc., also dancing, to amuse me" during the illness. Her mother was less nurturing: "Mamma, who regards me as a beautiful composite structure of sanctified air, & good cast iron, crowned with a large glove of imagination, cannot of course, understand that such a being ever has any but illusory aches" (Julia Romana Anagnos to Laura E. Richards, 1870, record group 20, folder "Letters: Julia Anagnos," YHPCC).

86. See Henry Marion Howe to Laura E. Richards, 27 December 1914, and to Florence Howe Hall, 24 December 1916, record group 32, folder "Letters: HMH to LER, 1914–1919," YHPCC.

87. Julia Ward Howe diary, 4 June 1876, bMS Am 2119 (814), HL. The question of Julia Romana's mental health is intriguing, and given the fact that various family members deliberately burned embarrassing family papers over the course of many decades (see the end of this chapter for more details), it is a topic that I cannot definitively settle. A review of the secondary literature yields the following results. First, Grant argues that Julia Romana had a nervous breakdown in 1859 and was not yet well by 1863 (*Private Woman, Public Person,* pp. 140, 186).

Second, Tharp contends that Julia Romana suffered a nervous breakdown at her father's death as well. The revelations about Chev's infidelities in the letters Michael Anagnos found and burned were, according to Tharp, exceedingly traumatic to Julia Romana (*Three Saints and A Sinner,* p. 352). I have found no evidence that Julia Romana read those letters or that her husband Michael shared their contents with her. But Tharp is a reliable source and had access to portions of the Howe archives while they were in the possession of Laura Richard's daughter Rosalind. Because Tharp included very few notes, however, there is no way to trace many of her contentions.

Third, historian Danny Smith catalogued the Yellow House Papers and is unquestionably the leading authority on Howe archival materials. He argues not only that Julia Romana suffered recurring bouts of insanity, but that Flossy's "intense jealousy of sister Laura drove her into periods of insanity requiring institutional care." See *The Yellow House Papers,* p. 110. I have absolute respect for Smith's expertise in all matters relating to the Howe family, but as yet I cannot confirm his claim from my own research.

As the complicated notes in this book suggest, Howe research is difficult. Records are scattered among many archives. Very few scholars have examined the Yellow House Papers. As Smith notes, the cataloguing was "in absolute abeyance" from the death of Rosalind Richards in 1964 until he undertook the task of inventorying and organizing the collection. Smith's inventory was published in 1991, but was never widely distributed, and is currently out of print. Therefore, a definitive answer to the issue of the mental health of Flossy or of Julia Romana potentially awaits a more intrepid (or observant) researcher than I. To quote Smith again: "That some scholar will have ample opportunity to expand the field is evident, not only through a more thorough exploration of the contents of individual Record Groups of the Yellow House Papers but in the collections of other historical societies, libraries, and archives. . . . To him, to her, and to them, the best of luck!" See *The Yellow House Papers*, pp. 21, 85.

88. Samuel Ward to Julia Ward Howe, 20 July 1876, bMS Am 2119 (1830), HL. Sam wrote to Julia that he had received a letter from Julia Romana announcing her recovery.

89. Maud Howe Elliott and Florence Howe Hall, *Laura Bridgman: Dr. Howe's Famous Pupil and What He Taught Her* (Boston: Little, Brown, 1903), p. 314.

90. *Proceedings of the Metaphysical Club*, pp. 21–22, 35–36. Ednah D. Cheney described Julia Romana's stubbornness in the gentlest possible terms. "She was not a child who acted from memory, or did things others told her to do; there was something creative about her. I think we felt it here. . . . If she made a remark, you felt it was her own thought, and not taken from others; and that was the reason she had such an enlivening effect upon everybody" (p. 34).

John S. Dwight provided insights into Julia Romana's management style at the Metaphysical Club she founded. "She had no idea of organization; that was not her nature; it was pure impulse. She said, I remember, 'You, Mr. Dwight, must be president.' Said I, 'On what authority; there is no society, no club yet that I am aware of; how can I be president?'. . . And so it went on week after week, she finding all the essayists, with a great deal of trouble of course, and arranging for the places of meeting with the lady friends. So it went on without any shape, scarcely, without anything like membership. Membership was always talked of, but no one knew who were members and who were not; it was simply a matter of more or less attendance" (pp. 9–10).

After Julia Romana's death, the club formed a committee to make recommendations for the future. Indecision reigned, as C. W. Ernst reported: "The committee, after meeting several times, and giving the subject full consideration, did not feel able to recommend any plan of reorganization. It was not empowered to make any full decision, or even to call a meeting of the Club. It could only preserve this memorial, and report its decision to the members, in the hope that some more competent source would come up with the means of carrying out the plans of Mrs. Anagnos" (p. 51).

Lectures presented at the club included "The Methods of Philosophical Study" (C. W. Ernst), "Nirvana" (Edna D. Cheney), "The Identity of the Anglo-Saxon Race with the Lost Tribes of Israel" (B. O. Kinnear), "Life Under Three Aspects, Appearance, Experience, Influence" (Julia Ward Howe), "Can We Know the Infinite?" (W. T. Harris), "Metaphysics of Scenery" (E. F. Hayward), "Immortality and Modern Thought" (T. T. Munger), and "Das Ewige Weibliche" (Edna D. Cheney). See pp. 69–73 of the Proceedings for a complete list.

91. Hall, *Memories Grave and Gay*, p. 3.

92. Richards, *When I Was Your Age*, p. 14.

93. Julia Ward Howe, *Reminiscences*, p. 442.

94. Richards, *When I Was Your Age*, p. 127.

95. Julia Romana Anagnos to Florence Howe Hall, South Boston, n.d., Women's Studies Manuscript Collection, Julia Ward Howe Family, series 3, no. 74, reel 10, Schlesinger Library.

96. Julia Ward Howe, *Reminiscences*, p. 440.

97. Julia Romana Anagnos, *Philosophiae Quaestor; Or, Days in Concord* (Boston: D. Lothrop, 1885), pp. 14–15, 26–31. I have found no record of Julia's response to her daughter's satirical description of the Concord School. A diary entry for September 2, 1886, recorded Julia's disapproval of a letter in the paper by Mrs. Harriet Stanton Blatch. According to Julia, Blatch ridiculed the Concord School of Philosophy and covertly derided the Dante lecture Julia had read at Concord. Julia was displeased. "This young woman is pretty, and pretends to be amiable. She is a graduate of Vassar. Her diatribe is silly & shallow, as well as insolent." Julia might as well (except

for the Vassar detail) have been describing the author of Philosophiae Quaestor (Julia Ward Howe diary, 2 September 1886, bMS Am 2119 [814], HL).

98. *Proceedings of the Metaphysical Club,* p. 7. There are times when the club's Proceedings (see also n. 90) sound like a satire that Julia Romana herself might have written. In their bubbling earnestness, John S. Dwight and C. W. Ernst seem almost to have emerged from the pages of *Philosophiae Quaestor.*

99. Julia R. Anagnos, *Stray Chords* (Boston: Cupples, Upham, 1883), p. 71.

100. See Anagnos, *Stray Chords,* pp. 66–67.

101. Julia Ward Howe, "Mind Versus Mill-Stream," *Passion-Flowers,* 1st ed., p. 81. I am indebted to Williams for the interpretation of the "crimson weed" as a reference to Julia's hair. See *Hungry Heart,* p. 157.

102. Maud Howe Elliott to Florence Howe Hall, Sunday [1893], Women's Studies Manuscript Collection, Julia Ward Howe Family, series 3, no. 75, reel 10, Schlesinger Library.

103. Richards and Elliott, *Julia Ward Howe,* vol. 2, p. 119.

104. Maud Howe Elliott, "Notes on the Last Summer of J. W. H.'s Life," p. 8, record group 18, YHPCC.

105. Even Flossy was not so poor that she could not afford a servant. The Howe poverty was of a genteel nature.

106. Maud Howe Elliott to Laura E. Richards, n.d., n.p., record group 15, folder "Letters from MHE to LER, 1910–1919," YHPCC. Julia did leave behind one poem chastising those who complained of poverty entitled "On Hearing One Complain 'There is no one to die and leave us money'"(Julia Ward Howe, *From Sunset Ridge: Poems Old and New,* p. 161):

ᴏᏽᴄ

Live, my beloved ones! live, and make us rich
With Life's sweet treasures of humanity.
Feed not the cruel agony and itch
Of souls distrained to Luxury's sharp pitch,
But let us earn our modest joys, and be
Richer in service than its moneyed fee.

ᴏᏽᴄ

107. The first meeting of the united bodies (called the National American Woman Suffrage Association) was in February 1890. See Clifford, *Mine Eyes Have Seen the Glory,* pp. 249–50.

108. Sandra Van Burkleo and Mary Jo Miles, "Julia Ward Howe," in John A. Garraty and Mark C. Carnes, eds., *American National Biography,* vol. 11 (New York: Oxford University Press, 1999), p. 332; and Paul S. Boyer, "Julia Ward Howe," *Notable American Women,* p. 228.

109. Boyer, "Julia Ward Howe," p. 229.

110. Ibid.; and "Mrs. Howe in Florence," repr. from the *New York Times* in the *Woman's Journal* 9, no. 30 (July 27, 1878): 236; Sarah Knowles Bolton, *Famous Leaders among Women* (New York: Thomas Y. Crowell, 1895), p. 297.

111. Julia Ward Howe, manuscript fragment, p. 4, box 5, folder "Miscellany/Notes and Fragments," Julia Ward Howe Collection, Library of Congress.

112. Julia Ward Howe, "The Liberty Wherewith Christ Has Made Us Free," n.d., box 3, Julia Ward Howe Collection, Library of Congress. I estimate this to be a relatively early sermon because it refers to the emancipation of the slaves as a sign of hope for the empowerment of women (a popular theme after the Civil War) and because some of the pages are written on the

back of Perkins Institute stationery that includes "187__" as part of the letterhead. The references for the material in this note come from a section of the sermon in which the pages are not numbered.

113. Julia Ward Howe, "The Liberty Wherewith Christ Has Made Us Free," pp. 20–25, 35–37, box 3, Julia Ward Howe Collection, Library of Congress.

114. Julia Ward Howe, "Moral Equality of the Sexes," 1893, Women's Studies Manuscript Collection, Julia Ward Howe Family, series 2, no. 33, reel 8, Schlesinger Library.

115. Julia Ward Howe, "Marriage and Divorce," pp. 5–10. Typescript copy of a speech delivered in Louisville for the Association for the Advancement of Women, 1888, bMS Am 2214 (320), box 8, HL.

116. Ibid., pp. 24–26.

117. Julia Ward Howe, "Benefits of Suffrage to Women," A.A.W. convention, Chicago, 1883, pp. 10–13, 30, bMS Am 2214 (320), box 1, HL.

118. Julia Ward Howe, "What the 19th Century Has Done for Women," *New York World* (winter 1898–99), Women's Studies Manuscript Collection, Julia Ward Howe Family, series 2, no. 34, reel 8, Schlesinger Library.

119. Julia Ward Howe, "Address of Mrs. Howe at the Annual American Woman Suffrage Association," *Woman's Journal* 41, no. 43 (October 24, 1885): 344.

120. Julia Ward Howe, "The Industrial Value of Women," repr. from *North American Review* in response to Charles W. Elliott's "Woman's Work and Woman's Wages," *Woman's Journal* 12, no. 43 (October 28, 1882): 338. Julia despised Elliott's suggestion that education made women too critical to be good spouses, and went to great lengths in this article to deny that woman's prime function was to bear children. "There is an insincerity as well as a falsity in the statement so often forced upon us, that the function of maternity should be the paramount theme of woman's thoughts, and the supreme end of their lives. We have tried to show that, for civilized women, child-bearing is only justifiable under strict conditions of respect, refinement, and sympathy. Does any man of education desire to link to himself this creature trained to marry the first man who asks her, to bear as many children as possible, and to limit her interests and activities to the sphere of the kitchen, the table, and the wardrobe? Does any man in his senses wish to see this *muliebrous* animal take the place of the women who are the intelligent companions of men, who appeal to their most chivalrous sentiments, and stimulate their highest capacities?"

121. Julia Ward Howe to Annie Ward Mailliard, 30 July 1883, bMS Am 2119 (679), HL. Neither Maud nor Julia Romana had children either, but if Julia made similar observations about her daughters, those remarks have not been preserved.

122. Julia Ward Howe, "Culture," n.d., p. 20, box 2, Julia Ward Howe Collection, Library of Congress.

123. Julia Ward Howe, *Reminiscences,* pp. 216–17.

124. Elmer C. Adams and Warren Durham Foster, *Heroines of Modern Progress* (New York: Sturgis & Walton, 1913), pp. 212–13.

125. "Mrs. Howe's Eightieth Birthday," *Woman's Journal* 30, no. 21 (May 27, 1899): 162.

126. Boston Authors Club, "Birthday Tributes to Mrs. Julia Ward Howe" (Winthrop B. Jones Press, 1905), pp. 5–8; T. W. Higginson, "Julia Ward Howe," *Outlook* (January 16, 1907), p. 177.

127. "Boston Warmed Up," *Philadelphia Press,* May 1899. Clipping pasted into Julia Ward Howe diary, 29 May 1899, bMS Am 2119 (814), HL.

128. Nathan Haskell Dole, "Julia Ward Howe and Her Talented Family," *Munsey's Magazine* (February 1910), p. 614.

129. Julia Ward Howe diary, 13 June 1910, and 3 August 1910, bMS Am 2119 (814), HL. Maud was convinced that the fall Julia suffered in June ultimately caused her death. According to Maud, Julia suspected that her maid was emptying her chamber pot down the set basin in Julia's bedroom, rather than in the bathroom. So Julia began emptying the vessel herself, early in the mornings. Julia's bedroom was darkened at that hour, because she thought that morning sun was harmful to her eyes. One morning, when Julia was carrying the chamber pot to the bathroom, she noted an effervescence inside, probably due to the reaction of urine to the cleaning powder residue in the pot. Julia was so startled by the foaming that she fell against the side of her bed. Though a doctor was summoned, the broken rib was not immediately diagnosed. Once the break was detected, Julia endured the ministrations of a private nurse until she felt well enough to dismiss her. Maud Howe Elliott, "Notes on the Last Summer of J. W. H.'s Life," pp. 1–6, record group 18, YHPCC.

130. Maud Howe Elliott, "Notes on the Last Summer of J. W. H.'s Life," pp. 4–6, 10.

131. Ibid., pp. 23–24. See also Richards and Elliott, *Julia Ward Howe,* vol. 2, pp. 412–14.

132. Julia Ward Howe diary, 24 May 1889, and 12 April 1892, bMS Am 2119 (814), HL.

133. Mayor Fitzgerald, "Opening Address," *Memorial Exercises in Honor of Julia Ward Howe* (City of Boston, 1911), p. 6.

134. Miss Mary E. Woolley, "Address," *Memorial Exercises in Honor of Julia Ward Howe,* p. 11.

135. Hon. Curtis Guild, Jr., "Address," *Memorial Exercises in Honor of Julia Ward Howe,* p. 38.

136. William H. Lewis, "Address," *Memorial Exercises in Honor of Julia Ward Howe,* pp. 23–24.

137. Laura E. Richards, *Letters and Journals of Samuel Gridley Howe: The Servant of Humanity* (Boston: Dana Estes; London: John Lane, 1909).

138. Laura E. Richards, "Woman in Literature," in Maud Howe Elliott, *Art and Handicraft in the Woman's Building of the World's Columbian Exposition, Chicago, 1893* (Paris: Goupil & Co., Boussod, Valadon & Co., Successors, 1893), p. 103.

139. Maud Howe Elliott to Florence Howe Hall, 25 February, n.d., Women's Studies Manuscript Collection, Julia Ward Howe Family, series 3, nos. 77–78, reel 10, Schlesinger Library.

140. In discussing Helen Keller's work with Annie Sullivan, the text indicated, "Helen Keller's early education was conducted on the same lines as Laura's." Before working with Helen, the text observed, Annie had studied Dr. Howe's reports, associated with Laura Bridgman, and spent five years at the Institute as a pupil, "using the books and appliances of the school and receiving constantly information from its teachers." Sadly, Maud and Flossy concluded, Annie Sullivan failed to apply the methods she had learned. "The exact and minute daily record, which is of such value in Laura's case, is unfortunately wanting in Helen's. It is deeply to be regretted that, owing to the lack of reliable scientific data, it has proved inexpedient to give a fuller account of this interesting case" (*Laura Bridgman: Dr. Howe's Famous Pupil and What He Taught Her,* pp. 332–33).

Annie Sullivan returned the Howe's enmity. As an impoverished student at the Institute, she had found the Howes arrogant, and in particular had no patience with Julia, who would occasionally read to the blind children. Because Annie succeeded in teaching Helen how to speak, the Howes were apprehensive that the public might regard Helen as superior to Laura Bridgman. Michael Anagnos's 1888 report on Annie Sullivan's work with Helen was glowing; by 1889 he had moderated that opinion considerably, noting that Annie had invented no techniques but had merely done a superb job of applying the methods of Samuel Gridley Howe. See Dorothy Hermann, *Helen Keller: A Life* [New York: Knopf, 1998], pp. 19–20, 26, 36, 55–85. The Howes suspected that Annie Sullivan was doing a great deal of Helen's communicating for her and felt vindicated when a children's book published by Helen turned out to be overly dependent on a story Annie had once read to her. Julia wrote that she had suspected, when she had watched Helen at age eleven making remarks about Rome at a public exhibition at the Institute, that Helen's words were not wholly her own (Women's Studies Manuscript Collection, Julia Ward Howe Family, series 2, no. 53, reel 9, Schlesinger Library).

For more details (and there are *many* more details) of the Howes' feud with Annie Sullivan, see also Nella Braddy, *Annie Sullivan Macy: The Story Behind Helen Keller* (Garden City, N.Y.: Doubleday, Doran, 1933); and Joseph P. Lash, *Helen and Teacher: The Story of Helen Keller and Anne Sullivan* (Boston: Addison Wesley, 1980). Records in the Perkins Institute archives are also of much value on this issue.

141. Henry Marion Howe to Laura E. Richards, 3 November 1910, and 8 November 1910, record group 32, folder "Letters: HMH to LER, 1909–1913," YHPCC.

142. This story is hard to trace, as the remaining documents are sketchy. Many pages from Maud's diary entries for January and February 1911 have been torn out. Maud was struggling mightily with this issue in those days—she called January 28, 1911, the worst day since Julia died, noting that a "dagger, poisoned, was driven into my heart—et tu Brute!" The pages that have been torn out of the diary presumably dwelled at greater length on her fury at brother Harry. She said on January 6 that she felt that she had been stabbed in the back by Harry and Flossy (who endorsed Harry's letter) (Maud Howe Elliott Papers, John Hay Library).

Harry's letter to Laura on January 2, 1911, indicated that he was not opposed to Jack Elliott's painting the portrait, but that he was convinced it would never be hung if Jack painted it (for reasons Harry did not specify). Harry's letter was intended to suggest to the commission that the family would not protest if a different artist were chosen (record group 32, folder "Letters: HMH to LER, 1910–1913," YHPCC).

143. Maud Howe Elliott diary, 8 February, 16 February, and 12 May 1911, John Hay Library. Maud wrote in her entry for February 8 that she was destroying many of her own papers during this housecleaning: "Dust and germs! Must avoid in future so much accumulation. Much of my papers are being burned every day. They are a menace to the future!"

144. Laura E. Richards to Maud Howe Elliott, 20 October 1913, file 42, YHPGPL. Letters in this folder are copies of the originals in the Colby College collection.

145. Maud Howe Elliott diary, 26 December 1911, 31 December 1911, 27 May, 1912, 2 June 1914, 17 October 1914, Maud Howe Elliott Papers, John Hay Library. Part of the way in which the family remembered Julia was by visiting her grave (and those of Chev, Sammy, and Julia Romana) on Decoration Day, which fell near Julia's birthday on May 27. For Maud, the day of mourning for Julia was not the day she died, but her birthday—a continuation, in a sense, of the old birthday week Maud had so despised. Maud's husband Jack died on May 26, 1925, and from then on Maud regarded the last days of May and early days of June as her own private Passion Week (Maud Howe Elliott diary, 19 May 1933).

146. Henry Marion Howe to Laura E. Richards, n.d. but ca. December 1910, red notebook, "Correspondence, HMH to LER, 1876–1922," YHPGPL. This letter is a typed copy of the original. Maud's diaries indicate concerns about exercise and losing weight. I do not know what she weighed in 1910, but her diary entries for 8–10 May 1936 list her weight as fluctuating between 166 to 168 pounds and her goal of reducing to 165 (Maud Howe Elliott diary, Maud Howe Elliott Papers, John Hay Library).

147. Smith, *The Yellow House Papers,* p. 26. According to Smith, who knows the Richards family well, Laura's daughter Betty (Laura Elizabeth Wiggins) "told me in March 1980 that the

knowledge revealed by MHE [Maud] about JWH's last year was the blackmail used to force her name as joint author of Julia Ward Howe, the first biography ever to bring a Pulitzer Prize to its authors."

148. Florence Howe Hall to Laura E. Richards, 24 July 1917, YHPCC.

149. Henry Marion Howe to Maud Howe Elliott, 22 November 1910; and to Laura E. Richards, 6 and 11 February 1911, record group 32, folder "Letters: HMH to LER, 1910–1913," YHPCC.

150. Laura E. Richards to Maud Howe Elliott, 10 March 1914, folder 41, "LER to MHE, 1901–1907," YHPGPL. This citation comes from a typed copy of the original letter.

151. Florence Howe Hall to Laura E. Richards, 24 July 1917, YHPCC.

152. Laura E. Richards to Henry Marion Howe, 22 July 1914, record group 32, folder "LER to HMH, 1913–1920," YHPCC.

153. Laura E. Richards to Maud Howe Elliott and Henry Marion Howe, 5 September 1914, record group 32, folder "LER to HMH, 1913–1920," YHPCC.

154. Henry Marion Howe to Laura E. Richards, 27 December 1914, record group 32, folder "HMH to LER, 1914–1919," YHPCC.

155. Maud Howe Elliott diary, 4 May, 6 May, and 18 October 1914, Maud Howe Elliott Papers, John Hay Library.

156. Maud Howe Elliott diary, 15 and 29 January 1915, Maud Howe Elliott Papers, John Hay Library. Maud noted in her diary in 1929 that Laura could not "endure any approach to serious advice, if it implies the remotest criticism of herself or family. I once said to her in our youth, 'What is the difference between you & the Virgin Mary? You have had seven immaculate conceptions, she only one.' Profane, but true. Her children cannot make a mistake nor any one she loves—except poor me!" (6 May 1929).

157. Maud Howe Elliott to Laura E. Richards, 14 January 1915, record group 15, folder "MHE to LER, 1910–1919," YHPCC. This may be the reason that the biography gives Julia's initial encounter with Chev as the day she saw him riding his noble black horse up to the Institute. Laura would have known, since she was using Julia's letters and diaries as sources for the biography, that Julia actually first met Chev prior to that summer day at the Institute. As discussed in chap. 1, Chev and Julia initially met at a February 1841 party at George Ticknor's, where Julia and Chev talked but did not dance because Chev disliked dancing. Laura may not have known about that initial meeting until she read her mother's correspondence after Julia's death—which could explain why she was in error in reporting that the initial meeting was at the Institute in *When I Was Your Age,* published in 1894.

158. Laura E. Richards to Henry Marion Howe, 18 January 1915, file 43, YHPGPL. This letter is a copy of the original.

159. Maud Howe Elliott to Laura E. Richards, 21 February 1913, and 14 July 1917, record group 15, folder "Letters from MHE to LER, 1910–1919," YHPCC.

160. Smith, *The Yellow House Papers,* p. 52.

161. Flossy may have been bolstered in this opinion by an April 30, 1899, letter that she received from her mother. There, Julia asked Flossy to delay making any use of old family letters until Julia's *Reminiscences* had a chance to sell. "I have some hope, not a very great deal," Julia continued, "that this book may prove to be literary property, and in that hope shall leave it to you three girls. Of course, it may not turn out so." Women's Studies Manuscript Collection, Julia Ward Howe Family, series 3, no. 72 reel 10, Schlesinger Library.

162. Florence Howe Hall to Laura E. Richards, 24 July 1917, YHPCC.

163. Laura E. Richards to Florence Howe Hall, [16] July 1917, record group 32, folder "HMH to LER, 1914–1919," YHPCC. This is a carbon copy of the original letter that was sent to brother Harry.

164. Henry Marion Howe to Laura E. Richards, 2 August 1917, record group 32, folder "HMH to LER, 1914–1919," YHPCC.

165. Henry Van Dyke to Maud Howe Elliott, 18 April 1918, box 3, folder 27, collected correspondence, Maud Howe Elliott Papers, John Hay Library. One can only hope that Maud was spared the pain of the various "Mine eyes have seen the glory of the burning of the school" parodies that have entered into common parlance.

166. Quoted in Smith, *The Yellow House Papers*, pp. 67–68.

167. Laura E. Richards to Katherine, 21 September 1934, bMS Am 2119 (1601-1611), HL. Katherine's last name is not given. This letter is one of the series of letters between numbers 1601 and 1611, but its exact number is not indicated in the accession lists.

168. Quoted in Smith, *The Yellow House Papers*, p. 71.

169. Laura E. Richards to Maud Howe Elliott, 7 October 1924, file 46, YHPGPL. This letter is a typed copy of the original housed in the Colby College collection.

170. Quoted in Smith, *The Yellow House Papers*, p. 74.

171. Laura E. Richards to Maud Howe Elliott, 24 June 1935, file 54, YHPGPL. This letter is a typed copy of the original housed in the Colby College collection.

172. Record group 20, folder "Correspondence between SGH and JWH," YHPCC.

173. Smith, *The Yellow House Papers*, pp. 28, 121. As Smith points out, the typed transcription of Julia's diaries was selective, omitting numerous embarrassing references.

174. "Terms of Availability" to the papers deposited by John and Rosalind Richards, 17 February 1956, bMS Am 2119, HL.

175. Smith, *The Yellow House Papers*, p. 89.

176. Anne Stokes Alexander, *Laura E. Richards, 1850–1843: A Critical Biography.* This 1979 Columbia University dissertation remains the most detailed treatment of Laura's life and work.

177. Smith *The Yellow House Papers*, pp. 89–90.

178. Jeanne Robert, "Julia Ward Howe as a Writer," *Review of Reviews* (February 1911), pp. 252–53.

179. Hall, *Memories Grave and Gay*, p. 336.

Selected Bibliography

PRINCIPAL ARCHIVAL AND MANUSCRIPT LIBRARIES

John Hay Library, Brown University

Houghton Library, Harvard University

Library of Congress, Washington, D.C.

Schlesinger Library, Radcliffe Institute, Harvard University

Yellow House Papers, Colby College (now at the Maine Historical Society, Portland, Maine)

Yellow House Papers, Gardiner Public Library, Gardiner, Maine.

PRINCIPAL SOURCES PUBLISHED BY HOWE FAMILY MEMBERS

Anagnos, Julia Romana. *Philosophiae Quaestor; Or, Days in Concord.* Boston: D. Lothrop & Co., 1885.

Anagnos, Julia Romana. *Stray Chords.* Boston: Cupples, Upham & Co., 1883.

Elliott, Maud Howe. *The Eleventh Hour in the Life of Julia Ward Howe.* Boston: Little, Brown, & Co., 1911.

Elliott, Maud Howe. *John Elliott: The Story of an Artist.* Boston and New York: Houghton Mifflin Co.; Riverside Press, Cambridge, 1930.

Elliott, Maud Howe and Hall, Florence Howe. *Laura Bridgman: Dr. Howe's Famous Pupil and What He Taught Her.* Boston: Little, Brown, & Co., 1903.

Elliott, Maud Howe. *Lord Byron's Helmet.* Boston and New York: Houghton Mifflin Co.; Riverside Press, Cambridge, 1927.

Elliott, Maud Howe. *Memoirs of the Civil War, 1861–1864.* n.p., n.d. Proceeds to Newport Chapter of the Red Cross.

Elliott, Maud Howe. *My Cousin F. Marion Crawford.* New York: Macmillan Co., 1934.

Elliott, Maud Howe. *This Was My Newport.* Cambridge, Mass.: Mythology Co./A. Marshall James, 1944.

Elliott, Maud Howe. *Three Generations.* Boston: Little, Brown, & Co., 1923.

Elliott, Maud Howe. *Uncle Sam Ward and His Circle.* New York: Macmillan Co., 1938.

Hall, Florence Howe. *Flossy's Play Days.* Boston: Dana Estes Co., 1906.

Hall, Florence Howe. *Julia Ward Howe and the Woman Suffrage Movement.* Boston: Dana Estes & Co., 1913. Reprint, Arno & New York Times, 1969.

Hall, Florence Howe. *Memories Grave and Gay.* New York and London: Harper & Brothers, 1918.

Hall, Florence Howe. *The Story of the Battle Hymn of the Republic.* New York and London: Harper & Brothers, 1916.

Howe, Julia Ward. *At Sunset.* Boston and New York: Houghton Mifflin Co.; Riverside Press, Cambridge, 1910.

Howe, Julia Ward. *From Sunset Ridge.* Boston and New York: Houghton Mifflin Co.; Riverside Press, Cambridge, 1899.

Howe, Julia Ward. *From the Oak to the Olive: A Plain Record of a Pleasant Journey.* Boston: Lee & Shepard, 1868.

Howe, Julia Ward, "Hippolytus." In *Monte Cristo and Other Plays,* edited by J. B. Russak. Princeton: Princeton University Press, 1945.

Howe, Julia Ward. *Is Polite Society Polite? And Other Essays.* Boston and New York: Lamson, Wolffe, & Co., 1895.

Howe, Julia Ward. *Later Lyrics.* Boston: J. E. Tilton & Co., 1866.

Howe, Julia Ward. *Leonora, Or The World's Own.* In *Representative American Plays,* edited by Arthur Hobson Quinn. New York: Century Co., 1917.

Howe, Julia Ward. *Margaret Fuller (Marchesa Ossoli).* Boston: Roberts Brothers, 1883.

Howe, Julia Ward. *Memoir of Dr. Samuel Gridley Howe.* Boston: Howe Memorial Committee; Albert J. Wright, 1876.

Howe, Julia Ward. *Modern Society.* Boston: Roberts Brothers, 1881.

Howe, Julia Ward. *Passion-Flowers.* 3 editions. Boston: Ticknor, Reed, & Fields, 1854.

Howe, Julia Ward, et al. *Proceedings of Peace Meeting Held at Union League Hall, New York, December 23d, 1879. For the Purpose of Free Consultation on the Subject of a Woman's Peace Congress for the World, As Proposed by Mrs. Julia Ward Howe of Boston.* Philadelphia: John Gilliam & Co., 1871.

Howe, Julia Ward. *Reminiscences, 1819–1899.* Boston and New York: Houghton Mifflin Co.; Riverside Press, 1899.

Howe, Julia Ward, ed. *Sex and Education: A Reply to Dr. E. H. Clarke's "Sex in Education."* Boston: Roberts Brothers, 1874.

Howe, Julia Ward, *Trip to Cuba.* Boston: Ticknor & Fields, 1860.

Howe, Julia Ward. *The Walk with God,* edited by Laura E. Richards. New York: E.P. Dutton & Co., 1919.

Howe, Julia Ward. "What Life Means to Me." In *The Cosmopolitan.* Rochester, N.Y.: Schlicht & Field, 1925.

Howe, Julia Ward, et al. *World's Peace Congress.* Boston: n.p., 1870.

Howe, Julia Ward. *Words for the Hour.* Boston: Ticknor & Fields, 1857.

Richards, Henry. *Ninety Years On: 1848–1940.* Augusta, Maine: Kennebec Journal Press, 1940.

Richards, Laura E., and Maud Howe Elliot, with assistance from Florence Howe Hall. *Julia Ward Howe, 1819–1910.* 2 vols. Houghton Mifflin, 1915.

Richards, Laura E. *Julia Ward Howe, 1819–1910.* 1 vol. Revised edition. Boston and New York: Houghton Mifflin Co.; Riverside Press, Cambridge, 1925.

Richards, Laura E. *The Julia Ward Howe Birthday Book.* Boston: Lee & Shepard, 1889.

Richards, Laura E. *Laura Bridgman: The Story of an Opened Door.* New York and London: D. Appleton & Co., 1928.

Richards, Laura E. *Letters and Journals of Samuel Gridley Howe: The Servant of Humanity.* 2 vols. Boston: Dana Estes & Co., 1906. London: John Lane, 1909.

Richards, Laura E. *Samuel Gridley Howe.* New York and London: D. Appleton-Century Co., Inc., 1935.

Richards, Laura E. *Stepping Westward.* New York and London: D. Appleton & Co., 1931.

Richards, Laura E. *Two Noble Lives: Samuel Gridley Howe, Julia Ward Howe.* Boston: Dana Estes & Co., 1911.

Richards, Laura E. *When I Was Your Age.* Boston: Estes & Lauriat, 1894.

Richards, Laura E. "Women in Literature." In *Art and Handicraft in the Woman's Building of the World's Colombian Exposition, Chicago, 1893,* edited by Maud Howe Elliot. Paris and New York: Goupil & Co., Boussod, Valadon & Co., Successors, 1893.

PRINCIPAL SECONDARY SOURCES WITH SIGNIFICANT FOCUS ON THE HOWE FAMILY

Alexander, Anne Stokes. *Laura E. Richards, 1850–1943: A Critical Biography.* Ph.D. diss., Columbia University, 1979

Bolton, Sarah Knowles, "Julia Ward Howe." In *Famous Leaders among Women.* New York and Boston: Thomas Y. Crowell & Co., 1895.

Boston Authors Club. *Birthday Tributes to Mrs. Julia Ward Howe,* May 27, 1905. Boston: Winthrop B. Jones, [1905].

Boyer, Paul S. "Howe, Julia Ward." In vol. 2 of *Notable American Women, 1607–1950: A Biographical Dictionary,* edited by Edward T. James, Janet Wilson James, and Paul S. Boyer. Cambridge: Belknap Press of Harvard University Press, 1971.

Braddy, Nella. *Annie Sullivan Macy: The Story behind Helen Keller.* Garden City, N.Y.: Doubleday, Doran & Co., Inc., 1933.

Brown, Emma E. "Julia Ward Howe and Her Club Work." *National Magazine,* March 1900, pp. 650–54.

Calhoun, Lucia Gilbert. "Mrs. Julia Ward Howe." In James Parton, Horace Greeley, et al., *Eminent Women of the Age; Being Narratives of the Lives and Deeds of the Most Prominent Women of the Present Generation.* Hartford, Conn.: S. M. Betts & Co., 1869.

Clifford, Deborah Pickman. "'The Last Letter to Sammy' by Julia Ward Howe." *Harvard Library Bulletin* 25, no. 1 (January 1977): 50–62.

Clifford, Deborah Pickman. *Mine Eyes Have Seen the Glory: A Biography of Julia Ward Howe.* Boston and Toronto: Little, Brown & Co., 1979.

Dole, Nathan Haskell. "Julia Ward Howe and Her Talented Family." *Munsey's Magazine,* February 1910, pp. 613–20.

Field, Margaret. "Julia Ward Howe and Her Daughters," *Munsey's Magazine.* February 1895, pp. 527–29.

Freeberg, Ernest. *Laura Bridgman: First Deaf and Blind Person to Learn Language.* Cambridge and London: Harvard University Press, 2001.

Gitter, Elisabeth. *The Imprisoned Guest: Samuel Howe and Laura Bridgman, The Original Deaf-Blind Girl.* New York: Farrar, Straus & Giroux, 2001.

Grant, Mary H. *Private Woman, Public Person: An Account of the Life of Julia Ward Howe from 1819 to 1868.* Brooklyn: Carlson Publications, 1994.

Grant, Mary H. "Domestic Experience and Feminist Theory: The Case of Julia Ward Howe." In *Woman's Being, Woman's Place: Female Identity and Vocation in American History,* edited by Mary Kelley. Boston: G. K. Hall, 1979.

Hermann, Dorothy. *Helen Keller: A Life.* New York: Alfred A. Knopf, 1998.

Higginson, T. W. "Julia Ward Howe." *The Outlook,* 16 January 1907, pp. 167–78.

Jennings, John. *Banner against the Wind.* Boston and Toronto: Little, Brown & Co., 1954.

"Julia Ward Howe." *The Independent,* 27 October 1910, pp. 993–94.

Lash, Joseph P. *Helen and Teacher: The Story of Helen Keller and Anne Sullivan.* Radcliffe Biography Series. Reading, Mass.: Addison Wesley Publishing Co., 1980.

Mead, Edwin D. *Woman and War: Julia Ward Howe's Peace Crusade.* Boston: World Peace Foundation, 1914.

Memorial Exercises in Honor of Julia Ward Howe. City of Boston, 1911.

Parkman, Mary Rosetta. "Julia Ward Howe: The Singer of a Nation's Song." In *Heroines of Service.* New York: Century Co., 1917.

"Presentation of the Portrait of Mrs. Julia Ward Howe." *Proceedings of the Bostonian Society,* 21 January 1913, pp. 35–48.

Proceedings of the Metaphysical Club, at a Meeting Held March 24, 1886, in Memory of Its Late President, Julia Romana Anagnos. Boston: Henry H. Clark & Co., 1886.

Robert, Jeanne. "Julia Ward Howe as a Writer." *Review of Reviews,* February 1911.

Schriber, Mary Suzanne. "Julia Ward Howe and the Travel Book." *The New England Quarterly* 62, no. 2 (June 1989): 264–79.

Schwartz, Harold. *Samuel Gridley Howe: Social Reformer, 1801–1876.* Cambridge: Harvard University Press, 1956.

Smith, Danny. *The Yellow House Papers: The Laura E. Richards Collection: An Inventory and Historical Analysis.* Gardiner, Maine, 1991.

Tharp, Louise. *Three Saints and A Sinner.* Boston: Little, Brown & Co., 1956.

VanBurkleo, Sandra, and Mary Jo Miles. "Howe, Julia Ward." In vol. 11 of *American National Biography,* edited by John A. Garraty and Mark C. Carnes. New York and Oxford: Oxford University Press, 1999.

Wilkie, Katherine Elliott, and Elizabeth R. Moseley. *Teacher of the Blind: Samuel Gridley Howe.* New York: Julia Messner, 1965.

Williams, Gary. *The Hermaphrodite: Or, The Laurence Manuscript.* Lincoln: University of Nebraska Press, 2004.

Williams, Gary. *Hungry Heart: The Literary Emergence of Julia Ward Howe.* Amherst: University of Massachusetts Press, 1999.

Wagoner, Jean Brown. *Julia Ward Howe: Girl of Old New York.* Indianapolis and New York: Bobb-Merrill Co., 1945.

Walker, Cheryl. *The Nightingale's Burden: Women Poets and American Culture before 1900.* Bloomington: Indiana University Press, 1982.

Whiting, Lillian. "Julia Ward Howe." In *Women Who Have Ennobled Life.* Philadelphia: The Union Press, 1915.

Woman's Journal. Boston, 1870–1911.

Index